MAN, MYTH, AND MAGIC

MAN, MYTH,
AND MAGIC

Witches and
Witchcraft

Cavendish
Square

New York

Published in 2014 by Cavendish Square Publishing, LLC
303 Park Avenue South, Suite 1247, New York, NY 10010

Library of Congress Cataloging-in-Publication Data

Baroja, J.C.
Witches and witchcraft / by J.C. Baroja.
p. cm. — (Man, myth, and magic)
Includes index.
ISBN 978-1-62712-572-7 (hardcover) ISBN 978-1-62712-573-4 (paperback) ISBN 978-1-62712-574-1 (ebook)
1. Witches — Juvenile literature. 2. Witchcraft — Juvenile literature. I. Title.
BF1566.B37 2014
133.4—d23

Editorial Director: Dean Miller
Editor: Fran Hatton
Art Director: Jeffrey Talbot
Designers: Jennifer Ryder-Talbot and Amy Greenan
Photo Researcher: Laurie Platt Winfrey, Carousel Research, Inc
Production Manager: Jennifer Ryder-Talbot
Production Editor: Andrew Coddington

Cavendish Square would like to acknowledge the outstanding work, research, writing, and professionalism of Man, Myth, and Magic's original Editor-in-Chief Richard Cavendish, Executive Editor Brian Innes, Editorial Advisory Board Members and Consultants C.A. Burland, Glyn Daniel, E.R Dodds, Mircea Eliade, William Sargent, John Symonds, RJ. Zwi Werblowsky, and R.C. Zaechner, as well as the numerous authors, consultants, and contributors that shaped the original Man, Myth, and Magic that served as the basis and model for these new books.

Printed in the United States of America

Contents

A Reader's Guide to *Man, Myth, and Magic: Witches and Witchcraft*

Wherever cultures have grown up, there are common universal themes running through their religions, storytelling, and mythologies. Throughout history, societies have often placed the blame for poor crops, unexplained illnesses, and other bizarre phenomenon at the feet of witches, conjurers, and sorcerers. When there was no natural explanation, civilizations often ascribed these happenings as magic. For some societies, there were attempts to curry the favour of those that seemed to wield this power of magic, either through payment in the form of offering or sacrifices, or giving these individuals positions of power and influence.

Although we often think of witches as female, in fact many cultures have male witches. As people who claim to manipulate the natural world for good or evil, witches have traditionally carried great authority as seers and wise advisers to people with problems. Witches have inspired not only respect but fear, and this led to such appalling reactions as the witch hunts in Europe and America, in which thousands of witches were put to death. Witchcraft continues to thrive in many cultures around the world—in recent years there has been a remarkable revival in Europe and America.

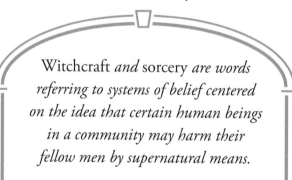

Witchcraft *and* sorcery *are words referring to systems of belief centered on the idea that certain human beings in a community may harm their fellow men by supernatural means.*

Man, Myth, and Magic: Witches and Witchcraft is a work derived from a set of volumes with two decades of bestselling and award-winning history. It is a fully comprehensive guide to over two millennia of the history of witchcraft throughout most known civilizations. While this book in the *Man, Myth, and Magic* series provides an excellent perspective on the historical persecution of witches throughout world, particularly in Europe and the United States, it discusses as well the recent revival of interest in Wicca and its practices.

Objectives of *Man, Myth, and Magic*

The guiding principle of the *Man, Myth, and Magic* series takes the stance of unbiased exploration. It shows the myriad ways in which different cultures have questioned and explained the mysterious nature of the world about them, and will lead teachers and students to a broader understanding of their own and other people's beliefs and customs.

The Text

Within *Man, Myth, and Magic: Witches and Witchcraft*, expert international contributors have created articles, which are arranged alphabetically, and the depth of coverage varies from major articles of up to 10,000 words to concise, glossary-type definitive entries. From Aberdeen Witches to the Witch of Endor, the major events from the global history of witchcraft are covered, with different articles focusing on how different countries viewed—and still view—witches and witchcraft in their society, and the choices made to either honour or persecute those (most often incorrectly) as witches. In addition to the numerous articles on the views of witchcraft, there are also several entries on key figures throughout history, such as Cornelius Agrippa, Aleister Crowley, Marie-Josephte Corriveau, and Dion Fortune, as well as the items and attributes associated with witchcraft, including broomsticks, plants, amulets, familiars, and coverage of both black and white magic.

The work is highly illustrated, and subjects of major interest are provided with individual bibliographies of further reading on the subject at the end of each article.

What made it possible to create this work was the fact that the last century has seen a powerful revival of interest in these subjects at both the scholarly and the popular levels. The revival of scholarly interest has created the modern study of the occult and a modern fascination with the Wiccan beliefs and practices. At the same time there has been a flourishing revival of popular interest in ancient

Examination of a Witch, Thompkins H. Matteson (1853)

civilizations, mythology, magic, and alternative paths to truth. This interest has shown no sign of diminishing in the present century; on the contrary, it has grown stronger and has explored new pathways. Scholarly investigation of these subjects has continued and has thrown much new light on many of the topics. The present edition of *Man, Myth, and Magic* takes account of both of these developments. Articles have been updated to cover fresh discoveries and new theories.

With all this, *Man, Myth, and Magic* is not intended to convert you to, or from, any belief or set of beliefs and attitudes. The purpose of the articles is not to persuade or justify, but to describe what people have believed and trace the consequences of those beliefs in action. The editorial attitude is one of sympathetic neutrality. It is for the reader to decide where truth and value may lie. We hope that there is as much interest, pleasure, and satisfaction in reading these pages as all those involved took in creating them.

Illustrations

Since much of what we know about myth, folklore, and religion has been passed down over the centuries by word of mouth, and recorded only comparatively recently, visual images are often the most powerful and vivid links we have with the past. The wealth of illustrations in *Man, Myth, and Magic: Witches and Witchcraft* is invaluable, not only because of the diversity of sources, but also because of the superb quality of colour reproduction.

Back Matter

Near the end of the book is a glossary that defines words that are most likely new to students, edifying their comprehension of the material. The A–Z index provides immediate access to any specific item sought by the reader. This reference tool distinguishes the nature of the entry in terms of a main entry, supplementary subject entries, and illustrations.

Skill Development for Students

The books of the *Man, Myth, and Magic* series can be consulted as the basic text for a subject or as a source of enrichment for students. It can act as a reference for a simple reading or writing assignment, or as the inspiration for a major research or term paper. The additional reading at the end of many entries is a stellar resource for students looking to further their studies on a specific topic. *Man, Myth, and Magic* offers an opportunity for students that is extremely valuable; twenty volumes that are both multi-disciplinary and inter-disciplinary; a wealth of fine illustrations; a research source well-suited to a variety of age levels that will provoke interest and encourage speculation in both teachers and students.

Scope

As well as being a major asset to social studies teaching, the book provides students from a wide range of disciplines with a stimulating, accessible, and beautifully illustrated reference work.

The *Man, Myth, and Magic* series lends itself very easily to a multi-disciplinary approach to study. In *Man, Myth, and Magic: Witches and Witchcraft*, students of literature will find interest in themes of good and evil, belief and betrayal, real and imagined. History students will be fascinated to read the accounts of, and trends toward, witch hunts, as well as the laws that made all the persecution and prosecutions possible. Students of art will find the images of paintings, old etching and woodblock prints, and sculpture particularly helpful in understanding how the representations of the magical and demonic have evolved over time. Readers looking to delve into the mystic will gravitate to the discussions of supernatural events and persistent ideologies regarding what can only be explained as magic.

Conceptual Themes

As students become involved in the work, they will gradually become sensitive to the major concepts emerging from research. Students can begin to understand the role that the beliefs and practices of witchcraft played in the development of major themes, patterns, and motifs underlying much of the world's mythologies, as well and society's judgments upon individuals as a result. For example, the concept of how humans communicate with and are guided by animals is covered by all major civilizations and belief systems, including the fear that witches use familiars as pawns to accomplish their nefarious ends.

The concept of magic appears in folklore tales all over the world. The stories and myths throughout all societies include witches, from ancient times to early American history. What similarities and differences exist in the concept of witchcraft among all cultures? The continuum of innocence and wickedness provides for the implementation of healing and corruption. The proverbial witches in Western culture and the revered shamans on nearly all the continents—whether in the practice of Native American or Polynesian totemism, Caribbean voodoo, or Shinto ceremonies for communication with the dead—exist because we humans want interaction with a power greater than ourselves. Faith and doubt, in the individual or a religion, pervade society as a whole, and allow for a wide range of explanations for what occurs—or merely seems to occur—in the world. The history of witchcraft and its effects is a reflection of our need to believe in unseen influences, and the hope and fear that they can be controlled

Aberdeen Witches

In the archives of the city of Aberdeen is a remarkable collection of documents (*Records of the Dean of Guild, 1596–1597*) which give details of the proceedings against many persons accused of 'the detestable practice of witchcraft and sorcery'. Marginal notes indicate that the documents were those used in court, most of them consisting of 'dittays', or charges against the accused.

The collection of evidence against those suspected of witchcraft and sorcery was made by the ministers and elders of the Reformed Church in the various parishes. Unhappily, suspects could be named by anyone—a feature that afforded full scope to the malicious—and many harmless old people were named. Suspects were summoned before the Kirk Sessions for examination and those considered guilty were remanded to Aberdeen Assizes. Even

when allowance is made for the ignorance and superstition of the time, it is difficult to excuse the ministers of the Gospel, educated men, whose evidence was the means of sending many innocent people to a horrible end.

However, some of the evidence suggests that there existed a definite organization practicing the black art in northeast Scotland; the group known to history as the Aberdeen witches.

Two main points can be estab-

> *He was appointed official witch-finder to the Assizes and with a three-inch needle pricked the suspects' bodies for the 'Devil's Mark'.*

lished concerning the group. First, the practice of witchcraft was a confidential cult, almost a family concern, its secrets handed down from generation to generation. Secondly, it was well organized, and although each of its members operated individually in

their own localities each was required to attend general meetings, to take part in the ceremonies and for instruction in 'working woe' (doing harm).

The Devil and the Queen of Elphen

The witches were organized in covens—groups of thirteen. At the general meetings the Devil himself presided, usually 'in the likeness of a great grey stag, boar, or dog'. Presumably he was a man dressed as an animal. The meetings were said to involve dancing and sexual relations with the Devil who went under the name of Christsonday and with a woman called the Queen of Elphen (queen of the elves) who, 'is said to be very pleasant, and she can seem old or young when she pleases, and she makes whoever she likes king, and lies with whoever she likes'. They were accused of saluting the Devil and the Queen by kissing them on the buttocks. There seems to have been no age limit on entrance and many of the accused testified to having been introduced as young children.

Each member of a coven specialized in some particular form of sorcery and these covered a wide range. Isobel Cockie bewitched mills and livestock, while Margaret Ogg devoted her attentions to butcher-meat with dire results; Helen Rogie brought illness and death by modeling figures of her victims in lead or wax, and Isobel Strachan was notorious as a fascinator of nice young men; Isobel Ritchie made a special line in confectionery for expectant mothers, while Isobel Ogg's forte was the raising of storms. It would seem that the witches had one faculty which was common to all, that of causing 'the sudden sickness' whereby their victims lay 'one half of the day roasting as if in an oven, with an unquenchable thirst, the other half of the day melting away

The burning of convicted witches in Scotland was merely the final part of a brutal, prolonged death sentence.

with an extraordinary cold sweat'.

Perhaps the most dramatic moment in the Aberdeen Assizes came when Andrew Man turned king's evidence against his colleagues. A witch from boyhood and the father of several children by the Queen of Elphen, he convinced the Court that, with his long and extensive experience, he was in the unique position of being able to identify any witch or warlock brought before him. Accordingly, he was appointed official witch-finder to the Assizes and with a three-inch needle pricked the suspects' bodies for the 'Devil's Mark'—a spot insensible to pain and believed to be inflicted by the Devil.

Strangled by the Executioner

While awaiting trial, the suspects were confined either in the cells of the Tollbooth or in Our Lady's Pity-vault, for the Reformation had brought degradation to this place of worship. A number of the accused took their own lives in prison and their bodies were thrown outside to be dragged through the streets until their battered, shapeless carcasses were unrecognizable.

When the Assizes closed in April 1597, twenty-four people—twenty-three women and one man—had been found guilty of witchcraft. All were condemned to death—'to betaken out between the hills, bound to a stake, strangled by the executioner, and their bodies burned to ashes'. The few whose guilt was 'not proven' were ordered to be branded on the cheek and banished. The final tragic scene took place 'between the hills', in the grassy hollow lying between Aberdeen's Castle Hill and the neighbouring Heading Hill—the depression now covered by Commerce Street—and the 'black reek and stench from the burnings hung over the burgh for many weeks'.

At one stage in the Assizes, it appeared that the number of executions would increase and the Dean of Guild,

fearing rising costs might prejudice the burnings, took it upon himself to lay in a supply of coal to the value of £26 4s. His foresight paid dividends as shown by the final entry in the records dated 21 September 1597, which states that the provost, baillies, and council 'considering the faithfulness shown by William Dun, the Dean of Guild, in the discharge of his duty, and, besides this, his extraordinary taking pains on the great number of witches burned this year and to encourage others to work as diligently in the discharge of their office, grant and assign to him the sum of £47 3s 4d'.

Before the end of the year and while

the subject of witchcraft and sorcery was still in people's minds, King James VI of Scotland (later James I of England) published his book *Demonologie* in defense of witch hunting. It proved to be a bestseller.

FENTON WYNESS

Cornelius Agrippa

At the age of twenty-three, Heinrich Cornelius Agrippa wrote *Three Books of Occult Philosophy*, devoted to the study of the three parts of the Universe: Elemental, Celestial, and Intellectual. The work addresses in detail the practice of

Heinrich Cornelius Agrippa (1486–1535/1538)

magic in these three spheres, including spells, symbols, and ceremonies.

Agrippa was well educated, having earned a master's degree from the University of Cologne at the age of 16 and continuing his career through Germany, Italy, and France, moving from one post to another, practicing both law and medicine while continuing to write on many topics, usually challenging the Church or accepted thought of the time. In an age when scholars and artists required a rich patron for support, Agrippa managed to acquire patrons time and again but then lost them, sometimes in a matter of months. He was especially concerned with the Church's stance on witchcraft, and successfully defended a woman against charges of witchcraft in Metz when he served as that city's legal counsel.

He was denounced as a heretic many times, and his own later writings often contradicted earlier ones. Practically anything that is known about him is questioned by one scholar or another, but his books remain in publication and have often been translated and annotated. Although *Three Books* was written early in his career and widely circulated, it was not formally published until 1531, four years before his death.

Amulet

An object worn or carried to ward off evil or to attract good luck; usually a jewel, a stone, or a piece of metal or parchment, inscribed with magic signs.

Astrum Argentinum

There are many variations of spelling, including Astrum Argentinium and Argeneteum Astrum, all of which translate roughly as Silver Star.

After Aleister Crowley's experience in Cairo (The Great Revelation) he quarreled with MacGregor Mathers, the founder of the Golden Dawn, and either was expelled from the ranks or resigned about 1904. In 1907 he founded the Astrum Argentinum along with his new partner George Cecil Lewis, who had also left the Hermetic Order of the Golden Dawn.

The A. A. was modeled upon other secret societies, including The Rosicrucians, Freemasons, and the Illuminati. There were three Orders within the society, and ranks within those Orders.

These vary from time to time, but the Orders were The Order of the Golden Dawn (the original group of which Crowley had been a member), The Order of the Rose-Cross, and The Order of the Silver Star.

Crowley published his periodical The Equinox after the A. A. was organized, and through it he instructed his followers in the ways of the new society. Upon his death in 1947, he appointed a student, Karl Germer to take charge of the order. However, Germer died and left no successor. Various threads of the group are still extant, but not one that seems to be a legitimate extension of the original.

Bamberg Witches

Dominating the minds of witch hunters in the time of the great persecutions in Europe was the belief that it was the duty of Christians to rescue heretics and pagans from the hideous fate which awaited them after death. Long before, St. Augustine had stated his conviction that 'not only every pagan but that every Jew, heretic and schismatic will go to the eternal fire . . . unless before the end of his life he be reconciled and restored to the Catholic Church'. The outcome of this attitude was the imposition of a veritable hell on earth upon thousands of human beings with the object of saving them from the terrors of hell in the next world.

The horrors of the persecution were probably worse in Germany than in any other part of Europe. Witch trials began there in the mid-fifteenth century but the bulk of the trials date from after 1570, at the time of the Counter Reformation, when the Roman Catholic Church began to roll back the tide of Protestantism and every form of heresy, including witchcraft, came under fierce attack.

Between 1609 and 1622 over 300 people were executed for witchcraft in the state of Bamberg alone. The accused were tortured without regard for age or sex. In 1614 a woman of seventy-four died undergoing torments 'up to the third grade'.

The Witch Bishop

From 1623 to 1632 the state of Bamberg, later described as 'the shrine of horror' was ruled by a fanatical witch-hater, the Prince-Bishop Gottfried von Dornheim. Known as 'the Witch Bishop', he established an extremely efficient witch hunting organization, under a subordinate, Suffragan Bishop Friedrich Förner, assisted by a council of lawyers. Special prisons were set up, the most notorious being the *Hexenhaus* or Witches House, where the captives were interrogated and tortured. A minimum of 600 people were burned as witches during this decade.

It was considered essential that the accused should confess to witchcraft, and no efforts were spared to obtain confessions. The means employed included roasting on an iron chair, rending the flesh with red-hot pincers, crushing the legs, dislocating the shoulders, and applying thumbscrews.

It was exceedingly dangerous to express the slightest doubt as to the guilt of anyone who was accused or to question the methods of the courts for, as

Woodcut illustrating types of torture used in Bamberg witch trials

soon became obvious, the authorities were determined that, once arrested, no prisoner should escape the stake. This the liberal-minded Dr. Haan, Vice-Chancellor of Bamberg, who had shown signs of leniency in his dealings with accused witches, discovered to his cost when he in turn was denounced as a witch. Under torture he admitted his guilt in full and denounced five leading burgomasters as fellow sorcerers. This did not save him, for in 1628 the kindly Vice-Chancellor and his wife and daughter were burned as witches.

The dreadful situation in which the five burgomasters now found themselves is revealed in a letter written by one of their number, Johannes Junius,

who had occupied this position of honour since 1608. Now, at the age of fifty-five, he was suddenly denounced as a witch on the testimony of Dr. Haan and others. He was accused of worshipping Satan, desecrating the sacred host, having sexual intercourse with a succubus (a demon in female form), and riding to the witches' sabbath on the back of a black dog.

His letter, addressed to his daughter and smuggled out of prison by a bribed jailer, conveys the agony of mind and body of an innocent man caught up in the mesh of the witch hunters, and the sense of hopelessness that soon destroyed all power to resist. 'For whoever comes into the

witch prison,' he wrote, 'must become a witch or be tortured until he invents something out of his head and, God pity him, bethinks him of something.' Junius described the torture of the thumbscrews, the mildest of all the engines of torment. 'And then came also—God in his highest heaven have mercy—the executioner, and put the thumbscrews on me, both hands bound together, so that the blood spurted from the nails and everywhere, so that for four weeks I could not use my hands, as you can see from my writing.'

During his examination a blemish was discovered on his right side, which being impervious to pain was assumed to be a Devil's mark, the sign of the Christian's submission to Satan. This further evidence seems to have been hardly necessary in view of the fact that under torture he confessed in full to the charges against him, and on 6 August 1628 he died at the stake.

Father Friedrich von Spee, a Jesuit whose hair had turned prematurely grey as the result of his experiences as a confessor of witches in neighbouring Würzburg, revealed the effects of torture on the human mind in a book which he wrote in 1631: 'the most robust who have thus suffered have affirmed that no crime can be imagined which they would not at once confess to if it could bring down ever so little relief and they would welcome ten deaths to escape repetition.'

The Witch Industry

The speed and efficiency of the court procedure would be unbelievable if one were not aware that the machinery was generously lubricated with money exacted from the estates of the accused. Within a matter of three weeks from the date of her arrest in June 1629,

Opposite page:
A woman accused of witchcraft,
from the Middle Ages

Frau Anna Hansen had been interrogated and tortured, had confessed, had ratified her confession and had been beheaded and burned. A prisoner who displayed any tendency to delay his inevitable death by obduracy could always be persuaded otherwise by the application of those Bamberg specialties, flaming feathers dipped in sulphur applied to the armpits and groin, or a scalding bath to which lime had been added.

Witch hunting in Bamberg, as elsewhere in Europe, involved a whole industry of interested parties whose income depended on a steady flow of victims. They ranged from the judges who tried the cases down to the merchants who supplied the timber for the execution fires. The whole cost of trial, imprisonment and execution was borne by the estate of the prisoner or, if he had no property, by relatives or by the local authority.

Anyone unfortunate enough to be accused had to contend not only

> *Many people confessed to having spoken to the Devil, who sometimes appeared as a male goat and at other times as a handsome mule.*

with the genuine belief in the existence of witches of a majority of the population, and with the clergy's determination to save his soul from hellfire, but also with the vested interests of those whose pockets were lined by his execution. The result was a vicious circle of torture, death, and the betrayal of friends. Whenever the confiscation of the property of the accused was suspended, the number of executions always declined.

End of the Terror

Refugees from the terror fled to the court of the Holy Roman Emperor, where they attempted to arouse concern about the travesties of justice at Bamberg. Father Lamormaini, the Emperor's confessor, told him of the disquiet created by the atrocities, and another Jesuit said that the victims, far from being execrated as witches, were rapidly becoming the objects of popular sympathy. Councillor Dümler of Bamberg described to the Emperor how his wife had been cruelly tortured and burned at the stake even though she was pregnant.

In time, the Emperor responded to the general clamor by ordering certain legal reforms, including legal representation of the accused and the ending of the confiscations of property. Torture, however, was not abolished.

After 1630 the witch hunt declined in intensity. In that year Bishop Förner died. He was followed two years later by his master, the Witch Bishop. The invasion of Germany by Gustavus Adolphus, the Protestant King of Sweden, distracted attention from witchcraft to the problems created by the presence of a victorious arch-heretic on Catholic soil. In 1630 there were twenty-four executions and in the following year there were none.

The horrors of German witch hunting, however, were perpetrated by Protestants as well as Roman Catholics. It is on record that a Lutheran named Benedict Carpzov admitted ordering the executions of at least 20,000 victims in Saxony.

With the gradual decline of belief in the Devil, the fear of witchcraft subsided. Concurrently, the burning need to rescue the heretic or witch from the terrors of hellfire by the infliction of agonies in this life gradually lost its relevance.

ERIC MAPLE

Basque Witchcraft

During the later fifteenth century, the whole of the sixteenth and the early years of the seventeenth, the witches and wizards of the Basque region were intensely active and acquired a reputation which spread all through Europe. The Basques are a people of mysterious origin, living along the coasts of northern Spain and southern France, under the shadows of the Pyrenees. As early as the 3rd century BC they were famous for their skill in predicting the future from the flight of birds. Later, their conversion to Christianity was a slow process and forms of worship which are nonCatholic and not centred on the Church have continued to appear right up to the present time.

A Spanish royal edict of 1466

Man in Black

Hans Petz from Steinbach, a court official in the district of Untermain, finally confessed after he had been subjected to such tortures as the application of thumbscrews and leg vises and the stocks. For three and a half hours he was suspended by a rope, 8 feet from the ground, while a stone weighing 20 pounds hung from his toes. He admitted the following:

'That he had committed adultery more than 100 times with Priestiklin of Steinbach and had copulated with her standing and in other ways. One day, while standing near her at a fountain and touching her on the body, she was suddenly transformed into the terrifying black figure of a man. His hands were rattling and on his right leg he had a cloven hoof, by which Petz recognized with whom he had been trafficking. This character called on Petz to deny God and to fetch the sacred host when he went to supper . . . Some time later she met him, when she had regained her natural form and they continued their sexual relationship, but by now it had become cold and lacking in love. In all he went to five witches' dances and at one of them it was discussed how the crops could best be spoiled.'

Graf von Lamberg,
Hexenprozessen in Bamberg

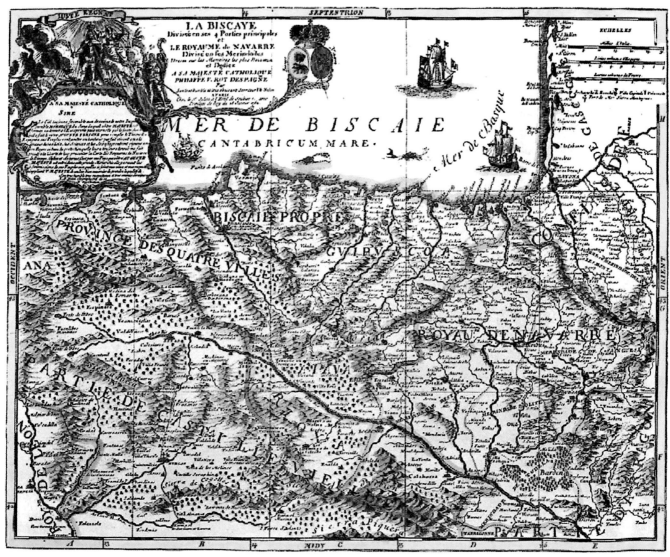

A region in the northeast corner of Spain, the Basque area secludes itself geographically as well as linguistically and culturally.

indicates that in the province of Guipuzcoa, on the southern shore of the Bay of Biscay, there were a number of men and women who practiced witchcraft and black magic. They were known as *bruxos* and *xorguinos*. The activities attributed to them included damaging property, causing harm to other men and women, inducing sterility and difficult childbirths, and causing bad vintages and bad harvests of other crops. The witches and wizards were also believed to deny God and the Virgin Mary. This was the period in which the Basque country was torn by warring nobles and factions. Armed men killed each other mercilessly, and blood relations disposed of each other by poisoning.

In a social environment such as this, where friendship could turn to violent enmity, where blood relationships produced both strong alliances and great family dramas, it is understandable that the public authorities shrank from intervening in incidents attributed to supernatural forces.

The Lady of the Caves

The next pieces of evidence about the sect of the witches known to the great historians of the Inquisition and heresy in Spain also come from Vizcaya. They date from 1500, by which time the Spanish Inquisition had already been functioning for many years, and there are two of them: that of Archdeacon Pedro Fernandez de Villegas,

in his commentary on Dante's *Inferno*, and that of Fray Francisco de Vargas. The archdeacon's text indicates that the 'centre for the witches' meetings or *conciliabules* was in the mountain range of Amboto, a place which is famous in Basque folklore, as it is said to contain some caves in which lives a deity known as *la Dama* (the lady), who was considered to be the patron of the witches.

Many people confessed to having spoken to the Devil, who sometimes appeared as a male goat and at other times as a handsome mule. But those who confessed to having seen this also admitted that he sometimes appeared as a man, though always bearing some sign which indicated his evil nature, for instance, a horn in his forehead or long protuberant teeth.

This form of 'witches' sabbath' must be related to those which took place somewhat earlier in the south of France and the Catalan Pyrenees (to the east of the Basque region). The first appearance of the 'sabbath' in Inquisitorial trials was in Carcassonne and Toulouse between 1330 and 1340. In the Catalan valleys it is first recorded about 1424.

Judged by the Left Eye

The trial of 1500 was considerably influenced by what had been written about witchcraft in different parts of Europe throughout the fifteenth century. The most famous text was the *Malleus Maleficorum,* which had such a pernicious influence in Europe from its first appearance until well into the seventeenth century, although it is true that there were some inquisitors and theologians in Spain who followed certain earlier, far less credulous doctrines about the reality of the activities attributed to witches and wizards. Among these must be counted Martin of Arles, who disagreed with those who believed witches to be capable of flying through the air and performing other similar acts, although he did believe that it was possible, by means of spells, to cause sterility in married couples, injure people, destroy fields and crops, all through the help of the Devil. But in spite of these exceptions it seems that in 1507 the Inquisitor of Calahorra burned some thirty witches and a few years later the kingdom of Navarre experienced a wave of terror and repression.

In 1527 the Inquisition, established on the frontier of Navarre, carried out an intensive investigation into the activities of witches. Two girls, aged nine and eleven, appeared before the court at Pamplona to denounce the abomi-nable acts they had taken part in. They offered their help in the administration of justice if they were pardoned. Accepting this condition, the judge went from village to village accompanied by 50 soldiers. The two girls were put in separate houses and suspects were summoned before them in turn. The children looked the suspects in the left eye and decided whether or not they were

> *The ointment they used was made from toads which had been skinned alive and pulverized.*

witches. They were looking for a 'sign' in the eye, resembling a frog's foot. It appears that over 100 men and women were discovered to be sorcerers, having been judged so independently by both the children.

The Devil's Communion

According to documents discovered by the city clerk of Pamplona a similar investigation was carried out in 1525 with Graciana de Izaroz as the witness, in the region of Ituren and Zubieta. Four hundred people presented themselves voluntarily and only twelve were picked out as sorcerers: two men and ten women. These were subjected to a second inspection by the same Graciana (whose grandmother had been burned as a witch) and she remained doubtful about two of them. Some of those convicted formed a family group (a married couple and an uncle); others, more sinister, were the classic solitary witch with a strong background of erotic activities, such as Maria of Ituren. The group of witches and wizards of Elgorriaga and Urroz were accused of making ointments with toads' blood and babies' hearts. Maria of Ituren was tortured and confessed to having celebrated a *conventiculo* (clandestine gathering) with her companions. There they ate and drank until cock-crow. Having anointed themselves, they changed into horses and galloped through the air. The ointment they used was made from toads which had been skinned alive and pulverized, and a herb called in Basque *usainbelar* (water plantain).

While Maria of Ituren confessed to all these activities, others flatly denied everything, and when subjected to ducking said that they believed in God and were telling the truth when they pleaded innocence. The Inquisitor Avellaneda evolved a theory of witchcraft which coincides almost exactly with the theories of other judges and theologians engaged in similar activities in different parts of Spain. The letter in which he expounds this theory is a monument of credulity. The classic argument 'seeing is believing' is of little use to us in judging what he saw and believed, for in the letter already mentioned he claims to have seen a witch flying, before reliable witnesses: and a witch smeared with ointment being transported by the Devil, who was then frightened off by the name of Jesus.

According to Avellaneda, the witches first deny the Christian faith. Then new witches are presented to the Devil by an initiate, in a particular place on the day appointed for such gatherings. On this day (it is usually Friday night) there is a horrible banquet and a kind of communion. Then there are great sexual orgies and evil acts against society. The Devil appears in the form of a black male goat and is worshipped in an indecent manner. The bait offered is the promise of riches and pleasures. The gatherings were sometimes very large: at one, between Pamplona and Viana, there were nearly 1,000 people.

The Horned Horse

The activities of Avellaneda must have caused a considerable disturbance amongst the high functionaries of the Inquisition, for in 1529 several of them met to discuss the question of whether witches flew or not and whether they went to their gatherings in reality or only in their imaginations. In fact six voted for their doing so in reality, three for their imagining it, and one remained doubtful. It can be said that opinions remained divided in similar proportions throughout the sixteenth century. The country suffered waves of terror and panic at the activities of witches and wizards. A succession of children and adolescents appeared, providing the most terrifying pieces of information and confessing themselves to be repentant sorcerers.

From 1530 to 1555 there was a veritable battle between those who called for heavy penalties against witches and wizards, and the Inquisition, which was disinclined to accept mass accusations. At times the civil authorities acted individually and on their own initiative, as happened in Vizcaya in the years 1555 and 1556, where proceedings were started against a family group of witches and wizards. The trial is significant because it indicates the existence of local rivalries, of disputes between families which may lie behind the accusations of witchcraft, and also in the importance given to the testimony of an eight-year-old girl, Catalina de Guesala, and of other minors.

The Crying Dog

They spoke of gatherings in houses, initiations, flight by means of ointments, worship of the Devil in specific places (in this case in Pretelanda) and the appearance of the Enemy in the form of a jet black horse with horns, seated on a chair. They described orgies of eating, drinking, and unnatural sexual practices. The sorcerers of Vizcaya caused harm to men and crops and appeared in one case as suckers of blood. The civil judge, however, did no more than condemn the accused to torture by ducking and flogging.

In 1575, several functionaries of the Inquisition were active in the territories of La Burunda, Echarri-Aranaz and Huarte Araquil. In Ciordia there was an outcry against Gracia Martiiz of Urdiain, who was accused of having been seen near her house one night with ten or twelve other people, all dressed in white. On being seen, all except for Gracia flew off on a sheet which was also white. One man, aged seventy, claimed to have seen all this when he was thirty. Another accuser declared that one night he saw animals emerging from the house of the same Gracia: deer, dogs, male goats, galloping and making a great commotion. Also a dog came out of another old house crying, from which it was inferred that the other noisy animals were 'witches and malefactors'. The ageing Gracia was put in prison. She

The Sabbath of the Witches, **Francisco de Goya (1746–1828)**

was over eighty and at one point it was decided to torture her. Several other women in the prison said she was no more than a skeleton. The Royal doctor of Navarre, Doctor Zalduendo, confirmed that if she was tortured she would die. Added to this was the testimony of two priests who proclaimed her Christian virtues. She was finally exiled from the kingdom.

In the valley of Araiz c. 1595 Maria Miguel de Orexa, twenty-six years old, submitted to a carefully prepared interrogation in which it came out that she had been initiated into the art of witchcraft at the age of ten by her grandmother, who was on her deathbed (in accordance with a tradition preserved to this day, that witches cannot leave this world without transmitting their condition to someone else). The girl went to a sabbath, which she reached, after having been smeared with ointment, by flying through the air with three female companions. They met fifteen others on the coast of Urrizola and from there flew to a large plain. In the middle of the plain were two seats which appeared to be of gold, with two black forms: one was a man with a head of a male goat, the other was his wife. In her confession, Maria Miguel identified them as Beelzebub and his spouse. The rest of her story tells us little which is new: dancing to the sound of tambourines and rebecks, worship of the Devil (in a nearby cave), and then an orgy till cock-crow.

Lives Dominated by Horror

According to the report of a trial in Logroño in 1610, the sect of witches and wizards had a very solid structure and a systematic organization. The art of witchcraft was handed down from one generation to another: It was not easy to join the sect. A master wizard sponsored a new convert and presented him on a night chosen for the occasion. Once the convert had abandoned

Christianity and made his new profession of faith in the Devil, he was branded and sworn to secrecy. Then came indoctrination under the tutelage of a master wizard, and an initiation ceremony.

The different grades formed by those attending a sabbath appear to have been as follows: 1, Children (who were under the guardianship of another member); 2, Initiates (also with their guardian); 3, Performers (without a guardian): makers of poisons and evil spells; 4, Masters: propagandists, initiators and tutors; 5, The leaders of the meetings or sabbaths: the King and Queen, the guardian of the children, and the executioner.

The organization was monarchic. The Devil appeared on his throne. At the sabbaths there were always banquets, dancing, and sexual orgies. But all this was subject to the principle of inversion to such an extent that what should have appeared agreeable, from a sensual point of view, was in fact repugnant.

The practice of evil was an important feature of the lives of these witches and wizards: to carry out their evil deeds they had recourse to shape-changing and flying. They blasted crops, livestock, and people: they practiced necrophagy (the eating of dead bodies) and vampirism. Not even their own families were safe from them, for the members of the sect murdered their relations. In addition they celebrated black masses and committed all kinds of sacrilegious acts.

The Logroño trial paints a picture of lives dominated by horror. The sorcerers seem to live like condemned men. However great the fear inspired by the Devil in Spain in the seventeenth century, the accumulation of so much evil proved something of a strain on even the most serious and balanced minds. The report of the trial was read by the humanist Pedro de Valencia, who wrote two critical essays about it

asking questions such as: Was all this true? Could these be orgiastic cults like those of classical times? Human excesses and strong passions could explain what was described to a certain extent, but was it not due rather to the effects of the imagination? Pedro de Valencia emphasizes the mental states which can be attained by the use of drugs, and also touches on the theme of a predilection for what is repellent, as described by some doctors.

The Devil's Priests

The priests and cures of Laboured and of the neighbouring districts of Navarre are for the most part sorcerers. They are so respected that no one is scandalized by their habits, frequenting the taverns, the dances, the ball games with swords by their side . . . or going on pilgrimages in company with three or four pretty girls. Their privileges are such that at first no one dared to accuse them, but Satan could not at last prevent an old priest of good family from being denounced. He confessed that some fifteen or sixteen years before he had wanted to quit this abomination, but the devil so tormented him that he was almost out of his senses . . . He was condemned to death . . . and he requested the Bishop of Dax to perform the degradation, after which he was duly executed . . .

This made a great sensation and there was no longer hesitation in accusing priests. Some of them feigned vows to Monserrat and other places and fled; others took to the sea. At first we looked on the accusations with suspicion as the result of enmities, but little innocent children and persons from other parishes bore testimony to seeing them in the Sabbat. We arrested seven of the most notable in the land, most of them having cure of souls in the best parishes of Laboured. One of them, Pierre Bocal of Siboro, aged twenty-seven, had celebrated the devil's mass in the Sabbat the night before he sang the first one in his church . . . For the service in the Sabbat the devil gave him 200 crowns, while that in his church brought him only about 100.

Pierre de Lancre,
Tableau de l'Inconstance des Mauvais Anges (1612)

Where does the truth lie?

As a man well versed in the ways of the world, Pedro de Valencia considered that the meetings of witches must be real, 'that their chief object is that which has been pursued by all such people in all ages, namely carnal self-indulgence'. In other words, witches and wizards were dominated by sensual passions rather than by any religious or antireligious beliefs and motives.

Deserted Sabbaths

According to the findings of Alonso de Salazar y Frias, one of the judges of the Logroño trial who became sceptical about the report some years later, 1384 children aged from six to fourteen had made confessions which were full of defects. There was no consistency of opinion as to where the sabbaths took place, nor on the question of the ointments used. Some of the sorcerers 'pottages' as the Inquisitor disdainfully refers to them, were tried out on animals and found to have no effect. He also proved to the witnesses and the sorcerers themselves that the things which they described had not in fact happened. He even sent two secretaries to one notorious sabbath on the appointed day and they found no proof that anything happened there.

Everything which the Logroño report had held to be true was exposed as a series of hoaxes and fairy tales. The Inquisitor saw the results of the previous trials as being due to the ignorance and malicious intent of witnesses, the mentally confused state of the accused and the incomprehension or laziness of the judges. He himself confesses to having put pressure on some of the accused, and of not having punished two witnesses who were responsible for the majority of the denunciations and who afterward boasted of having told lies.

The Church of Satan

The French Basque coast was, like the adjoining territories, a prey to fear of the activities of witches and wizards; and in Navarre, Guipuzcoa, and Vizcaya the French Basques were believed to be even more notorious sorcerers than the Spanish. There was a succession of trials there between 1576 and 1605.

In 1609 came an explosion of panic on the French Basque coast which is

She has a woman's face of extraordinary beauty. She sometimes flies through the air surrounded by fire and is the president and directress of witches.

describing a secret society organized on monarchical lines, with a court of the French type having its grades and hierarchies, de Lancre imposes a whole ecclesiastical system on the sorcerers' society, so that the sabbath appears as an imitation of the Catholic faith, with temples, altars, diabolical saints, and decorations. There were also, according to him, ecclesiastical grades among the sorcerers, from subdeacons to bishops.

Basque Witch Beliefs Today

Even today in one or two rural communities, one can find a wealth of traditions about the activities of witches and wizards. Little is said in these traditions of sabbaths or diabolical gatherings, though in Vizcaya the witches are said to meet in a so-called partridge field and in caves. Here and there caves, springs, dolmens, and other specific places are considered to be the haunts of witches.

not easily explained. The people of Labourd, as those of Guipuzcoa before them, demanded the punishment of the sorcerers, who were becoming a veritable plague. King Henry IV of France commissioned the president of the *parlement* of Bordeaux and two councilors to take action. One of them, a lawyer named Pierre de Lancre, worked with terrifying zeal. He was prejudiced from the start against the Basques. Besides being a hostile observer, he had at his fingertips the books of former well-known judges of witches and the harsh laws which had been applied elsewhere in Europe in the past. Thus equipped, and with a total ignorance of the language, he succeeded in reducing the region to a state of terror worse than any previously recorded.

Here again there were hysterical declarations by crowds of children. The image of witchcraft which de Lancre held is similar to, but more complex and lurid than, that given by the report of Logroño. The number of sabbaths grew, and the abundance of demons was matched by the number of different forms they took. Besides

But as significant as this, or more so, is the fact that in Vizcaya and Guipuzcoa a belief has existed right up to the present time in a goddess who is supposed to live in the mountains. She has a woman's face of extraordinary beauty. She sometimes flies through the air surrounded by fire and is the president and directress of the witches. This deity is called 'la Dama' or 'la Senora' (the lady). This name, as in la Dama de Emboto, is sometimes followed by the name of the place where she resides in a cave filled with gold and illusory precious objects which are transformed into coal when exposed to daylight. Thus beliefs current before the fourteenth century are closer to the present day than those of the sixteenth or seveenth centuries.

J. C. BAROJA

FURTHER READING: J. C. Baroja. The World of Witches. (Weidenfeld, 1964).

Benemmerinnen

Also known as Lilin, these witches of Hebrew mythology steal newborns. They are bald but have hair covering their bodies, including their faces.

One of the manifestations of Lilith, who in Hebrew mythology was Adam's first wife and was formed from earth just as he was and was thus his equal. Lilith rebelled and chose to leave the Garden of Eden and align herself against God and mankind. When God sent three angels to retrieve her, she refused to return and, in later versions of the myth, was transformed into a demon who swore to take vengeance upon the children of Adam. She is associated with difficulty in childbirth and harm to newborns.

Newborns were vulnerable to attack by the benemmerinnen until they had received their names. For boys this happened at circumcision, for girls on the first Sabbath after their birth. Amulets inscribed with the names of the three angels sent to bring Lilith back were considered protection against Lilith until the naming ceremony.

She is known as the night hag (Isaiah 34. 8–14 [Revised Standard Edition]). Also associated with the owl, the serpent in the Garden of Eden, and possibly with Sophia, the Greek goddess of Wisdom, and with Lamashtu, a Babylonian demoness who caused infant death.

The benemmerinnen is first mentioned in a book published in 1648 in Amsterdam, called *Emek HaMelech* (Valley of the King), by Rabbi Naftali Hertz ben Ya'akov Elchanan.

Black Magic

Magic attempts to make use of mysterious forces which most people cannot control or do not believe in. A black magician is one who does this for evil purposes. Power is the black magician's guiding light. It is the hope of obtaining limitless power which spurs him on, and the exercise of power which he enjoys. He exalts dominance, cruelty, hatred, lust, all fierce and hard emotions, while he scorns kindness, humility, sympathy, and self-sacrifice. He often takes a double-edged attitude to his own activities, convincing himself that his intention to kill or terrify is the highest good, while simultaneously wriggling with glee at his own delicious evilness.

Black magicians exist today, as in the past, but they are few and far between. The number of people so dedicated to the total reversal of the accepted rules of the society they live

European witches were said to keep familiar spirits in animal form which sucked their blood.

in that they consistently practice evil magic is, and always has been, very small. But human reluctance to believe in a universe so disorderly, and so out of sympathy with man that important events can occur by mere chance, has caused all sorts of misfortunes, deaths, illnesses and accidents to be put down to hostile magic. And so the term 'black magic' includes both the practices of a limited number of deliberate sorcerers and the much wider field of illusory practices and powers attributed to nonexistent ones.

The Left-Hand Path

Both in fact and in popular belief, black magic is intensely antisocial, rejecting all accepted values and proclaiming their opposites. This is why it is connected with things which are inverted, upside down or the wrong way round. In the Ozark hill country of the United States the ceremony of initiating a witch ends with the recitation of the Lord's Prayer backward. In southern France in 1932 an American writer, W. B. Seabrook, found a witch-doll, pierced with pins and smeared with toad's blood, intended to kill the person it represented. Near it, resting on a Bible, was an inverted crucifix on which a toad had been crucified head downward. Today, some of the people who dabble in Satanism wear inverted crosses.

Black magic is called 'the Left-Hand Path' because right-handedness is normal and left-handedness is reversal of the normal. Witches were accused of dancing widdershins, to the left, at their meetings. And the principal charge against witches in Europe was that they had leagued themselves with the Devil, the arch-enemy of God and man, the rebel against divine order.

The same connection between black magic and the reversal of accepted values appears outside the European tradition. Navaho Indians say that to obtain his power a black magician must murder one of his younger brothers or sisters. In the Congo, the Logo and Keliko people say that witches walk about upside down. The night-dancing witches of the Kaguru in East Africa go about naked, walk on their hands, and turn their black skins white with ashes.

Black magicians, real or alleged, are sexually perverse and they love dirt. In Africa the Azande associate lesbianism with witchcraft. The Mandari of the Sudan say that wizards practice homosexuality, bestiality with cows and goats, and intercourse with immature girls. In Europe witches were accused of committing every conceivable sexual perversion, with each other and with demons, and the words 'filthy', 'lewd', and 'unnatural' appear constantly in descriptions of their behaviour. Aleister Crowley, a notorious modern black magician, performed perverse rituals with male and female partners, and took a marked interest in human excrement.

Incest and cannibalism are commonly associated with black magic, and so are unnatural relationships with animals. European witches were said to keep familiar spirits in animal form which sucked their blood; like Jane Bussey of Kent, accused in 1583 of keeping three imps: 'Pygine resembling a mole, Russell resembling a grey cat, and the other called Dunsott resembling a dun dog, with intent that she might enchant and bewitch men as beasts and other things'.

The Methods of Black Magic

The black magician's armoury is as various as his purposes. He may use his own inner powers; spirits, demons, or forces outside himself; mimicry, words, and gestures; 'weapons' like the magic wand or circle, and 'medicine'.

Evil 'medicines' can be herbs or plants, roots, parts of the bodies of animals or human beings, pieces of paper with words or symbols written on them, knots tied in string, stones or almost anything else. Whether they are actually harmful, like snake venom, or outwardly harmless but having sinister associations, like bat's blood, they are not usually expected to work by themselves. There must be a link between the charm and the victim. His nail clippings or hair, clothes he has worn, or bedding he has slept in, are believed to retain a connection with him, so that what is done to them is done to him. Less tangible things, a man's name or his shadow or his footprint, are also linked with him and can be used against him. An eighteenth century French magical textbook, the

Witches add ingredients to a cauldron

Grimorium Verum, says that you can harm an enemy by driving into his footprint a nail from an old coffin, saying *Pater noster upto in terra,* which seems intended to mean 'Our father which art on earth', parodying the Lord's Prayer and appealing to the Devil. You hammer the nail well in with a stone and say, 'Cause harm to so-and-so until I remove you.'

If there is no natural link with the victim, the magician must create one. He may bury an evil charm in a path where his victim will walk over it, or he may hide it in his enemy's house. When the Roman general Germanicus died in 19 AD, under the floor and behind the walls of his room were found human bones, rotting bits of dead bodies and pieces of lead, the metal of death, with his name written on them.

The Weapon of Language

Language is one of the great magical weapons because of the belief that words, infused with the power of the magician's will, make what is stated in the words happen. In some societies, as among the Maori in New Zealand, the words which make a particular spell work must never be altered. The correct forms are handed down from magician to magician, for the words themselves have magical force. But more often a magician is free to vary his incantations and he experiments with them until he finds those which seem to work best. Through mimicry, words, and gestures the magician works up his own inner fury of hatred or lust to a frenzied pitch, and through them he externalizes his frenzy and directs it at his target. The sorcerers of the central Pacific islands list all the parts and organs of the victim's body, saying over and over again in a torrent of rage, 'I break, I twist, I burn, I destroy'. When a bone or a stick is pointed at a man to kill him, the magician jabs it in the air with an expression of violent hatred, and turns and twists it as if in the wound.

In the same way, a European black magician acts out hatred for his victim, stabbing the air with a sword or a knife and whipping or wounding an animal or another human being, filling his mind with images of blood and pain, and working himself into a state of frenzy in which, he believes, he draws into himself all the forces of violence and destruction in the universe. He becomes these forces; he masters them, and he launches them against his enemy with scarifying force.

To what extent a magician's magical power comes from inside himself or from outside is a matter which magicians themselves are often vague about. The European magical textbooks are mainly concerned with rituals for summoning up spirits and demons which will obey the magician's orders.

Quiche Indians in Guatemala say that a man who wants to become a witch sleeps in a cemetery for nine nights and prays to the Devil, from whom he can obtain power. In Africa the Nyoro black magicians send evil spirits to attack people and the Lele sorcerers force the spirits of dead babies to foretell the future.

When Magic Works

When magic works, as it sometimes does, it usually appears to be explicable in terms of its effects on the minds of the magician and his victim, without any necessity to assume the presence of mysterious outside forces. A black magician of dominating personality can have a terrifying effect, even on the sceptically inclined, and when a sor-

cerer puts a fatal spell on a man who believes in his power it is not unknown for the victim to fade away and die. But it is probably the belief which kills him, not the spell.

In European ritual magic a small group of magicians perform a long and exhausting ceremony in which they attempt to conjure up to visible appearance a spirit or occult power of some kind. During the ceremony they gradually whip themselves up into a state of intense excitement. They have

A witch . . . possesses inner magical power and can injure a person by concentrating malice upon him.

a clear mental picture of the demon they expect to see, and often a drawing or painting of it. It is not very surprising if at the climax of the ceremony they actually see it, but the demon seems more likely to be a creation of their own minds than something existing independently.

Some anthropologists studying African beliefs have drawn a rough distinction between a sorcerer and a witch. A sorcerer uses 'medicine', plants, roots, nails, hair and the rest. A witch, on the other hand, possesses inner magical power and can injure a person by concentrating malice upon him. Anyone who takes the time and trouble can learn to become a sorcerer, but not everyone has the innate power possessed by a witch.

This distinction is not always clear in practice and is not accepted as generally true by all anthropologists. Certainly it does not fit the European tradition, in which both black magicians and witches are credited with innate power and both use noxious substances and potions. In Europe the

distinction between them is based on the difference in their characteristic attitudes to the forces with which they deal. Broadly speaking, the black magician seeks to dominate and control occult powers, while the witch worships them. This is reflected in the fact that the majority of European black magicians have been men and the majority of witches women.

Black Magic and White

The distinction between black and white magic is simple enough in theory: a black magician works for evil ends and a white magician for good. But in practice the distinction is frequently blurred. For one thing, it rests in the eye of the beholder and very often white magic is what you work and black magic is what other people work. For another, a man who believes he has magical powers is likely, being human, to use them sometimes to help and sometimes to harm.

Among North American Indians the medicine man who can cure a disease can also inflict it. A Papago Indian recalled a year in which 'we lynched a medicine-man. He had been killing people.' Similarly, modern witches and white magicians will usually admit their readiness to turn their powers against rival occultists who attack them.

For magicians themselves, magic is morally neutral. It works automatically, like a tap. If you turn the taps on in the bath, you get water. You may be filling the bath to wash the baby or to drown him, but your motives do not affect the water supply.

The most startling thing about the European *grimoires* or magical text books is their use of fervent and sincere prayers to God, asking his help in operations intended to kill people, to cause pain or to stir up hatred. One example from many is the long process in the *Grimoire of Honourius*, dating from the seventeenth century or earlier. It purports to have been written by a pope, and the magician who uses it should be a priest. It involves the slaughter of a lamb which is ritually identified with Christ as the Lamb of God, and it bristles with impassioned appeals to God and solemn sayings of Mass. But its purpose is to summon up the Devil.

The authors of the grimoires inherited an old magical tradition that the power of a god can be captured and 'turned on' like a tap, regardless of the magician's motives. They also inherited a deeper tradition still, that the true goal of the magician is to find and identify himself with an ultimate unity underlying and pervading all things. All things are grist to the magician's mill and all experiences are necessary to him. He must experience and master hatred as well as love, cruelty as well as mercy, evil as well as good. This is the path of the 'magus' and it is the magus perverted who makes the master black magician.

Black Mass

It is important to make a clear distinction between the Black Mass and the activities of witches as they were investigated by the Inquisition from the thirteenth century onward.

'Witchcraft', as it was identified, was in essence the survival of folk beliefs that were regarded as heretical by the Church, and was practiced largely in peasant communities. The Black Mass, on the other hand, was supported by members of the moneyed classes, who could afford to pay for its performance, who believed in the teachings of established religion—and who therefore believed in the existence of evil entities that could be suborned to work against the power of God.

Since 'witchcraft' retained many elements of pre-Christian religion, it became a widespread, loosely defined cult that might be practiced fairly regularly. But the Black Mass was seldom performed more than once or twice for any individual, and most of

The Temptation of St. Anthony, Hieronymus Bosch (c. 1450–1516)

its practitioners were at the same time members of the established Church.

However, each kind of practice, having been condemned as sacrilegious, gradually adopted aspects of the other's ritual—while the Church, and most particularly the Dominican inquisitors, who regarded all equally as heretics, attributed the same perversions to both.

The Obscene Goat

The hairy goat, for instance, is clearly a survival of the bucolic rites of Dionysus. It took the Church a long time to identify it with the Devil, but once this was done we soon find accounts of a giant goat squatting obscenely on the altar during the Black Mass, and this idea has passed into modern folklore. Conversely, the country witches were accused of the same dualist beliefs that lay behind the practice of the Black Mass.

The Black Masses said by the abbé Guibourg in the house of La Voisin have been reported in greater detail than any other, and indeed the ceremony seems to have been practiced more widely in France than in any other country. However, over the past six centuries, there have been many occasions on which the powers of evil have been deliberately invoked.

In 1303 the bishop of Coventry was accused before the Pope of doing homage to the Devil; and in 1324 Lady Alice Kyteler was accused in Ireland of ritual witchcraft, and 'in rifling the closet of the ladie, they found a Wafer of sacramentall bread, having the divels name stamped thereon in stead of Jesus Christ'.

The Mass of St. Secaire

J. F. Bladé, in his book *Contes de Gascogne*, gives details of the Mass of St. Secaire, which (it is said) was still performed occasionally in the Basque country within living memory. Intended to bring about the wasting and death of its victim, the mass is of a kind that was condemned by the council of Toledo as early as the ninth century.

The celebrant enters a disused church at 11 pm, so timing the ceremony that it ends on the stroke of midnight. His server should be a woman with whom he has copulated. Prayers are said backward, the Host is black and triangular, and the chalice contains water from a well in which an unbaptized child has been drowned.

A similar, but more horrific, mass was said to have been held by Catherine de Medicis in January 1574 in an attempt to save the life of her son Charles IX, King of France. The Host was black and white, and the chalice contained human blood. The blood was that of a young boy, whose head was cut off after he had taken communion of the white part of the Host, the black being retained for the subsequent ceremonies of the mass.

After the trial of La Voisin, and of the many corrupt priests associated with her, the Black Mass became little more than a rumour in France. Only late in the nineteenth century, fol-

The Black Ceremony

When the Paris chief of police, La Reynie, searched the premises of the abortionist La Voisin in 1679, he made a disquieting discovery. In a corner of the grounds, partly hidden by trees, stood a pavilion. Inside, its walls were hung with black, and at one end stood an altar, behind it a black curtain embroidered with a white cross. Black candles stood on the altar, which was covered with a black cloth; beneath the cloth was a mattress. La Voisin's daughter, Marguerite, eventually made a statement describing what occurred in a Black Mass held there in January 1678.

The woman at whose request the Black Mass was celebrated was Francoise Athenais de Mortemart, marquise de Montespan, one of king Louis XIV's mistresses. She believed that previous Black Masses had resulted in the defeat of her rival Louisa Frances de la Baume Le Blanc, duchesse de Vallière, and now she desperately needed to regain the affections of the king, who had fallen in love with Marie Angelique de Scoraille de Rousille.

Naked, she lay on the altar mattress, her legs spread wide, her head supported on a cushion and her arms outstretched. The priest, abbe Guibourg, and his clerk (a woman) were dressed in white vestments embroidered with black pinecones.

The priest approached the altar so that he stood between the marquise's legs, and laid the black cloth, the corporal, on her belly, placing a chalice upon it. Then he kissed her body, we may guess where, and commenced the ceremony, repeating the obscene kisses at moments throughout the mass.

Few details of the office are available, but the chalice and the Host were elevated in a parody of consecration, and then, we are told, 'the consecrated elements were subjected to manipulations of a very gross and obscene character'.

Finally a young child was sacrificed, and its blood mixed with the contents of the chalice, and the offering made with the words:

'Astaroth, Asmodeus, I beg you to accept the sacrifice of this child that we now offer to you, so that we may receive the things that we ask.'

It is possible, of course, that the child was obtained by abortion: La Voisin confessed to having consigned 2,000 bodies of unwanted children to the flames of her furnace. Among the women known to have visited her house were Anne-Marie Mancini, duchesse de Bouillon; Marie-Louise of Luxembourg, of whom it was said that she was 'as ugly as she was loose'; Marie-Louise Pot de Rhodes, duchesse de Duras; and Olympe Mancini, comtesse de Soissons, who was strongly suspected of having poisoned her husband, and was another of the king's mistresses.

It is not known whether these women also took part in the Black Mass, or whether they had attended La Voisin's house to obtain abortions, or potions and poisons for the fulfillment of their sexual desires.

lowing a revival of interest in occult matters that began in France but soon spread to most of the countries of the western world, did highly-fanciful accounts begin to appear.

The first to attract wide attention was the novel by H. K. Huysmans, *La-Bas* 'Down There' (1891), in which the hero, Durtal, attends a Black Mass in the Vaugirard district on the southwest side of Paris. It was later claimed that Huysmans had based his account upon his personal experiences.

However, the appearance the following year of an even more sensational work, *The Devil in the 19th Century*, which claimed to be factual, reinforces the suspicion that Huysmans's description was the product of a fevered imagination. This latter book was the work of 'Dr Bataille' a pseudonym for a former ship's doctor named Charles Hacks; he was inspired by an extraordinary character named Gabriel Jogand-Pagès, whose life's ambition was no less than the destruction of the Roman Catholic Church. Finally came Jules Bois's *Satanism and Magic* (1895), with its hysterical descriptions of Black Masses drawn largely from old witch hunters' accounts.

Crowley's Rituals

In England, the 'wickedest man in the world' Aleister Crowley developed his own esoteric cult. He was accused of performing the Black Mass, but his own writings show that the ceremonies which he performed—although they had a strong sexual content—had little or no connection with the Catholic mass, in no matter how perverted a form. To this day, there are those who claim to celebrate Black Masses; but, with the steadily declining belief in the corporeal existence of the powers of darkness, these are little more than obscene play-acting.

FURTHER READING: H. T. F. Rhodes. The Satanic Mass. *(Rider,*

Salem Witch on Her Broom. **Salem, Massachusetts (c. 1925)**

1954); Montague Summers. Geography of Witchcraft. *(Routledge & Kegan Paul, 1978).*

Broomstick

The humble broomstick has played an intriguing part in the social, sexual, and psychic life of mankind. In popular belief witches invariably fly through the air on broomsticks, though in fact the number of witches who confessed to doing so is remarkably small.

Brooms were originally made of a stalk of the broom plant with a bunch of leaves at the head. As an indoor, domestic implement, the broom became a symbol of woman. The equivalent symbol for man is the pitchfork, and in many medieval pictures of witches' gatherings the women hold brooms and the men or the devils hold pitchforks. In some parts of England until quite recently a woman would prop up a broom outside her door when she went out, or she might push the broom up the chimney with its end sticking out at the top, as a sign that she was out.

But perhaps originally her purpose was to guard her home by being symbolically present there in the form of the broom, for the seventeenth century Scottish witch Isabel Gowdie said that before leaving to go to the witches' sabbath, a woman would put her broom on the bed to deceive her husband. The witch would say, 'I lay down this besom in the Devil's name; let it not stir till I come again.'

In the Middle Ages it was believed that witches traveled on an infinite variety of flying objects, including animals, hobby horses, shovels, eggshells, bunches of straw, and wisps of grass, or without any visible means of support at all. A forked stick was a particularly popular witch-vehicle.

She Ambled and Galloped

A famous Irish witch of the early fourteenth century, Alice Kyteler, was said to own a staff 'on which she ambled and galloped through thick and thin, when and in what manner she listed, after having greased it with the ointment which was found in her possession.' There is no clear indication here of flying through the air, though the mention of the ointment suggests it. According to an anonymous tract from Savoy, *Errores Gazariorum,* written c. 1450, a stick anointed with flying ointment was presented to every witch on her initiation. The earliest known case of a witch confessing to flying on a broom was in 1453, when Guillaume Edelin of St. Germain-en-Laye, near Paris, stated that he had done so. A witch of Savoy, tried in 1477, said that the Devil gave her a stick 18 inches long and a jar of ointment. She would grease the stick and, putting it between her legs, say 'Go in the Devil's name, go!' and at once she was carried through the air to the sabbath.

One hundred years later, in 1563, Martin Tulouff of Guernsey said that he saw his aged mother straddle a broomstick and whisk up the chimney and out of the house on it, saying as she went, 'Go in the name of the Devil and Lucifer over rocks and thorns.' In 1598 Claudine Boban and her mother, witches of the province of Franche-Comte in eastern France, also spoke of flying up the chimney on a stick. The belief that witches usually left their houses by way of the chimney became firmly embedded in popular tradition, in spite of the rarity with which it appears in witches' own confessions: there may be some connection with the custom, mentioned earlier, of pushing a broom up the chimney to indicate the housewife's absence.

The lawyer and witch hunter Jean Bodin, in his *Démonomanie* of 1580, maintained that witches flew on either a broom or a black ram but that it was only the woman's spirit that flew through the air, while her body remained at home to perplex investigators. There is evidence that the 'flying' of witches was a dream or hallucinatory experience, and most witches said that they went to their meetings in the ordinary way, on foot or on horseback. It is also possible that the belief that witches flew on broomsticks was partly based on the fact that they danced with a stick between their legs, jumping high in the air. This may explain the curious statement of a Somerset woman named Julian Cox at her trial in 1664, that 'one evening she walked

out about a mile from her own house, and there came riding toward her three persons upon three broomsticks, born up about a yard and a half from the ground.' Two of the three persons she knew, the third 'came in the shape of a black man'.

Freedom of the Air

An effective form of defence against aerial witches was considered to be a peal of church bells. Stronger methods were sometimes used: in Slav countries people used to fire muskets at the clouds, screaming as they did so, 'Curse, curse Herodius, thy mother is a heathen damned of God', while others bestrewed the ground with scythes and billhooks, edge upward to ensure that there should be no soft landing for the witches.

Toward the end of the eighteenth century the whole question of the flying of witches was thrashed out in an English court of law. The judge, Lord Mansfield, delivered his famous judgment: that he knew of no law of England that prohibited flying and that, as far as he was concerned, anyone so inclined was perfectly free to do so. It remains a mystery, therefore, why from the moment of its sanction by British law, flying by British witches appears to have stopped almost immediately, except for isolated reports of East Anglian witches skimming church spires on flying hurdles throughout the next fifty years.

Broomstick Wedding

Once grounded, the broomstick survived only as one of the props in the Mummers' play, in the now extinct broomstick dance of the Fen country, and in the long discarded comic dance of the weird sisters in Macbeth. Its eclipse appears so complete that only 150 years ago Collin de Plancy wrote in his *Dictionary of Demonology:* 'The idiots who imagined that sorcerers and demons celebrated the Sabbath also

argued that witches traveled to the Sabbath on broomsticks. Nowadays everyone knows there are no sorcerers and no one rides on broomsticks.'

A rite which survived, however, in Wales and among gypsies, was the old custom of the broomstick wedding. The happy couple solemnized their union by leaping from the street into their new home over a broom placed in the doorway. This had to be done before witnesses and without dislodging the broom. At any time within a year the marriage could be dissolved by reversing the process, the couple jumping backward out of the house over the broom, again before witnesses and without touching the broom.

For a single girl to step over a broomstick, however, was a most unfortunate omen, for it meant that she would be a mother before she became a wife. Lighthearted wags used to delight in putting broomsticks in the paths of unsuspecting virgins. It was also very unlucky to make a broom in May, by long tradition an antifertility month and unsuitable for weddings, or during the Twelve Days of Christmas. It was disastrous to sweep dust out of the front door, which meant dispersing all the luck of the house. On the other hand, in India, a sweeper's broom is still often tied to the mast of a ship, as a charm to 'sweep' storms away. In recent years the witch's broomstick has regained significance with the revival of witchcraft itself. The ritual importance of 'wand, riding-pole, or broom stick' is stressed in the manuals of the modern witch covens. Man, it seems, finds it impossible to escape from the dreams of his childhood, perhaps influenced by the nursery rhyme of the

Witch on a broomstick

old woman who ascended in a basket to brush the cobwebs from the clouds with her broom. But it is still surprising that an object specifically designed for sweeping the floor should also be in fantasy a vehicle on which to swoop through the skies.

FURTHER READING: M. A. Murray. The Witch-Cult in Western Europe. (Oxford University Press, rep. 1967); Charles A. Hoyt. Witchcraft. (Southern Illinois University Press, 1981); M. Summers. History of Witchcraft and Demonology. (London: Routledge & Kegan Paul, rep. 1973).

Caroline Code

Based on the German Bambergensis of 1507, the *Constitutio Criminalis Carolina*, or the Caroline Code, the law code of the Holy Roman Empire, was ratified under Charles V in 1532.

The Carolina code established that burning at the stake was the proper punishment for witches as well as for blasphemers, heretics, sodomites, arsonists, counterfeiters, poisoners, and other perpetrators of what were considered heinous crimes.

Although the code was meant to unify all the states that were part of the Roman Empire, it was interpreted and administered locally, so there was some variance in how punishment for crimes was meted out. Germany was particularly cruel in its punishment of accused witches and in the very number of such punishments, with thousands being put to death after they were tortured until they confessed.

Interestingly, when Christianity was first imposed upon the people of Saxony in the eighth century, Charlemagne decreed that anyone who believed in witchcraft and burned an accused witch should be executed. The pagan belief in witchcraft was forbid-

den by the Church in the Early Middle Ages, so that the belief was the crime, not witchcraft itself. By 1300, the tide had begun to change and by the time of the Carolina Code, the Church had come full circle and was now itself promoting the burning of witches.

FURTHER READING: Julius R. Ruff. Violence in Early Modern Europe 1500–1800 (New Approaches to European History). (Cambridge University Press, 2001); Ronald Hutton. The Pagan Religions of the Ancient British Isles: Their Nature and Legacy. (Oxford: Wiley-Blackwell, 1993).

Marie-Josephte Corriveau

The facts of the life of Marie-Josephte Corriveau are short and dismal. She was a young widow with three children in the Canadian province of Quebec when she married Louis Etienne Dodier in 1761. Two years later, he was murdered and Marie and her father were accused of the crime. Her father received the death sentence, but then accused his daughter of acting alone. Another trial was held and she was found guilty and hanged.

Her corpse was placed on display in an iron cage, or gibbet, referred to as 'hanging in chains,' which was a British form of degradation reserved for traitors and others of especially ill repute.

For the next 200 years, her life and untimely death were memorialized to suit the fashion of the time. In oral tradition, La Corriveau was rumoured to have been a witch who poisoned seven husbands.

Later her story was amended to portray her as an example of English oppression in Quebec, and emphasis was placed on the fact that she could not read, did not understand English, and was a victim of spousal abuse. She confessed to murdering her husband in his bed with a hatchet after her father turned state's evidence against her (likely because he feared the gallows himself and thought the court would be more lenient in judging a woman).

In *The Golden Dog*, a novel of Quebec by William Kirby, La Corriveau is portrayed as a witch, a wise woman, the daughter and granddaughter of witches from France; in the novel, unlike her real life, she lives to be an old woman and is both feared and hated by all.

Finally, in the play La Cage by Anne Hebert, Marie-Josephte is portrayed as an example of what she was in the beginning, a victim of abuse rather than a symbol of British cruelty or a powerful witch.

Illustration showing a witch offering a young woman a charm.

Coven

A word that has now come to mean exclusively a group of witches, 'coven' is derived from the same root as 'convent', and originally had an equivalent meaning. As early as AD 1290 we read of a preaching friar, who 'hadde a covent of freres . . . his twelve freres before him comen . . .' and Chaucer used the same word in *The Canterbury Tales* to mean a group of thirteen people.

Ecclesiastical Memorials (1536) speaks of religious houses 'whereof the number in any one house is or of late hath been less than a covent, that is to say under thirteen persons'; and an early fourteenth-century poem, *Handlyng Synne*, describes a 'coveyne' of thirteen people who danced in the churchyard while the priest was saying Mass, and were duly punished.

In Scotland the word coven came to mean a group of friends, and in fact the word was not recorded as being applied to an assembly of witches until 1662, when the Scottish witch Isobel Gowdie confessed to meeting with twelve others, with the words (as they are spelt in the report of her trial): 'Ther is threttein persones in ilk [each] Coeven'.

There is an obvious line of development from the group composed of Christ and his twelve apostles, through the establishment of religious communities in direct imitation, to the secular use of the term in description of a number (not necessarily thirteen) of like-minded individuals. From at least Roman times thirteen has been a sinister number, and Isobel Gowdie's confession excited the popular imagination.

However, it was not until the twentieth century that thirteen as the number of witches in a coven was finally established firmly in common belief by the anthropologist Dr.

Margaret Murray in two books: *The Witch-Cult in Western Europe* (1921) and *The God of the Witches* (1931). Following the publication of the first of these, her figures were challenged by Alex Keiller, who 'after detailed study of Miss Murray's lists of Scottish and Irish witches designed to evidence the prevalence of covens of thirteen, found in a number of instances the arrangement to be unfounded and the count to be of no value'.

In her second book, Dr. Murray returned to the attack, reproducing, among other illustrations, an old woodcut from a broadsheet ballad. It shows a horned and ithyphallic Robin Goodfellow, the folk survival of the pagan earth god, in the centre of a ring of dancing men and women; there are eleven figures in the ring, outside sits a twelfth, providing music on a pipe.

Dedicated research uncovered other examples. In the trial of Dame Alice Kyteler for witchcraft in Kilkenny, Ireland, in 1324, the names of the accused totalled twelve; the thirteenth

was one Robin Artisson, who escaped. Joseph Glanvil, in his *Sadducismus Triumphatus* (1681), describes two assemblies of witches who were tried in Somerset—one at Wincanton and the other at Brewham; each assembly numbered thirteen.

There is, however, no evidence of the survival of witches' covens—of whatever number—through the eighteenth and nineteenth centuries. The concept of modern witchcraft as an alternative religious practice is due almost entirely to the Englishman Gerald Gardner, who retired from his career in Malaya in 1936, soon after the publication of *The God of the Witches*, and took up the study and practice of the subject. In 1951, the last of the Witchcraft Acts was repealed in Britain, and Gardner's *Witchcraft Today*, with an introduction by Margaret Murray, was published in 1954.

So it is to Gardner, as much as anybody, that we owe the present formalization of the coven. Gardner's rituals incorporated elements taken

Witches' Sabbath (The Great He-Goat), Francisco de Goya (1746–1828)

from Charles Leland's study of Italian sorcery, *Aradia, or the Gospel of the Witches* (1899); from Masonic initiation ceremonies; and from the writings of Aleister Crowley. They cannot be regarded as traditional in any way.

One of Gardner's disciples, Doreen Valiente, has written:

> *The coven of thirteen is the best-known of the witches' cult groups; but there is also a lesser-known coven of eight. This consists of more experienced initiates than the coven of thirteen. In fact, the latter might be called the fertility coven, invoking and worshipping the powers of life and luck in a general way; whereas the coven of eight is the magical coven, which concentrates on deeper things . . .*

Gardner, on the basis of his reading of *Aradia* and his own interest in nudism, was responsible for the doctrine that covens perform their rituals naked. There is no evidence that western European medieval witches were ever other than fully clothed.

FURTHER READING: Margaret Murray. The Witch Cult in Western Europe. *(Oxford University Press, 1921);* The God of the Witches. *(Sampson Low, 1931); Gerald Gardner.* Witchcraft Today. *(Rider, 1954); R. E. Guiley.* Encyclopedia of Witches and Witchcraft. *(Facts on File, 1989).*

Aleister Crowley

Poet, novelist, writer of books on magic, eccentric—Crowley (1875–1947) was all this and more. He strove hard to assume the mantle of magician, and long before he died he knew that he had succeeded. He is thus in direct line of descent from Sir Edward Kelley, Cagliostro, the Comte de Saint-Germain, Eliphas Levi, and Madame Blavatsky, all of whom were credited with remarkable, if not miraculous powers. Crowley's father was a successful brewer, the manufacturer of Crowley's Ales, but whose main interest by the time Aleister was born was that of traveling about the English countryside preaching the doctrines of the Plymouth Brethren and trying to gain converts to his sectarian views. The first important fact, therefore, about Aleister Crowley is that he was brought up amid the mysteries of the Christian religion; at the age of eleven, however, when his father died, he grew to detest the faith in which he had been brought up and, without knowing why, went over to the side of Satan. While still a Christian and subjected to daily Bible readings in the Crowley household, he had taken a fancy to the 'False Prophet', 'the Beast whose number is 666', and the 'Scarlet Woman', characters or archetypes

Making Do as They Can

I think that I must make it clear that, as far as my experience goes, while the coven should traditionally have six couples and a leader in the circle, nowadays it may often have less. At a meeting, if there were more than thirteen initiated people present they would sit outside with any uninitiated and watch the religious rite. If for certain reasons they were required in the circle, others would step outside to make room, and those without would then be purified and taken inside. When the rites were finished and the circle closed, all took part in the dance and feast. If there were, say, twenty initiated and enough room, they would probably form two covens, each in their own circle, with one leader or timekeeper. If there were still more, they would form three circles. Nowadays, no unititiated persons are ever present and the ceremonies are usually indoors, where there is seldom room for more than one circle. Also, though the witch ideal is to form perfect couples of people ideally suited to each other and so in perfect sympathy, and to cause people to be suited to each other, nowadays this is not always possible; the right couples go together, the others go singly and make do as they can.

Gerald Gardner, *Witchcraft Today*

Few people in living memory compare to English writer and occultist Aleister Crowley (1875–1947) as a practitioner of the dark occult.

which were to play a prominent and decisive part in his later life.

Educated at Malvern and Tonbridge schools, and later at Trinity College, Cambridge, as a young man Crowley began to write verses after the manner of Swinburne. His real seat of learning, however, which suited his peculiar talents, was the magical society known as the Hermetic Order of the Golden Dawn, the leading light of which was a man of considerable magical potential, Samuel Liddell Mathers, known as MacGregor Mathers.

The Secret Chiefs

The Golden Dawn, which had about 100 members, spread among several lodges, taught the use of magical weapons, how to consecrate talismans, set up magic circles, travel astrally and so on. It also gave instruction in the use of that ground plan of Western magic, the Cabala. In a word, it taught and practiced ceremonial magic as opposed to magic which used other aids such as drugs or sex.

Although one member at that time, 1900, described the Golden Dawn

to the present writer as 'a kind of club, like any other club', it was quite unlike any other club in one respect: its constitution was not derived from its governing body but from superior beings or intelligences called (following Madame Blavatsky) Secret Chiefs. Mathers, it was said, had met the Secret Chiefs one night in the Bois de Boulogne in Paris. Crowley joined the Golden Dawn in 1898. Accepting all the vows and obligations, he took the magical title of Perdurabo (I will endure to the end).

At this time, Crowley was living in a flat in London's Chancery Lane and describing himself as Count Svareff, a Russian nobleman. Under this and other names, he published at his own expense several books of verse and, anonymously, a work of pornography entitled *White Stains* (1898).

Mathers was also a scholar, and translated and edited three important works: *The Kabbalah Unveiled*, *The Key of Solomon*, and *The Book of the Sacred Magic of Abra-Melin the Mage*, 'as delivered by Abraham the Jew unto his son Lamech, AD 1458'. *Abra-Melin* inflamed Crowley's spirit; he described the book as one which is in marked contrast with all the puerile nonsense written on the subject. The technique of this magic has something in common with yoga; a secluded spot and a long period of purification are necessary before one's Holy Guardian Angel or Higher Intelligence can be invoked. Crowley searched the Lake District and Scotland and found what he wanted in Boleskine House, near the village of Foyers, in Inverness. He dropped the title of Count Svareff, assumed that of Lord Boleskine, constructed his oratory and began the operation. But instead of his Holy Guardian Angel appearing, he merely attracted a host of evil spirits.

He quarreled with Mathers and was expelled from the Golden Dawn.

Crowley retaliated by denying that Mathers had met the Secret Chiefs in the Bois de Boulogne and been confirmed by them as Head of the Order. Mathers, he said, had only bumped into some evil demons. He continued to pour out a torrent of verse and to climb mountains, in Mexico and in the Himalayas. He acquired a wife, Rose, and wrote for her the pornographic *Snowdrops from a Curate's Garden.* His greatest need was to make his own link with the Secret Chiefs or Mahatmas; without such a link he was a negligible force.

This uncertain state of affairs did not last long. Toward the end of 1903, when Crowley was twenty-eight, he went with his wife on a trip to Ceylon. In the new year, he decided to return home, and on the way back stopped for a while in Cairo. Wearing a turban with a diamond aigrette, a silken robe, and a coat of cloth of gold, he gave out that he was Prince Chioa Khan. He was driven with Princess Khan (formerly Rose Kelly, the daughter of the Vicar of Camberwell) about the Cairo streets, with 'two gorgeous runners to clear the way for my carriage'. Despite his style of living, Crowley was undecided about his future and growing short of money. Then an event occurred which put at last some magical ground under his feet. This was 'the Great Revelation in Cairo'. The old world of Christianity came to an end for Crowley and a new world, of which he was prophet, was born.

Aiwass, also spelt *Aiwaz,* the name of his Holy Guardian Angel whom he had tried with only partial success to invoke at Boleskine House, appeared to him in his Cairo flat and commanded him to take down a message for mankind. After an hour's dictation, Aiwass disappeared, but he was back again the following day at the same time, noon. Aiwass described himself as the minister of Hoor-Paar-Kraat

(the Graeco-Egyptian god Harpakrad or Harpokrates), that is 'a messenger from the forces ruling this earth at present'. Aiwass came on three occasions and each time dictated a chapter of *The Book of the Law,* as the work is called. In other words, a new era, or rather aeon, in the world's history had begun, one which will last for 2,000 years. The heart of Crowley's magic is derived from this work; it is the text behind his magic and his philosophy which he summed up in the phrase 'Do what thou wilt shall be the whole of the Law.'

Cultist Aleister Crowley

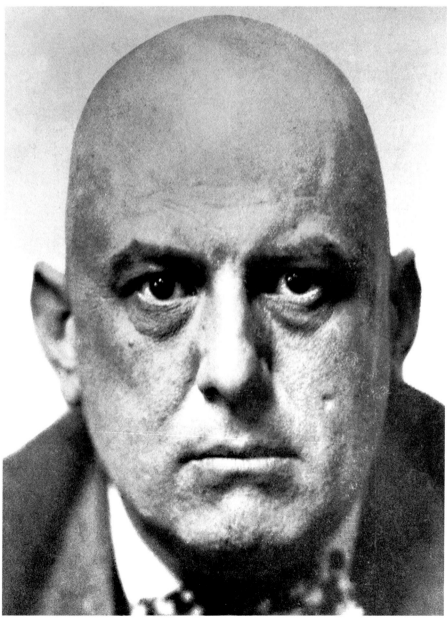

The Number of the Beast

Just before Aiwass appeared in Crowley's Cairo flat, a curious incident occurred in the Boulak Museum (now the National Museum). Rose had been in a strange, dazed state of mind and in this condition she had been mumbling something about Horus. 'Who is Horus?' asked Crowley, who was not aware that his wife knew anything about Egyptian religion. 'There', said Rose, pointing, 'there he is'. She was indicating an ancient Egyptian stele on which was painted Horus in the form of the hawk-headed Ra-Hoor-Khuit (Ra-Hara-khte). Crowley went forward, then fell back in amazement. The exhibit bore the number 666, the number of the Beast, his number!

Many years later, in 1946, I asked Crowley, 'Why do you call yourself the Beast?'

'My mother called me the Beast,' he replied briefly, presumably not wishing to go into the deeper aspects of the subject. Crowley's mother was a pious woman and the behaviour of her son reminded her of the Beast of the book of Revelation that came out of the depths of the sea, with horns on his head, blaspheming God.

The cosmology of *The Book of the Law* is explained by Crowley thus: there have been as far as we know, two aeons in the history of the world. The first, the aeon of Isis, was the age of the domination of the woman, of matriarchy. The choice of Egyptian names for these aeons is purely arbitrary and does not imply that they are confined to Egypt. The second aeon, that of Osiris, was the aeon of the man, the father; it coincides with the Christian period, also with that of Judaism, Buddhism, Mohammedanism. It was superseded in 1904 by the aeon of Horus, the child. He explained that the emphasis for this present period, that of Horus, is on the will (*thelema*) or true self in man as opposed to external authority, priests and gods. 'Be strong, o man! lust, enjoy all things of sense and rapture: fear not that any God shall deny thee for this.'

The Silver Star

On his return to Europe in the spring of 1904, Crowley wrote to Mathers informing him that the Secret Chiefs had appointed him the head of the Order and declared a new magical formula—thelema. 'I did not expect or receive an answer,' said Crowley, 'and I declared war on Mathers accordingly.'

The following year Crowley led a disastrous climbing expedition to Kanchenjunga and added to his evil reputation by deserting his comrades on the mountain. In 1910, he published the curious and obscene *Bagh-I-Muattar* or 'The Scented Garden of Abdullah the Satirist of Shiraz'. This was a volume of homosexual love poems, from medieval Persia.

But all this was marginal activity; his work was to spread the good tidings. A new world had been born and a new aeon had arisen. To this end, he founded his own magical association, the A. A. (*Argenteum Astrum*, the Silver Star) which constituted the Inner Order of the Great White Brotherhood; the Outer Order was the Golden Dawn. And he brought out his own publicity organ, *The Equinox*. This was issued for several years at the rate of two bulky volumes

A cohort of English writer and occultist Aleister Crowley, wearing the mark of the beast (19 November, 1955)

a year. Its articles and reviews were mainly written by Crowley under a variety of names. The series titled 'The Temple of Solomon the King' contains details of Perdurabo's ascent in the Great White Brotherhood. Number 7 contains *The Book of the Law* with his first brief comment; he thought it time to give it out to the world, but it caused no stir whatsoever. Between whiles he went off on any magical adventure which offered itself, during which he probed the gods for further guidance.

One night during 1912 Crowley received an unexpected visit at his flat in Victoria Street, London, from Theodor Reuss, a high ranking German Freemason. They were strangers to each other and Reuss had apparently come over from Germany for the express purpose of meeting Crowley. Without beating about the bush, he accused Crowley of giving away magical secrets. Reuss wore a handle-bar moustache and pince-nez; he was alleged to be a member of the German Secret Service. Crowley denied the accusation. Reuss replied by going to the bookshelf and taking out Crowley's *Liber CCCXXXIII: the Book of Lies*. He opened it at the page which begins, 'Let the Adept be armed with his Magical Rood and provided with his Mystic Rose,' and showed it to Crowley.

The secret that Crowley had been giving out to all the world was that sex can be used ritually or magically; but as he had been expressing it in veiled language, as in this extract, Reuss's point is difficult to see. The previous head of the order to which Reuss belonged, a wealthy German ironmaster called Karl Kellner, had learned this so-called secret from Tantric yogins in India during the last decade of the nineteenth century. He had been introduced to the ritual of *maithuna* (sexual union), in which the mind, the breath, and the semen are held

British writer and 'magician' Aleister Crowley, whose interest in the occult and suggestions of involvement in human sacrifice led to his expulsion from Italy

still. And on his return to Germany, he had expounded the delicate subject to his fellow Freemasons, among whom was Franz Hartmann, one of the companions of Madame Blavatsky, and proposed that they should start a new magical society to embody these sex and yoga teachings. Thus in 1902 the *Ordo Templi Orientis*, or Order of the Templars of the East, was founded. It claimed that it could communicate in nine degrees the secrets not only of Freemasonry but of the Rosicrucians, the Illuminati, the Order of the Hidden Church of the Holy Graal, the

Knights of the Holy Ghost, and those of St. John, of Malta, and of the Holy Sepulchre—in fact, of every mystic order that they could think of. 'Our Order possesses the KEY which opens up all Masonic and Hermetic secrets, namely, the teaching of sexual magic, and this teaching explains, without exception, all the secrets of Nature, all the symbolism of freemasonry and all systems of religion.

'Be strong, O man! lust, enjoy all things of sense and rapture: fear not that any God shall deny thee for this.'

In 1904 Crowley proclaimed the advent of a new era in which the emphasis would be on man's true inner self, as opposed to the external authority of gods and priests.

Sexual Magic

Crowley and Reuss talked long into the night. 'Since you know our hidden sex teachings,' said Brother Merlin (Herr Reuss's magical name), 'you'd better come into our Order and be its Head for Great Britain.' Crowley, who never declined a dinner, an adventure, or a title, readily agreed. After a journey to Berlin, he was transformed with due ceremony into 'the Supreme and Holy King of Ireland, Iona, and all the Britains that are in the Sanctuary of the Gnosis.' And with that keenness and audacity of mind which sees and seizes the main point, he gave himself the magical name in this secret society of Baphomet; this was the name of the idol which the original poor Knights of the Temple were accused of worshipping.

One could not join the Order and start attempting to perform maithuna. The aspirant had to work his way diligently up to the IX°. One more degree was added by Crowley, the XI°, that of homosexual workings (or IX° inverted). In Paris during 1914 he worked this XI° O. T. O. with his pupil Victor Neuburg on twenty-four different occasions, the whole being known as The Paris Working. The X° was of an honourary character to distinguish the 'Supreme and Holy King' of the Order in each country where the Order was established.

The *Ordo Templi Orientis* claimed that the teachings of the Knights Templars (whose Order was disbanded amid a great scandal at the beginning of the fourteenth century) were known and continued by them, but this is wishful thinking. And the prostitutes whom Crowley frequently took as partners in his practice of sexual magic, apart from their not being trained in this form of worship, were completely ignorant of what he had in mind. His descriptions in *The Magical Record of the Beast* of these activities are quite out of keeping with the tone and

> Whoever penetrates into the inner city will find there Perdurabo, the false god, choking with guilt from having set himself up in God's place.

elaborations of maithuna.

At the outbreak of the First World War, Crowley transferred his activities to the United States. The one important magical event which happened to him at this time, apart from his meeting with Leah Hirsig, the Scarlet Woman—who outdid all other Scarlet Women in the Beast's life—was his assumption during 1916 of the Grade of Magus.

Since 1909, he had been a Master of the Temple, an exalted grade which enabled him to join the Secret Sanctuary of the Saints or the abode of the Secret Chiefs; now he went one higher. These upper stages in his career were implied in the Great Revelation in Cairo, that is to say in his being the vehicle of *The Book of the Law*. At last, he was ready to assume the throne and proclaim his word, *thelema* or 'do what thou wilt,' which ushers in the new aeon of liberty, as opposed to the old aeon of suffering (Christianity and other slave religions).

The words of the ceremony which he performed, and during which he crucified a frog, make this clear.

'Night being fallen, thou shalt arrest the frog, and accuse him of blasphemy,

sedition and so forth, in these words: Do what thou wilt shall be the whole of the Law. Lo, Jesus of Nazareth, how thou art taken in my snare. All my life long thou hast plagued me and affronted me. In thy name—with all other free souls in Christendom—I have been tortured in my boyhood; all delights have been forbidden unto me; all that I had has been taken from me, and that which is owed to me they pay not—in thy name. Now at last I have thee; the Slave-God is in the power of the Lord of Freedom. Thine hour is come; as I blot thee out from this earth, so surely shall the eclipse pass; and Light, Life, Love and Liberty be once more the law of Earth. Give thou place to me, O Jesus; thine aeon is passed; the Age of Horus is arisen by the Magick of the Master the Great Beast.' And so on and so forth.

Do What Thou Wilt

With the end of the war, Crowley returned to England; he did not stay in England for long but departed with small means and two mistresses, one of whom was his Scarlet Woman, Leah Hirsig, for Sicily. At Cefalu, he rented a villa, consecrated a temple to the New Aeon in one of the rooms, and painted on the front door the words DO WHAT THOU WILT. This was his famous 'abbey', his *Collegium ad Spiritum Sanctum*; here, during three years, he had time to add copious details to his diary, to paint pictures which reveal his remorseless vision, and to try to fuse together the bits and pieces of his life. His aim at Cefalu was to create a world centre for the study of occultism, but few availed themselves of the opportunity of going there. Furthermore, the Beast's increasing dependence on heroin undermined his driving-force and the discipline of the abbey. However, during this period, he was revived by a commission from Collins, the publisher, to produce a novel about the drug traffic and to write his confessions; he set to work with unexpected vigour. The good produces the bad: *The Diary of a Drug Fiend*, 1922, was the initial cause of his expulsion from his abbey following the review of the novel, and a general attack on Crowley and his creed in a Sunday paper.

But Crowley had uttered his word, *thelema*, and done his work; it remained only for him, the Logos (word) of the New Aeon, to publish some more magical writings and attend to the affairs of the Order. The turn of the wheel of fortune produced new followers in Germany, and the Mandrake Press which brought out during 1929 two of the projected six volumes of his Confessions which Collins had dropped. He also published about this time his magnum opus, *Magick in Theory and Practice*.

Crowley, who behaved as if the world was only an exhalation of his own being, wound the vast subject of magic round himself and the petty incidents of his life, with the result that *Magick* is a city within a city. Whoever penetrates into the inner city will find there Perdurabo, the false god, choking with guilt from having set himself up in God's place.

JOHN SYMONDS

FURTHER READING: J. Symonds and K. Grant ed. The Confessions of Aleister Crowley. *(Hill & Wang, 1970); J. Symonds.* The Great Beast. *(Roy Publishers, 1952); K. Grant.* Aleister Crowley and the Hidden God. *(Weiser, 1974).*

Aleister Crowley in the later years of his life.

Martin Antoine Del Rio

Martin Antoine Del Rio (1551–1608), born in Antwerp, was a Jesuit theologian, lawyer, historian, and careful scholar. He was known as 'the miracle of his age,' spoke nine languages, received the degree of Doctor of Law, and served as senator, auditor of the Army, and other public service offices before becoming a Jesuit in 1580.

His most famous work, published in three volumes in 1599 and 1600, was called *Disquisitionum magicarum libri sex,* or *Investigations Into Magic*, and it was the most academic treatise on the subject of magic since the publication of *Malleus Maleficarum* in 1487. He was also the author of treatises on civil law and theology, but it is his work on magic for which he is remembered.

Del Rio's work covered all aspects of the occult, including alchemy, witchcraft, and possession, as well as conjuring tricks and illusion. His work was used as a guidebook for judges and is said to have been influential in the Salem Witch Trials in Massachusetts.

Doruchów Witch Trial

The Doruchów witch trials may have been the last mass execution of witches in Europe, and may have led to new laws being passed in 1783 making witch trials illegal. Or it may not have happened that way at all.

The original story is that fourteen women in the city of Doruchów were tried, found guilty, and burned at the stake for the crime of witchcraft after the wife of a leading citizen became ill for no discernible (at that time) reason. The women were accused of making her ill through the practice of witchcraft, and eventually they were executed; their executions led to laws in Poland that made the execution of witches illegal. That is the original version of the story, but it has been refuted in recent years.

It is a matter of historical record that laws were passed in Poland in 1776 banning torture and the burning of witches. If the Doruchów trials took place in 1775, they may have been a catalyst for the new law. Whether they took place before or after the law was passed is a matter of some dispute.

Later historians have determined that there is evidence supporting a trial in Doruchów in 1783 in which six alleged witches were sentenced, but there is no proof that they were actually executed. Furthermore, if this account is true, the Doruchów witch trials could not have been responsible for the change in Polish law that took place in 1776.

The original account (of fourteen witches executed in 1775) was written by Konstanty Majeranowski, a Polish journalist and poet, many of whose historical accounts were later proved to be hoaxes.

East Anglian & Essex Witches

The traveler through the eastern counties of England and particularly East Anglia will observe on village greens and in market places certain monuments dedicated to the victims of religious persecutions during the reign of Mary I in the first half of the sixteenth century, in which no less than 277 Protestants were burned by the Romanists. After Elizabeth I had succeeded to the throne an implacable hatred for all things popish exploded into a violent demand for radical reform. A primary objective of the Reformers was the elimination of the practitioners of magic and sorcery who had been permitted to function almost unchecked by the Church of Rome, and it was no accident therefore that Essex, heartland of dissent, should have become foremost in the demand for a house-cleaning involving every aspect of superstitious usage. At the same time the voices of the returned Marian exiles from the Continent, where witches were being persecuted in many countries, added still further to the clamor for action against the alleged sorcerers.

In a sermon delivered by Bishop Jewel before Elizabeth in 1560, he stressed the need for legal action against the magicians. 'Witches,' he declared, 'had marvelously increased within your Grace's realm,' and he went on to demand that 'the laws touching such malefactors be put in due execution'. At that time there were laws upon the statute book prohibiting witchcraft, for the first abortive Witchcraft Act of 1542 had been repealed in the reign of Edward VI, while a subsequent attempt to introduce legislation had failed in the reign of Mary. The year 1563 witnessed the Convocation of the Church of England urging stronger penalties upon the practitioners of witchcraft and in that same year the Elizabethan Witchcraft Act passed into law. This imposed the penalty of death for murder by sorcery, and the pillory and imprisonment for witchcraft of a less lethal character.

The first person known to have been executed in England after the new Act had come into force was sixty-three-year-old Agnes Waterhouse of Hatfield Peverel in Essex; she was hanged at Chelmsford in 1566 for the alleged crime of bewitching William Fynee to death. Her principal aid and accomplice was her familiar, a cat named Sathan. It is significant that no less a personage than Sir Gilbert Gerard, the Attorney General, participated in the trial of the accused. The first of the victims, like so many who were to follow her to the gallows, was of peasant stock. The English rich, unlike their Continental counterparts, were secured by their wealth from the wild accusations of witch-hating fanatics, for they retained the power as well as the legal right to sue any detractor for defamation of character. In Sir George Croke's *Reports of Select Cases* at law during the Elizabethan period (published in 1661), there occurs the significant instance of Fortescue v. Hext in 1593, in which the court held it to be 'very heinous and actionable' for a woman to say of a man 'He is a witch and bewitched my husband to death for he made his picture in wax and roasted it every day by the fire until he roasted my husband to death'.

So much for the Witchcraft Act as it affected the well-to-do, and it was no doubt due to this and other circumstances such as the absence of both Inquisition and official torture, that English witchcraft preserved its traditionally peasant characteristics throughout the whole period of the persecutions. The victims were mainly

Opposite page:
Close-up of East Wretham village sign in Norfolk, England

confined to the social outcast or the village scapegoat. The offenses with which they were charged were mostly acts of simple *maleficia*—baleful acts attributed to the vindictiveness of witches—without any signs of the elaborate sabbaths conjured up by the Inquisitors of France and Germany.

It was the misfortune of the county of Essex to remain the scene of continuing persecutions during the whole of this period, the major sixteenth century trials occurring in 1566, 1579, 1582, and 1589. The notorious trial of the witches of St. Osyth, near Bright-lingsea, was held in 1582; fourteen women were charged with various acts of witchcraft, including murder, upon the evidence of children of six to nine years of age. The tragedy began as a village quarrel with the exchange of such insults as 'old trot' and 'old whore' and the bewitching of cows and geese. It was the St. Osyth trial which in all probability impelled Reginald Scot to publish his famous *Discoverie of Witchcraft* (1584) in which the manifest absurdities involved in the witch hunts were exposed to the acid test of ridicule. Even the most casual survey of the evidence provided by the old court records reveals that the outbreak of the witch mania in East Anglia bore all the characteristics of mass hysteria, with the whole folklore of witchcraft being hurled at the heads of the accused along with the 'evidence' based upon hearsay, and with the testimony of young children being freely accepted by the courts.

At the very heart of this conspiracy, it appears, were the village soothsayers, known as Cunning Men and Cunning Women. They were in fact witch doctors and had no hesitation whatsoever in denouncing unpopular individuals as witches. This had been their role from time immemorial when the punishment had been limited to ecclesiastical penances or the ritual drawing of the witch's blood to neutralize the spell. Now, however, with the state as official witch hunter, their influence in village life spelt misery and death to every suspect.

Although practitioners of magic themselves, the Cunning People only rarely fell foul of the authorities. They were universally respected, for they represented to the peasant mind the antiwitch principle and were therefore regarded as an integral part of the grand alliance of Church and State against black witchcraft. George Gifford, an Elizabethan clergyman of Maiden in Essex, left a contemporary account of their sinister role in Eliza-bethan times. Gifford, who regarded Cunning People as agents of the Devil and deluders of the people, observed: 'When the people fear a witch there is much running to the wizards to learn what to do. The Devil teaches these Cunning Men many horrible abominations and foul abuses of the name of God by which they are made believe that they are cured from their harms.' Gifford thus testified to the malevolent power of the practitioners of white witchcraft who were to his mind as guilty of witchcraft as those they so readily denounced, a fact that very few of those in authority were prepared to admit at the time.

An illustration showing Anne Baker of Bottesford, Joan Willimot of Goodby, and Ellen Greene of Stathern. All three women were taken for examination and revealed that they had visions and consorted with familiar spirits. They were accused of being involved with the witches of Belvoir. The witch trials took place between 1618 and 1619.

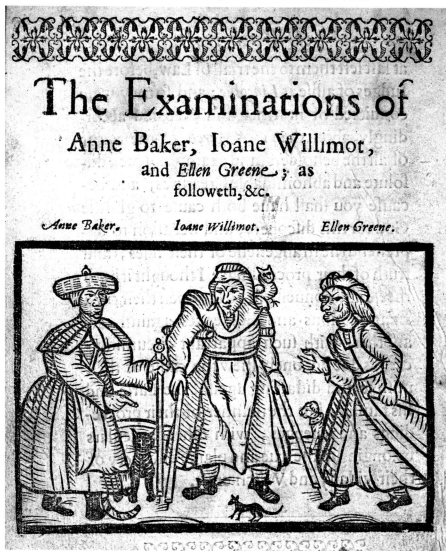

It was Gifford's contention that many of the rituals then employed to combat witchcraft were in reality forms of pagan sacrifice, particularly the burning alive of farm animals. He went on to point out that these village witch doctors were responsible for the arrest of perfectly respectable individuals: 'Within these last few years,' he said, 'the devil has by Cunning Men accused the very religious and godly of having secret marks upon them.'

How to Tell a Witch

The witch fever raged throughout Essex and East Anglia, overflowing into the adjacent counties. In Norfolk, ever-growing numbers found themselves dragged before the magistrates to be executed or confined in prison or the pillory until they were ready to confess their guilt. Suffolk also suffered its spate of denunciations, arrests, and hangings.

The death of Elizabeth and the accession of King James I, a witch-fearing fanatic, had little influence upon the general trend of the witch mania in the eastern counties, for wherever the extreme Protestants maintained their militancy witch hunting was likely to break out at any time and spread like a forest fire. In Catholic areas, needless to say, the magistrates were far less zealous in rooting out evidence of pagan practices and there the witch hunters were far less certain of their prey.

Handbooks for magistrates, as for example Michael Dalton's *Country Justice* (1618) and Richard Bernard's *Guide to Grand Jurymen* (1627), insisted that the primary evidence of witchcraft was the possession of an animal familiar. Bona fide physicians, as fallible as their unofficial allies, the Cunning People, were generally prepared to diagnose many of the illnesses that they were unable to cure as caused by witchcraft. At the same time the Puritan clergy sought everywhere for the least sign of any religious deviation that could be classed as a 'superstitious practice'.

Tainted Blood

The most primitive types of magic beliefs prevailed among the peasant

The prisoner was searched for witch's marks and tormented by being denied sleep, an apparently legitimate form of toture.

population, all of whom claimed to be staunch Christians. In 1624 John Crushe was presented to the Essex Archdeacon's Court accused of burning a bewitched lamb alive on Hawkwell Common in order to break the spell of witchcraft from which his flock were suffering. It was during this century that the people of East Anglia began to protect themselves against the malice of witches by the use of witch bottles, receptacles containing urine, and horseshoe nails which were heated on the fire as a form of counter-magic and which were probably introduced from the Low Countries. Good urine it appears was absolutely essential; bad urine (that of a witch) causing the bottle to blow the cork.

East Anglia underwent its second and infinitely more severe witch hunt in 1645, led by the self-styled Witchfinder General Matthew Hopkins, a lawyer who had become interested in witchcraft. It was in Manningtree, near the Suffolk border of Essex, that the persecution was revived with considerable intensity. Conditions were ripe, for with the Civil War still raging and its outcome far from certain the Puritan eastern counties had been reduced to a state of tension which only the punishment of a scapegoat could relieve. The population was, if anything, even more fanatically Protestant and therefore witch-fearing than in the times of the Elizabethan witch hunts and there existed in addition a further factor that has received scant attention from students of witchcraft in the past.

In many of the towns and villages of East Anglia there still lived the children and grandchildren of the victims of the trials of the 1560s and 1570s; and since witchcraft was generally assumed to be in the blood and therefore a hereditary taint, these became the automatic first choice, whenever fresh victims were required. In 1645 John Rivet, a tailor of Manningtree, troubled by the illness of his wife, sought advice from a Cunning Woman named Hoyve of Hadleigh in Suffolk, and was told that her sickness was due to witchcraft. Rivet, searching his mind for a likely suspect, remembered that the mother of Elizabeth Clarke, a neighbour, had been hanged as a witch. This information came to the ears of Matthew Hopkins, who seized upon the discovery as an opportunity for publicity and brought Elizabeth Clarke before a magistrate. The prisoner was searched for witch's marks and tormented by being denied sleep, an apparently legitimate form of torture, while Hopkins waited for her imps to visit her. In due course these put in an appearance, taking the form of a kitten, two dogs, a rabbit, a toad, and a polecat.

The unhappy prisoner was finally forced into making a full confession and named as her accomplice Anne West, a poverty-stricken widow who had long been suspected of witchcraft. The latter had the additional disadvantage of being denounced by her own daughter Rebecca, who freely admitted having attended a witch's meeting in company with a number of Manningtree women. What was to become the stock ritual of denunciation followed by prosecution leading to further denunciations then followed. St. Osyth village, scene of the terror in Elizabethan times, once again delivered up its quota of suspects into Hopkins's hands, as did many other villages in the vicinity.

Searched for Witch's Marks

Following their trial held at Chelmsford in the summer of 1645 before Robert Rich, Earl of Warwick, nineteen country-women died on the gallows. Arthur Wilson, the Earl's steward, who was present at the trials, set down as his opinion that the prisoners were no more than victims of their own imaginations being 'poor, melancholy, envious, mischievous, ill-disposed and ill-dieted,' confirming once again that it was the miserable poor who had become the victims of the witch hunts.

Hopkins claimed to possess the Devil's list of all the witches in England and, thus armed, set out to find further victims, accompanied by his own group of professional witchfinders. Amongst these were John Stearne, who searched the male prisoners for witch's marks, and Mary Phillips, who searched the women. They began systematically to comb the countryside of East Anglia, moving from town to town and village to village, often at the invitation of the authorities, who were by this time utterly overwhelmed by the witch panic. Among Hopkins's charges for his services were the sums of £23 0s 6d for a visit to Stowmarket and £15 for King's Lynn. Witch hunting had become an extremely profitable profession.

By a deliberate policy of terrorism in which prisoners were tied up, deprived of sleep, made to sit cross-legged on stools for hours on end, or marched backward and forward until they dropped from exhaustion, Hopkins secured the confessions he needed without crossing the official boundary between mere duress and illegal torture. There appears to have been no shortage of suspects; for to Hopkins witchcraft meant the possession of animal familiars, hence any unfortunate outcast possessing a pet

A suspect had even been known to volunteer to be searched for witch's marks in order to vindicate his good name in the eyes of his neighbours.

cat, dog, or mouse became particularly liable to suspicion. In the same way any sudden or inexplicable outbreak of disease among human beings or cattle could indicate witchcraft as most contemporary physicians would have been prepared to testify.

Not only Norfolk and Suffolk but also the counties of Cambridge, Northampton, Huntingdon, and Bedford became the stamping grounds of the Hopkins gang who took care never to venture beyond Puritan territory. The mechanism of witchfinding appears to have been in the main self-generating and the mere presence of a witch hunter in the vicinity usually sufficient to agitate a whole community into a frenzy of denunciations. So great was the terror engendered by the witchfinders that a suspect had even been known to volunteer to be searched for witch's marks in order to vindicate his good name in the eyes of his neighbours, as for example Meggs, a Suffolk baker, who offered himself for examination and, having failed the test, was sent to the gallows.

Witch hunting involved all manner of respectable citizens. Great Yarmouth, Norfolk, paid its local team of searchers for Devil's marks '12d per day to be divided among them'.

Ordeal by Swimming

With 200 of his victims packing the jails of East Anglia, Hopkins staged a great trial of witches at Bury St. Edmunds in 1645. Among the eighteen who died by hanging was John Lowes, a seventy-year-old clergyman who had been denounced as a witch by his own parishioners at Brandeston in Suffolk. Forced to undergo the walking torture until he fainted from exhaustion, Parson Lowes at last admitted to the ownership of familiars, one of which he had dispatched to sink a ship at sea. None of his accusers ascertained whether or not such a ship had existed, let alone had sunk on that day, and the old man was hanged after reading his own burial service, as no other clergyman could be persuaded to undertake it for him.

Among the best known methods used for the detection of witches at this period was the 'swimming test', an ordeal in which the suspect was trailed on ropes in a pool of water or a stream, the assumption being that if she floated she was guilty and that only if she sank could her innocence be presumed. Long pins were also plunged into the bodies of suspects in the search for Devil's marks. The swimming test was forbidden by a Parliamentary Commission in 1645 but no restraint was imposed by officialdom upon Hopkins's other enormities.

In 1645 Hopkins undertook a number of incursions into the county of Huntingdon. Here he came into conflict with a clergyman, the vicar of Great Staughton, Rev. John Gaule, who resented his presence in the county and who openly attacked him from the pulpit. Although compelled to recant Gaule returned to the attack, finally publishing a damning indictment in pamphlet form titled 'Select Cases of Conscience Touching Witches and Witchcraft' in which he exposed the cruel tortures used by the Hopkins gang, making the point that 'every old woman with a wrinkled face, a furrowed brow, a hairy lip, a gobber tooth, a squint eye, a squeaking voice, or a scolding tongue . . .' was liable to be pronounced a witch. Hopkins attempted a reply to the charges raised against him in his own pamphlet *The Discovery of Witches*, but by this time his star was beginning to wane and there was every sign that the day of the unofficial tribunal was over. In the first place the triumph of Parliament in the Civil War had created more settled conditions and, secondly, the voice of criticism was beginning to be raised against him from all quarters. In 1646 Hopkins retired to his house in Manningtree where he died in the following year.

The type of person selected by fate to fulfill the role of witch is a problem for the psychiatrist. Sir Charles Oman, the historian, divided English witches and wizards into four main groups: the conscious charlatans, the malignant persons who really believed they had the power to harm their enemies, the sheer lunatics, and finally the victims of torture and duress. There is not the least doubt that most of those who suffered in the great East Anglian witch hunts of the seventeenth century believed personally in the reality of witchcraft, and some possibly that they were guilty of the crimes with which they were charged, for belief in magic was universal among the peasantry. One Newmarket woman who sincerely believed her pet toad to be a familiar spirit received the scientific attentions of Dr. William Harvey, discoverer of the circulation of the blood and physician to King Charles I. The doctor, to the witch's disgust, cut open the unfortunate toad, demonstrating to his own satisfaction at least that there was nothing supernatural in its composition. Harvey was many years in advance of the majority of his profes-sion, who were perfectly prepared to use witchcraft as an alibi for their own medical deficiencies.

Livestock Burned Alive

A Dr. Jacob of Yarmouth, in the year 1664, basked in the glory of a reputation for 'helping children that were bewitched'. Jacob was involved in the notorious case of the Bury St. Edmunds witches of 1665 when Rose Cullenden and Amy Duny of Lowestoft were found guilty of bewitching a number of children, one of whom died. Given in evidence was the astounding fact that at the instigation of Dr. Jacobs a toad which had been discovered in the bedding of one of the children was thrown into the fire where it exploded, and that afterward Amy Duny was seen to have burns upon her arms, a sure sign of her guilt. During the court proceedings a number of children testified that Amy Duny and Rose Cullenden were attacking them 'spectrally' when it was quite obvious to those present that the women were doing nothing of the kind. This type of 'spectral evidence' was perfectly acceptable to the witch-fearing judge Sir Matthew Hale who, in spite of doubts raised by other members of the court, sentenced the prisoners to death. Contained in the indictment were the usual stock charges against seventeenth century witches: the conveying of nails and pins into the bodies of victims, the bewitching of farm carts, and the magical killing of cows and pigs.

There is a note of grim humour in the curious case of Abre Grinsett, a beggar woman who was charged in 1665 with bewitching Thomas Spatchett, bailiff of Dunwich, so that he suffered attacks of headaches, and fits. The fact that he had broken his skull as a child appeared to have little bearing on the evidence submitted to the court, which included a full confession, by Spatchett, of a compact with the Devil who had assumed the shape of a 'pretty handsome young man'. One of the magistrates observed that if Abre Grinsett chose to bewitch men like Spatchett she was free to do so, and she was discharged and sent home where she was later found dead, to all appearances murdered by her neighbours.

Throughout the seventeenth century and well into the eighteenth, witch hunting remained a popular sport in East Anglia and Essex. The repeal of the Witchcraft Act in 1736 had little effect upon the superstitious fears of the common people who continued to believe in witchcraft for a further century. Under the terms of the new Act witchcraft ceased to be a legal offence although punishment limited to imprisonment and pillory was reserved for those who claimed to have supernatural powers, as for example the Cunning People. To a considerable extent the situation had reverted to that existing before the Witchcraft Act of 1563 with witch hunting now a private matter between the bewitched and his adviser, the Cunning Man.

Faith in white witchcraft as prescribed by the Cunning People remained extremely strong in East Anglia until the 1850s when, following the decline in the belief in magic, witchcraft ceased to be a factor in peasant philosophy. Even as late as 1826 a huckster was swum as a witch at Wickham Keith, Suffolk, and at about this time Ipswich was honoured by the presence of its own Cunning Man 'Old Winter', a notorious white wizard. In 1857 *The Times* cited a not untypical case, in which a magistrate at Hockham in Norfolk was requested by a citizen to submit a suspected witch to the swimming test. Behind the scenes as prime instigator had been the inevitable Cunning Man.

Many magical practices belonging properly to the Dark Ages continued to be practiced in the remoter parts of the East Anglian marshlands until fairly recently. Livestock was burned alive throughout the first half of the nineteenth century as an antidote to witchcraft, while as late as 1866 crosses were nailed to barn doors in Norfolk during an epidemic of cattle disease, to protect the herds from devils and witches. Even in the twentieth century iron objects like knives and scissors were placed under cottage doormats to keep witches from the premises.

The marshland coastal fringes bordering the North Sea long remained an area of peasants who were dissenters almost to a man, and almost medieval in their acceptance of witchcraft. Until 1860 Essex possessed the most famous Cunning Man of all times, James Murrell of Hadleigh, an expert exorcist whose prowess with the witch bottle was proverbial. Even as late as the 1870s the witch bottle was not unknown among country labourers, although as often as not the refinements of the art had been forgotten, a jam jar of urine being used instead. Witch's imps in the shape of white mice were still feared in parts of Norfolk, Suffolk, and Essex until the close of the century and provided the theme of many macabre legends, some of which are remembered to this day.

The Devil's Harvest

Further north, in the Fenlands, country folk long believed in the satanic compact, considering it possible to secure the granting of material requests from the hands of the Devil by a rite called 'The Gathering of the Devil's Harvest', which was performed on St. Mark's Eve. Perhaps the best-known survival of witch fear in its most malignant form was the notorious incident of 1863 in which an old fortune-teller, after being accused of witchcraft, was forced to undergo the

swimming test at Sible Hedingham in Essex as the result of which he died. For this crime the two principals, a man and a woman, both shopkeepers, were sentenced to terms of hard labour. It transpired from the evidence given in court that the unhappy victim had been submitted to the cruel seventeenth century ordeal known as the walking torture, in an effort to persuade him to remove a spell he was supposed to have placed upon the woman. It was not far from here, at Dunmow, that one of the last known attempts to impose the swimming

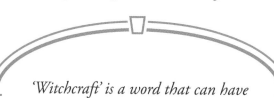

'Witchcraft' is a word that can have several meanings, and it can be feared and give rise to public panic.

test upon a witch was made by two country labourers in 1880. The offenders were brought before the courts and punished.

As a macabre postscript to the East Anglian witch hunts of the sixteenth and seventeenth centuries a St. Osyth resident discovered, when digging his garden less than a century ago, the skeletons of two women buried in a northsouth orientation and riveted limb to limb. Whether these were survivals of witch persecution it is not possible to say with absolute certainty, but it is reasonable to assume that the bodies had been so restricted after death to prevent them rising from the grave to haunt the community.

ERIC MAPLE

FURTHER READING: R. Trevor Davies. Four Centuries of Witchcraft Trials. *(Methuen, 1947); T. Gardiner.* Broomstick over Essex and East Anglia. *(Henry, 1981); Roberts.* Witches and Witch Hunters. *(Folcroft, 1973); Eric Maple.* The Dark World of Witches. *(A. S. Barnes, 1964); G. Morgan.* Essex Witches. *(Spurbooks, 1973).*

European Witch Persecutions

Witch scares and witch hunts in Europe began in the very late Middle Ages and culminated in the sixteenth and seventeenth centuries. Nothing of the kind is known to have happened before about 1300 AD. The whole historical problem involved in interpreting the phenomenon of these persecutions can be summed up in that one fact.

Sorcery—the use of, or pretending to, occult powers—was always against the laws of the Church. It was probably fairly common in early medieval society, but would have been handled by the ecclesiastical penitential system, which became vastly more ambitious in the thirteenth century. Secular legal codes of the period are mostly silent on the subject, not out of enlightened liberalism but because it was considered strictly the affair of the Church. The change to an atmosphere of public panic and the demand for violent solutions came quite slowly, and at a time which we are accustomed to think of as one of intellectual progress, although the same period saw an apparent increase in the practice of astrology and alchemy.

Geographically, the first witch hunts of all were probably on French soil, but the centre shifted eastward later. In the early stages the panic seems to have been most deeply rooted in the Alpine region. It lingered longest in the Danube basin where quite large scale persecutions occurred as late as

De Heks van 's-Heerenberg (The Witch of 's-Heerenberg) by Patrick Beverloo, the Netherlands

experts in the field. In the age of the Reformation, Italy and the Iberian peninsula were more completely under the Church's control than anywhere else, which may account for the fact that they seem to have been more peaceful than elsewhere in this respect.

The Work of the Devil

'Witchcraft' is a word that can have several meanings, and it can be feared and give rise to public panic, for more than one reason. In the Renaissance epoch it is probable that not all those who participated in the persecution of people they thought of as 'witches' attached the same meaning to the word or could have given the same reasons for their fears, but the body of literature which grew up around the subject, including manuals for witch-finders, gives a clear picture of what officials of Church and State understood themselves to be fighting against.

The type of witchcraft which men in authority were trying to stamp out—whether it existed or not, and whether the general public understood it or not—was something quite different from the furtive fortune telling and spell peddling, cursing, and blessing, which the Church had been trying to put down since the Dark Ages. This was looked upon as sinful, partly because many things that witches were believed to be able to do were obviously evil and partly because even their relatively benevolent practices implied disrespect toward Providence and the Church's own ministrations. It was almost irrelevant whether the culprits could or could not perform what they claimed, but probably most bishops and their judges thought that they could.

The new witchcraft, discovered and revealed to the world by zealous Inquisitors in the late Middle Ages, was something else again. The older kind indeed survived, and was taken into and absorbed by the new, but

the eighteenth century. Certainly the German-speaking countries suffered the most. After the Reformation persecution seems to have flourished predominantly in territory under Calvinist control, but a causal connection between Calvinism and witch hysteria has not been proved. In the British Isles the scare arrived very late—after the Reformation—and rose to a peak in the Civil War period. It then died down almost completely in England and Scotland; Ireland had scarcely been touched at all. In all three

countries individual witches might be punished from time to time until new legislation under George II made it impossible, but individual cases are not persecutions.

In countries controlled by the Inquisition (Roman or Spanish) there were no major witch hunts in the period when panic was highest elsewhere. There may have been a continuous stream of trials, and certainly the Inquisitors were not reluctant to punish witchcraft—in the early days of witch hunting they were the acknowledged there was one vital new element in the situation: witchcraft had come to be recognized as the work of the Devil.

Of course, all sin is the Devil's work in a sense, but the Inquisitors, and later Protestant witch-finders, meant something altogether more precise. They meant that the witches (who from this point onward begin to be of both sexes, although women, as in folklore, continued to predominate) had put themselves consciously under the guidance and command of Satan to work his nefarious will in the world, while gratifying depraved desires and ambitions of their own. Thus it followed that they really did enjoy occult powers, supplied them by their infernal master; it now became a mark of orthodoxy to believe in witchcraft, and a ground of complicity to deny it or express scepticism. Moreover, all witches being servants of one master were members of a huge all-pervading conspiracy. Eventually, the propagandists were to claim to know something about the details of the organization and by the time when we can reasonably use the phrase 'witch persecution' association of one suspect with another was sufficient evidence of guilt.

The Obscene Kiss
The associating together of witches had not been prominent in earlier beliefs so far as we can tell, but was not unknown. The two annual occasions when witches are supposed to foregather—Walpurgisnacht (30 April) and Hallowe'en (31 October)—are important in the folklore of most European countries and although it is impossible to be certain that those parts of folklore which are relevant to witches are not later accretions, it is unlikely. However, the older superstition most clearly involving the assembly of a number of witches is one that the Church had earlier tried

to suppress as delusory. This is the story of the witches' ride, recorded in the so-called *Canon Episcopi*. This famous document (first referred to c. 900 AD) denounced 'certain wicked women' who falsely claimed to have ridden by night, covering immense distances, with 'Diana', whose ser-

> *The Devil's mark might take many forms, it might even be invisible, but it was a spot somewhere on the body which was insensible to pain.*

vants they were. The suggestion was that they had dreamed it and that good Christians ought not to believe that such a thing could really happen. In later copies Diana changed her name; her best known aliases being 'Herodias', 'Holda-Perchta', and 'Dame Habonde'. Until the fifteenth century a succession of churchmen, lawyers, poets, and others continued to deny that this lady existed or that witches rode with her by night. None of them mention broomsticks. The witches rode on animals, presumably monstrous. As with other tales of supernatural journeys, it is very hard to guess whether in the teller's mind they actually flew or not. The witches' flying through the air eventually became an integral part of the idea of witch assemblies on such occasions as Hallowe'en. Witch hunters believed that it really happened, and the *Canon Episcopi* was definitely inconvenient.

One thing they knew which Regino of Prum, the earliest writer to use the *Canon Episcopi*, certainly did not know, was what happened at the assemblies. The real leader, of course, was Satan and not Diana. He appeared in the form of an animal—usually a goat—and required his devotees to kiss him under the tail—the *'osculum infame.'* The proceedings also included

a sexual orgy. The participants, apart from the Devil, were naked. These details are fairly constant. There might also be some act of conscious blasphemy, but the Black Mass dear to modern magicians does not play a conspicuous part in the picture drawn by the propagandists. The remarkable thing about all these accusations is that they had previously been used to blacken the reputations of heretical sects such as the Waldenses.

In the thirteenth century, especially in the South of France, a variety of heresies became sufficiently firmly established to require vigorous action on the part of the Church; the Dominican Order and the Inquisition were both founded at this time and for this purpose. By the time that the Albigensians, Waldenses, Picards, Patarenes, and so on had been thoroughly crushed, the Church's machinery of repression was stronger and more efficient than ever before, and Inquisitors and preachers had learnt a great deal about the way in which the Devil used dissident groups that fell under his control. By the end of the century, it quite suddenly becomes easy to document the idea that he requires everybody who has become his servant, not only heretics, to kiss his hindquarters.

Indeed only one major charge that was useful to witch hunters appears not to have been used by heresy-hunters. This was the charge that the Devil had physically marked the culprit as one of his own. The Devil's mark might take many forms, it might even be invisible, but it was a spot somewhere on the body which was insensible to pain. This belief differs from those already mentioned in being of very little use as a propaganda smear but useful as evidence; it suggested ways of detecting who was and who was not a witch.

This brings us to the subject of witch trials, about which remarkably little is known for certain. In all the countries of Europe, the survival of court records from the period of major persecutions is incomplete and dependent on chance, nor did official court records attempt to give a complete transcript of proceedings. Only occasionally and by accident do we know whether a confession was extracted by torture or not, and we can never hope to know what kind of ordeals were imposed on suspects by lynch mobs, although it is pretty obvious that much of the persecution took that form. The uneven survival of records makes it futile to attempt a statistical analysis of witchcraft cases. In addition to court archives, information about particular trials is sometimes found in general manuals for witch-finders such as the *Malleus Maleficarum* and often occurs in the numerous pamphlets that describe individual witch hunts.

The *Malleus Maleficarum*, was the most influential authority of all on the subject. It spawned a numerous progeny of handbooks, and nowhere else is the witch hunting temper, in its earlier, pre-Reformation phase, better conveyed. It was the work of two Dominicans, Heinrich Kramer or Institoris, and Jacob Springer, natives respectively of the Tyrol and Basel and thus of the same general region, from which nearly all their examples are drawn. Kramer had been active, as Inquisitor, in witch hunting in the Tyrol, where he had actually been removed from office for excessive zeal. The book was intended to vindicate him as well as to urge the necessity of witch hunting in general. Pope Innocent VIII in some sense commissioned the work by his bull *Summis Desiderantes* of 1484, in which he speaks of immense harm being caused by supernatural means and Satanic influence; this bull was afterward quoted as papal endorsement for the authors' views.

The *Malleus,* which ran into thirteen editions by 1520, became for Catholics the most authoritative manual available, so that later works tended to appeal to its authority or to that of the bull. It conveyed in fairly developed form the picture of the Satanic witch cult described above; it disposed of the inconvenient *Canon Episcopi* with the argument that what was a dream and a delusion on one occasion might be true experience on another, and it supplied detailed advice to judges on how to go about examining witches.

Joan of Arc, who was tried long before this, in 1431, was asked whether her angels came to her in the form of naked men and whether she had danced round a tree which was reputed to belong to the fairies.

Had she been tried after the *Malleus* and its imitators had gained currency she would probably have been asked as a matter of routine whether she believed in witchcraft. 'No' was the wrong answer, and almost proved one was a witch. Questions would follow about her more intimate relations with Satan, as well as any accusations that might emerge from neighbourhood gossip about actual wicked deeds. For witches, as for heretics, there was a presumption of guilt. The only authorized defense against any accusation was that the accuser was motivated by malice, but the accused had no right to know who the accusers were. Torture was highly recommended, even though it was sometimes held that the Devil could counteract its effects by anesthetizing his servants.

American actress Jean Seberg (1938–1979) burning at the stake as Joan of Arc in a scene from the film *Saint Joan* (1957).

Opposite page:
Sculpture of Lisbeth Nypan, the penultimate accused and sentenced witch of Norway

The familiar procedures of the Inquisition were of course normally employed on Catholic territory, and were reinforced by the technical advice of Kramer and Sprenger and their later disciples. Elsewhere secular courts with different procedures were sometimes involved. In England confessions were legally useless as evidence and therefore nobody troubled to extract them. The search for the 'Devil's mark' was accordingly more important. In the great panic of the 1640s in Britain, when witch-finders were encouraged by the Roundhead party in the Civil War, men such as the notorious Matthew Hopkins who specialized in locating the mark could charge £1 a head.

In a very famous case in Newcastle in 1649 the finder, having scared an hysterical subject out of her wits, stuck his pin into the chosen spot and duly demonstrated that the woman could not feel it. An unusually sceptical Roundhead officer insisted that the test be made again when she was calmer, and saved her. The finder eventually confessed that his method was a fraud.

Although they never had the same official sanction, there were of course other traditional ways of identifying a witch, such as the well-known practice of throwing her, bound, into water and seeing if she would float. If she was a witch, she would, because witches were believed to be preternaturally light. This could also be tested by weighing them against the big Bible in the parish church. This latter test was probably never accepted as evidence in a court; the water-test was occasionally accepted on the Continent, but most references to it are references to attempts to forbid it.

Contagious Hysteria

It seems safe to assume that people accused of witchcraft were rarely given a fair trial, both because of the spreading panic that the accusation inspired and because the accused were usually drawn from the poorer, more downtrodden and unpopular members of the community. What no court records can convey is the atmosphere of suspicion, inside and outside the courtroom. Yet this atmosphere, in which accusations breed further accusations, is the most outstanding feature of the witch persecutions.

It seems likely that popular hysteria was less important in the earlier part of the period and became a major factor later. The early Lutherans were relatively calm and sceptical, though they fell victims to the common dread about the 1580s. Calvin and his followers were zealous persecutors and in Geneva in the 1540s some hundreds were arrested, and thirty-four executed in less than a year. Calvin himself urged every severity, claiming that witchcraft was on the increase. He believed that the Devil, alarmed by the progress of the Gospel, was making a special effort to encourage sorcery in the territories of the Reformed Churches. Puritans of Calvinistic inspiration were active in the dissemination of horror pamphlets about witchcraft, and the persecution in Presbyterian Scotland was fiercer than in England.

A case could be made, however, that persecution was most virulent of all, if only for short periods, in the territories whose political and religious future was uncertain.

The Prince Bishop of Fulda in Germany recovered the city from the Protestants in 1602 and within five years he had burned 250 witches, and his witch-finder, Balthasar Ross, claimed to have achieved 700 executions in his lifetime. In another threatened Prince Bishopric, Bamberg, the decade 1623–1633 saw around 600 executions and they had been common enough before. At Quedlinburg, Saxony, in 1589, where the ruler was Protestant and the population mixed, 133 witches were burned in one day.

These are among the most dramatic figures to be found.

A new element in the post-Reformation phase is the much greater use of the printing press. Horror pamphlets could help spread hysteria among the general public in areas not previously affected. Some late scares look as if they were wholly stirred up by this means, notably that in Mohra, Sweden, in 1669. The evidence here supplied by children, was a fantastic mixture of standard anti-witch propaganda and local folklore, amounting to the tallest and most unbelievable tale in the whole literature of the subject. It was, however, believed. Three hundred were arrested, many of them children themselves, and 100 were punished, a minority receiving the death penalty. There are obvious similarities between this and the best known American scare at Salem, Massachusetts, in 1692.

On the other hand, the age that saw an increase in popular witch-baiting literature and an increase in the number of actual executions also saw the beginnings of counter-propaganda. The suggestion that witchcraft was a mere delusion, at one time a dangerous thing to say, was urged by many throughout the seventeenth century. Reginald Scot's *Discoverie of Witchcraft* (1584) provoked King James I to write his *Daemonologie* (1597) in reply, but James, when investigating witchcraft cases in person, was extremely cautious and sceptical.

In the last age of persecution the impetus to persecute came from the common people, and judges and officials tried to restrain it. All the evidence goes to show that this was a late development, and that it was the official, ruling and learned classes who were the original instigators of the witch hysteria.

ELLIOT ROSE

FURTHER READING: N. Cohn. Europe's Inner Demons. (Basic Books, 1975); C. A. Hoyt. Witchcraft. (Univ. Press, 1981); Christina Hole. Witchcraft in England. (Rowman, 1977); and A Mirror of Witchcraft. (Clarke, Irwin, 1957); H. C. Lea. Materials Towards a History of Witchcraft. (Yoseloff, 1958); Margaret Murray. The Witch-Cult in Western Europe. (Clarendon Press, Oxford, 1967 reprint); The God of the Witches (Doubleday, 1960); and A Razor for a Goat. (Univ. of Toronto Press, 1962); C. L'Estrange Ewen. Witch Hunting and Witch Trials. (Dial Press, 1929); R. Johnson. Witches and Demons in History and Folklore. (Johnson NC, 1978); R. Kieckhefer. European Witch Trials. (Routledge & Kegan Paul, 1976); J. Burton Russell. Witchcraft in the Middle Ages. (Cornell Univ. Press, 1972); and Malleus Maleficarum. (Hogarth Press, London, 1969); Scot's Discoverie of Witchcraft. (Univ. of Illinois Press, 1964); and Guazzo's Compendium Maleficarum. (Muller, London, 1970).

Familiars

The witch's black cat has become firmly entrenched in popular imagination in Britain. Storybook witches all have cats as henchmen to help them with their spells and traditionally her cat is the one creature to which the witch is attached. Yet in the history of witchcraft the small animal kept as a crony appears fairly late, part of the final phase of witchcraft belief. Nor was the cat the only, or even the commonest, of the witches' pets: ferrets, rabbits, hedgehogs, mice, or any small common animal, also figure in reports. Blackbirds and crows were fairly frequent, being traditional birds of augury. Toads and frogs were also regarded as suitable pets, being cold blooded, but fishes are never mentioned—perhaps because the fish is an ancient Christian symbol as well as an emblem of chastity. There were also more exotic 'familiars' like the one that was said to have appeared to Bridget Bishop of Salem during the outbreak of witch hysteria there in the late seventeenth century: 'A black Thing . . . the Body was like that of a Monkey, the Feet like a Cock's, but the Face most like a man's . . .'

Ideas of witchcraft at the Salem trials were a direct import from the England of a generation earlier. In the rest of Europe, the pattern and traditions were rather different. In the widespread Continental witchcraft persecutions of the fifteenth and sixteenth centuries, accusations concerning familiars seem to have played little part: the pet imp in the form of an animal was a typically, if not exclusively, British phenomenon. Accusations of familiar-keeping occur as corroborative evidence most frequently in the seventeenth century British witch-trials, possibly because witchcraft only became a capital offence under the second Witchcraft Act of 1604. This Act, which also provided harsher penalties for the 'wasting' of men's bodies or goods—an accusation easy to make and hard to disprove—was particularly unfortunate for the aged, the antisocial and the isolated who were most liable to become obsessively attached to small animals. Hence one of the modern stereotypes of the witch—the poor old crone, persecuted because she has only her cat for company.

The pet imp in the form of an animal was a typically, if not exclusively, British phenomenon.

A Detection
of damnable driftes, practized by three VVitches arraigned at
Chelmiffozde in Effex, at the
laste Affifes there holden, whiche
were executed in Apzill.
1 5 7 9.

Set foozthe to difcouer the Ambufhementes of
Sathan, whereby he would furpzife vs
lulled in fecuritie, and hardened
with contempte of Gods
vengeance thzeatened
foz our offences.

Imprinted at London for Edward White,
at the little North-dore of Paules.

A woodcut illustration of a cat. Image taken from *A detection of damnable driftes practized by three witches arraigned at Chelmisforde in Essex at the laste assises there holden whiche were executed in April* (1579). Originally published/produced in *Edward White*, London (1579).

Breast-Feeding the Familiar

While there is undoubtedly some truth in this image, the association between witches and the animal kingdom is far more complex and its roots go far back to the origins of sorcery. The use of animals' skins and masks in ancient witchcraft fertility rituals and the legends of werewolves are both reflections of the persistent idea that witches could, at will, turn themselves into animals. Tales of this kind crop up all over the world. In countries where the bear and the wolf (the oldest incarnations) died out during the Middle Ages, the cat, already associated with the witch for other reasons, was substituted in the myth.

There are many fifteenth and sixteenth century tales, chiefly from the Continent and from Scotland, of witches who became cats at night for their revels and turned themselves back again into their human form at daybreak. Often these witches were unmasked because wounds which had been inflicted on the cats would be evident the next day on the bodies of highly respected female members of the community.

Such tales, particularly those in which the practitioner assumed animal shape when she wanted to perform some evil deed unobserved, were confused by some authorities with the keeping of familiars, but there is a distinction: the true familiar spirit was an imp or minor devil kept by the witch and distinct from herself. It was also distinct from the Devil in person. It was sometimes given or sold to the witch by that gentleman, but here too confusions arose on account of the Devil's own habit of assuming a variety of animal forms. Thus Dame Alice Kyteler, a celebrated fourteenth century witch of good social standing, was said to be frequented by a dark man called Robert Artisson who also appeared to her on occasions in the shape of a cat or dog. Clearly this was thought to be the Devil-God himself—the name 'Artis' suggesting a possible derivation from a pagan deity of Mediterranean origin.

Three centuries later, however, when the ancient fertility rites were further decayed and forgotten, those who reported on the trial of Abre Grinsett in Suffolk were probably mistaken when they assumed that the witch considered it to be the actual Prince of Darkness 'who did appear in the form of a Pretty handsome Young Man first, and since Appeareth to her in the form of a blackish Grey Cat or Kitling, that it sucketh of a Tett which searchers since saw in the place she mentioned.' Suffolk was then a backward, rural area; elsewhere by that date (1665) informed opinion had begun to take the view that it was surely unlikely that the Devil in person 'would consent to be at the beck and call of poor, doting women.'

In other respects the description of Abre Grinsett's familiar is within the classic tradition of such cases. The suckling of the familiar by the witch is a typical detail which throws light both on the true nature of the relationship and on the evil interdependence which was popularly believed to characterize it. The modern reader, inclined to take the part of the 'harmless old women' may believe that this tale of suckling was a dirty-minded calumny spread by the, witch hunters, but it should be remembered that such events are set in an era when people lived closer to Nature, when infants were universally fed at the breast for want of any other alternative method, and thus many women went on being 'in milk' and casually nursing other babies besides their own for the greater part of their reproductive lives. It was apparently not uncommon for an old granny, left to mind a baby, to put it to her dry breast just to soothe it if it were fretful. It will be appreciated that in these circumstances to give the breast to a treasured animal would be seen as an exaggerated piece of petting but not necessarily as an unnatural or perverted action.

In Russia, as late as the nineteenth century, there are cases recorded of peasant women being ordered by their masters to nurse bear cubs that were being reared for sport. It therefore seems likely that much of the evidence about women suckling their pets was quite genuine, especially since they themselves frequently gave the animals nicknames such as 'Suckin' or 'Titty'. A sixteenth century Somerset witch, for instance, stated that 'her Familiar doth commonly suck her right Breast about seven at night, in the shape of a little cat of dunnish colour . . . and when she is suckt, she is in a kind of Trance.' It is probable that what alarmed our ancestors was not the intimacy of the relationship between mistress and familiar, but the supposition that the woman was thus rewarding her creature for malevolent services it performed for her.

Cats Burned as Devils

Some familiars were thought to carry the witch through the air to sabbath revels—a version of the common tradition that witches themselves could fly—though the evidence is further confused by the coincidence that 'cat' is also an old dialect word for 'stick' (broomstick). More commonly, the spirit was supposed to act as a medium for ill-doing. Elizabeth Device, one of the Pendle, Lancashire, witches, had a brown dog called Ball through whom

> *The christening and ritual sacrifice of cats was a piece of magic that related back to fertility cults and the ceremonial sacrifice of the god.*

she was said to attempt to kill people who had offended her. Another classic case was recorded in 1619, when a witch named Margaret Flower and her sister Philippa were hanged at Lincoln for using witchcraft to murder the eldest son of the Earl of Rutland. She said that among other rituals intended to kill the Earl's children and render the parents sterile, she had rubbed certain personal belongings of her victims, which she managed to steal, against the body of her cat. To ensure that no babies would be born, she had obtained feathers from the Countess's bed and had rubbed them on the cat's belly: this meant that the marriage would henceforth be barren. It seems probable that this witch, like many others, indeed regarded herself as a witch and actually performed the actions stated.

The cat employed—and doubtless cherished—by the Lincoln witch and her kind falls into a different category from the luckless animal that Agnes Sampson and her accomplices seized at random, christened and then cast into the sea, in an attempt to bring about the death by drowning of the future James I. The christening and ritual sacrifice of cats was a piece of magic that related back to fertility cults and the ceremonial sacrifice of the god; it survived as a rite in certain places, notably Aix-en-Provence, till the end of the fifteenth century. Elsewhere it was generally replaced during the Middle Ages by the burning of live cats as 'devils' on Good Friday or other significant day—a good example of a barbarous practice originating from pagan rites but later sanctioned by the Church, unchanged in essence, and adopted for a different purpose.

There are shades of the sacrificed cat in the latter-day witch's familiar—it was not uncommon for witches to make a small ceremony of naming their pets, often with a name suggested by the Devil their Master. It is also significant that cats seem to have been employed particularly, as in the Rutland case cited above, to bring about sterility: Bast, the cat-goddess of Egyptian origin, patron of fertility, became in the Christian world associated with sterility, that reversal of fertility that consists of 'taking' things for the Devil.

Most true familiars, far from meeting a sacrificial fate, seem to have been

Opposite page:
Statue of Alice Nutter, one of the accused Pendle witches, in Roughlee, Lancashire, England

particularly long-lived. Jennet Dibble, one of a company of witches who plagued the Fairfax family at Fuiston, Yorkshire, in the early seventeenth century, had 'her spirit in the shape of a great black cat called Gibbe, which hath attended her now above forty years.' Others were handed down from one witch to another, a circumstance which reflects the persistence of the sorcery tradition in one place or family for generations. Elizabeth Francis, one of the Chelmsford witches arraigned in 1556, had a white-spotted cat called 'Sathan' who had been given to her by her grandmother and to whom she talked in a special 'hollow' voice. At the recitation of the *Pater Noster* in Latin it would change into a toad — shape-shifting was attributed to many familiars. She kept it fifteen or sixteen years until, wearying of it, she passed it on to another witch, Agnes Waterhouse. It was kept in a basket fed on bread and milk, and given a drop of blood every time it did something for her.

The belief that the familiar fed not only on milk but also on blood was a common one, which lent a more sinister twist to the character of the suckling familiar. Abre Grinsett's imp sucked 'at a Tett which Searchers since saw in the place she mentioned' that is, a special teat or 'witch's pap' which might be anywhere on her body but most probably 'in the secretest part'. There is ample evidence concerning these unnatural teats, which came into the wider category of 'witch-marks' and were, for a time, infallible proof of a witch.

Matthew Hopkins, the notorious Witch-finder General who carried on his trade briefly but profitably between 1644 and 1646, employed a special female searcher to hunt out these 'paps.' Presumably some of them were quite genuine supernumerary nipples, which are not uncommon in either sex. Others were probably warts,

or seem from their position to have been piles, though the searcher usually declared that they were unlike any piles she had previously seen. There is a contemporary engraving of Hopkins standing in an admonitory way over two witches and their attendant imps, among them a kitten, a rabbit, a polecat, and a 'long-legg'd greyhound with a head like an Ox' called Vinegar Tom. Other names given to these familiars were Pecke-in-the-Crown, Grissel Greedigut, and Pyewackit. The outlandishness of these pet-names was considered at the time, by the unimaginative persecutors, proof of their Satanic origin.

It is hard to avoid the conclusion that many of the defenceless old women arraigned with their pets must have been pathetic indeed, particularly when they were so confused in their wits as to implicate themselves readily. Delusion is not confined to paranoiac witch hunters; it was found as often in the hunted, as a few of the more intelligent seventeenth century commentators pointed out.

There is also the fact that, though torture was never officially sanctioned for witches in England, many an arrested woman was certainly bullied and harassed—put in a cramped gaol, walked up and down, nagged at for a confession, kept awake, and watched continually to see if any small animal should creep into her cell to visit her, in which case it would, of course, be a devil. As many of the country gaols of the period must have been squalid and tumble down, infested with rats and cockroaches, it was all too likely that 'proof' should sooner or later appear.

This kind of circumstantial evidence on which a witch could be convicted (guilty unless proved innocent) is typified by the report of a trial at Bideford in 1682, a time when in better educated circles the whole reality of witchcraft was beginning to be called

in question: 'This informant saith he saw a cat leap in at her window, when it was twilight: and this informant further saith, that he verily believeth the said cat to be the devil, and more saith not.'

But the keeping of pets was not confined to poor old women. At various times even eminent men fell under suspicion on this count including Oliver Cromwell, who was said to have a familiar called Grimoald. Witchcraft seems to have been an issue—if a covert one—in the Civil War, each side suspecting the other of practising it. It was whispered that the great storm that occurred on the night the Protector died was raised by the Fiend come to fetch him.

The distinguished German scholar Heinrich Cornelius Agrippa (1486–1535) came under suspicion on the same count. A strange mixture of occultist and sceptic, worldly lawyer and genuinely original thinker, he made a thorough and intensive study of alchemy, astrology, and the occult arts and developed an analytical faculty which eventually led him to speak out against the whole unscientific basis on which the witchcraft hunts were carried out. He denounced the Inquisition at Metz, his home town, and was forced to leave. Only his previous eminence and prosperity saved his life, for the automatic assumption was, as always when a witch hunt is in process, that those who defend witches must be in league with them. At this point his pet, a much loved black poodle called Monsieur, naturally fell under suspicion as a familiar.

That Animal Attraction

It is perhaps not out of place to end this brief survey of the place of the pet in witchcraft with a quotation from a memoir which has nothing to do with witchcraft but is by a man who, throughout his life (he died in

1967) was an outsider of a modern kind, a highly promiscuous homosexual. After several decades in which, by his own account, he expended a disproportionate amount of time and energy in seeking ephemeral sexual gratification, he unexpectedly found peace and fulfillment in a close (but nonsexual) relationship with an Alsatian bitch.

'I don't believe there was anything special about her, except that she was rather a beauty . . . She offered me what I never had found in my sexual life, constant, single-hearted, incorruptible, uncritical devotion, which it is in the nature of dogs to offer. She placed herself entirely under my control. From the moment she established herself in my heart and home, my obsession with sex fell wholly away from me. The pubs I had spent so much of my time in were never revisited, my single desire was to get back to her . . . the fifteen years she lived with me were the happiest of my life.'

The witch in the seventeenth century sense of the term may have disappeared, the animal-magic on which the ancient rites were based may be virtually extinct in our civilization, but the human need of relationships with the animal world is not extinguished. The plane of spontaneous instinct and sensation which the animal represents continues to exert a powerful attraction for us.

GILLIAN TINDALL

FURTHER READING: C. Hole. Witchcraft in England. *(Rowman, 1977); and* A Mirror of Witchcraft. *(Irwin, Clarke, 1957);* C. A. Hoyt. Witchcraft. *(South Illinois University Press, 1981);* H. E. Wedeck. A Treasury of Witchcraft. *(Citadel Press, 1966).*

Finding of Witches

An important difference between witchcraft and sorcery in tribal societies (possibly also in pre-Christian Europe), and witchcraft in the Christian era is reflected in methods of finding witches and sorcerers.

Tribal beliefs in witchcraft attempted to explain why it was that, at a particular moment and in a particular place, a particular person suffered a particular misfortune—such as disease, the death of kin or animal stock, accident, the blighting of crops, and so on—when he had previously not been

> *After being denounced by some accuser, witches were then subjected to torture, under which they both confessed and implicated others.*

thus unfortunate and his fellows were still enjoying good luck. His ill-fortune was ascribed to the malevolence of a personal enemy, operating by occult or supernatural powers. But witchcraft was not the only possible hidden occult cause of such events: gods and other spirits, or ancestral spirits, or breach of taboo, might be the mysterious cause of ill-fortune.

Witches and sorcerers harmed those against whom they felt envy and jealousy, spite, malice, hatred, or anger. The ancestral gods usually sent misfortune to either a wrongdoer who had broken a rule of morality which came under their surveillance, or one who had failed to render to them appropriate offerings or sacrifices.

Oracles and Ordeals

Different tribal societies ascribed misfortunes to various occult causes in varying degrees: among the Azande of the Sudan it was primarily witchcraft

which was blamed; among the Tallensi of Ghana it was ancestral spirits or the earth goddess; among the Bantu of South Africa it was equally witchcraft or the ancestral spirits—though in all these societies there was some element of all these, and yet other, beliefs. Sometimes the occult cause of a misfortune was indicated by its very nature, but mostly it had to be sought by some form of divination or oracle (the latter might involve an ordeal).

There were many forms of divination. Some were mechanical devices, while others involved direct searching by specialist magicians (usually called witch doctors, but better named, following J. A. Barnes, witch-detectives). These magicians were often believed to be helped or possessed by spirits, frequently ancestral, who spoke through them, in their search for occult causes. The most famous of all were the Greek oracles of Apollo at Delphi and of Zeus at Dodona. Tribal diviners of this time, commonly called shamans after the Siberian model.

Evans-Pritchard's illuminating study of the systems of belief among the Azande analyzed the hierarchy of divinatory and oracular mechanisms. When a Zande suffered a misfortune, he was likely first to consult a rubbing-board oracle: it was believed that the boards stuck at the name of any man who might be the witch causing that particular misfortune. Or he might put two different kinds of twigs into a termite's nest, with the name of a suspected witch, and depending on which was the more eaten he received confirmation or not of his suspicion.

The most important form of Zande oracle involved giving a chicken a certain substance—a form of strychnine—which had to be collected with much hardship in enemy territory. Questions were put to the oracle-substance in the chicken; and the answer was 'no' or 'yes' depending on whether the form of the question called for the chicken to vomit the substance or to die.

If the misfortune were a continuing one, the consultant could then, through a neutral intermediary, send the wing of a chicken to a man thus accused of being the witch responsible. The accused had to blow water over the wing and state that, if it was his witchcraft which was at work, he was not aware of this, and by blowing cold water he 'cooled' his witchcraft. (Witchcraft in this context was a substance in the intestines, whose power could go out and harm others when it was animated by malevolent feelings, even if the alleged witch did not intend it to; immoral feelings set witchcraft power to work.) Should a man thus accused refuse to blow water, and merely assert his innocence, it would be taken as proof of his obdurate guilt.

The death of a kinsman on the father's side demanded that his fellows take vengeance. The verdict of their oracle had to be confirmed by the chief's oracle, and the person held by the chief's oracle to be responsible for a death had to pay compensation. However, after the then Anglo-Egyptian joint government prohibited such payments, the social demand for vengeance persisted, and the kin of the dead person made magic against the unknown witch responsible for the death: whenever any person died in the neighbourhood, the kin asked the oracle if they had been killed by the vengeance magic. If their oracle said 'yes', confirmation had to be obtained from the chief's oracles before they could cease mourning, with their vengeance completed.

Azande sometimes organized seances at which one or more witch-detectives would dance to work up the power of their magical substances, detect particular witches at work, or clear away a threat of witchcraft from around the organizer of the seance. He might give the witch-detective in advance the names of those he suspected.

The Personal Grudge

Certain important facts become clear in discussing the finding of witches and the threat of witchcraft within a single society. First, we see that in the example of most Azande techniques the sufferer controls the names of the persons put to the oracle, so that he is likely to point out some person who has a grudge against him, or against whom he has a grudge, as the cause of his misfortune. For this reason many early observers of these systems of belief and action considered them to be fraudulent. But we must remember that for people who believed in the system in which they had been reared, it seemed very reasonable that personal enemies should be responsible for one's misfortunes; and since one was deeply concerned to avoid the misfortune, one had a greater interest than anyone else in detecting the responsible witch accurately.

When a diviner or oracle spoke directly, in a trance, or through a possessing spirit, the clients were obviously much less in control of the course of divination. Such diviners—like the oracle—substance of the Zande, which could not be in human control (as the rubbing-board oracle might be)—were more trusted than others.

In most of the tribal societies described, witches were considered most likely to be relatives of the actual victim, or of the person who was guardian of the victim. More recent researches have brought out that each divination might have to be understood in terms of a long process of development of social relationships, as sections of a village or large group of kinsfolk, or individuals, competed for positions of authority over the whole. Hence one section might reject a divination acceptable to another, and go to its own diviner; or a divination acceptable at one time might be rejected some time later, and quite a different occult cause postulated for the misfortune.

Witch Hunts in the West

The search for witches in tribal societies was quite different from the great witch hunts in Europe in the sixteenth and seventeenth centuries, or the outbreak of accusations at Salem, Massachusetts, in 1692. In tribal societies accusations of witchcraft were specific to particular social relationships; these might be set in the development of relationships within a group of relatives, bound together with strong sentiments of love and cooperation, but also involved in competition for positions of authority and limited resources. A witch was usually a witch with reference to the particular misfortunes of a particular person; and other persons might not be interested in the question. But in the European hunts for witches the whole community, and more particularly the Church, would be deeply involved. For witchcraft was closely identified with heresy, and with Jewry, and in some areas with Islam; and it was the task of the Church to root out heretics and witches.

After being denounced by some accuser, witches were then subjected to torture, under which they both confessed and implicated others as partners with them in the witches' sabbath. Alleged spectral visions of others and admissions against themselves extracted under torture were the principal evidence; and those judges who showed any leniency, or thinkers who might question the sense of the outburst, became suspect themselves. The only ordeals akin to those in tribal societies required the thrusting of the arm into hot water and then judgment of its effects, or throwing the suspect into a pond: if she floated it was the Devil who bore her up, if she sank she

Witches' Sabbath, Johannes Praetorius (1668)

the witch-detecting of tribal societies and of the Christian world need to be understood in very different contexts, despite superficial similarities.

The outbreaks of witch-finding cults which periodically have swept through parts of Africa seem to be at least a first stage in the spiritual reaction of small-scale societies to their absorption in the economy and organization of the expanding Western world: hence they are in some ways akin to the situations of European witch hunts, or the Salem trials. But they were not carried out in the name of a Christian orthodoxy, nor did they hunt directly for witches. They demanded that their adherents purify their hearts and get rid of their charms of witchcraft and magic and, lacking the support of an organized Church and being opposed by government, they were far less searching or punitive. They appear to have been succeeded by millenary cults, which echoed Judaeo-Christian ideologies, but which included generally the idea of cleansing one's heart of vicious feelings against one's neighbours, and in societies which had indigenous beliefs in witchcraft this entailed cleansing one's heart of witchcraft. Hence we can describe them as a community method of finding out witches—and at the same time curing them of their evil.

MAX GLUCKMAN

FURTHER READING: E. E. Evans-Pritchard. Witchcraft, Oracles and Magic Among the Azande. *(Oxford: Oxford UP, 1937); M. Gluckman.* Custom and Conflict in Africa. *(Barnes & Noble, 1969);* Politics, Law and Ritual in Tribal Society. *(New American Library, 1968); J. Middleton.* Lugbara Religion. *(Oxford: Oxford UP, 1960); J. C. Mitchell.* The Yao Village *and W. Turner,* Schism and Continuity in an African Society *(both published by Humanities, 1972).*

was innocent, and lucky if she was rescued before being drowned.

It is true that the kinds of fantasies produced by persons subjected to torture who made confessions in European witch-trials, or the standardized beliefs and allegations of their accusers, bear similarities to the beliefs in tribal societies about the activities of the witches: riding in the air on familiars or objects, going naked, committing incest, and indulging in sexual promiscuity, and so on. But the sociological settings of these forms of witchcraft were quite diverse, and so therefore were the methods of detecting witchcraft and witches. Some of those who observed the witch hunts in Europe or in Salem commented that they reflected village hatreds and malice; and we have seen that malevolent motives in tribal personal relationships were believed to inspire witches to do harm. But this similarity of motives is too trivial to help us make sense of the quite different social and cultural systems of belief and action which share them, while the similitude of fantasies can be understood better by examining the limited number of emotional and moral themes open to human beings in society. Hence the witchcraft and

Witches Leaving the Sabbath, Charles Maurand

Flying Ointment

An ancient and very widespread belief held that witches could fly through the air, riding upon broomsticks, staves, forks, or upon the backs of demons in animal form, and sometimes, though more rarely, without any visible support. Usually they made ready for their journey by smearing their bodies, or the objects upon which they rode, with a magical ointment given to them by the Devil, or prepared according to his instructions.

It is known how some of these flying ointments are made because a number of English and Continental writers in the sixteenth and seventeenth centuries described the methods; all the recipes contained extracts from strongly poisonous plants. The ingredients most commonly listed were aconite, deadly nightshade, hemlock, and the boiled fat and marrow of babies who had been stolen from their homes before they were baptized, or dug up from their graves. Reginald Scot in his *Discoverie of Witchcraft* (1584), recorded that the 'bowels and members' of such children were seethed in a cauldron, and the thickest part of the resultant grease was used as a basis for the ointment. Other ingredients mentioned in various prescriptions were cinquefoil, sweet flag, poplar leaves, the blood of bats or lapwings, parsley, soot, and, if human fat was omitted, some sort of oil.

Francis Bacon who, like Reginald Scot before him, was inclined to ascribe the supposed witch flights to imagination or drug-induced delusions, noted in *Sylva Sylvarum* (1608) that 'the ointment that witches use is reported to be made of the fat of children digged out of their graves; of the juices of smallage (wild celery), wolfbane, and cinquefoil, mingled with the meal of fine wheat; but I suppose that the soporiferous medicines are likest to do it.'

Although the use of flying ointments was widely credited, there was curiously little evidence for it in the recorded confessions of the witches themselves. Claire Goessen, a Belgian witch, confessed in 1603 that she had flown to the sabbath on more than one occasion, riding upon a staff smeared with an unguent. In 1460, in northern France, five accused women admitted that the Devil gave them a salve which they rubbed on their hands and on a small wooden rod, and then placing the rod between their legs, they flew away, 'above good towns and woods and waters' to their meeting-place.

The Swedish witches of 1669, who rode 'over Churches and high walls' to Blocula upon a beast provided by the Devil, said that he gave them 'a horn with a Salve in it, wherewith we do anoint ourselves'. The members of two Somerset covens confessed in 1664 that, before they went to their meetings, they smeared their wrists and foreheads with a greenish oil, 'which smells raw', and which their Spirit gave them, 'and then they are carried in a very short time, using these words as they pass, Thout, tout a tout, tout, throughout and about.' The impression given in these, and other similar confessions, is that the occult properties of the ointment were essential to the power of flight, but evidently this was not always the case. Some witches spoke of flying without any preliminary anointment, simply by straddling a staff, or a straw, or a hollow stalk, and uttering an incantation. In *Disquisitionum Magicarum* (1599) Martin Delrio remarked that the Devil was able to carry witches to the sabbath without the help of any unguents, and that he often did so; but for several reasons, he preferred that his servants should first anoint themselves.

Learned opinion was never quite unanimous on the question of whether witches actually flew or merely imagined that they did. Most writers on the subject accepted that demonic transportation, with or without the use of flying ointments was possible, and

did in fact occur. There were however others who held that the witches' confessions of flight were due to hallucinations or vivid dreams. As far back as the ninth century, the document known as the *Canon Episcopi* condemned as demon-induced error the claims made by certain women that they had flown through the air with Diana, riding in large companies upon beasts over immense tracts of country in the dead of the night. Such women were deceived by sinful fantasies inspired by Satan, who 'deludes the minds of his subjects in sleep, so that the victim believes that these things, which only her spirit experiences, she really experiences in the body.'

A tale recounted by Nider in *Formicarius* (1517) suggests that flying dreams could be caused by the magical ointment itself. A certain woman anointed herself with an unguent while she was sitting in a kneading-trough. She fell asleep and dreamt that she was flying, rocking the trough so violently that she fell out of it and injured her head. John Cotta in *The Triall of Witchcraft* (1616) quoted an Italian story related by the natural philosopher Giambattista della Porta (1540–1615) concerning a woman who, having rubbed herself with ointment, went into a trance, from which she could not be roused, even when shaken and beaten. When she finally woke of her own accord, she declared she had been flying over seas and mountains, and could not be convinced that she had been asleep in her own room all the time.

In an appendix to Dr. Margaret Murray's *Witch-Cult in Western Europe,* Professor A. J. Clark pointed out that the strong poisons contained in flying ointments would have definite physiological effects, especially if rubbed into skins broken by scratches or the bites of vermin. Aconite produces irregular action of the heart; hemlock and belladonna (deadly nightshade) produce

excitement and delirium. An unguent containing a combination of these drugs could cause delusions which, in some cases, might account for the witches' confessions of magical flight.

Dion Fortune

Occultist, psychoanalyst, and novelist, Dion Fortune—whose real name was Violet Mary Firth—was born in 1891 and died in 1946. At a very early age she showed signs of extreme sensitivity to people and places and it soon became evident that she possessed strongly developed psychic faculties. Brought up in a Christian Science household, her marked independence of spirit and penchant for prolonged daydreaming caused much anxiety. The power of imagination plays a great part in occultism, and in later years she learnt to make use of reverie, properly controlled and directed, in the kind of occultism she was to teach and practice.

When she was about twenty years old, Violet Firth suffered a traumatic experience which determined the course of her life. It occurred while she was working at an educational establishment. Her employer, the principal, was a domineering, unscrupulous woman of a particularly malevolent disposition, who had studied the techniques of yoga for many years in India. When Violet unwittingly antagonized her, she responded by attacking her with a form of yoga resembling hypnosis, perverting the process so as to produce destructive emanations. The attack left the girl shattered in mind and body. 'It was this experience which led me to take up the study of analytical psychology, and subsequently of occultism,' she wrote in her most characteristic book, *Psychic Defense* (1930), a study of the abuses of occult power and the ways in which the victim can protect himself.

Violet Firth first trained as a Freudian psychoanalyst and throughout her life retained a strong interest in psychology, publishing several books on the subject under her own name. 'As soon as I . . . watched the dissection of a mind under psychoanalysis, I realized that there was very much more in the mind than was accounted for by the accepted psychological theories'; it was in order to understand these unexplained aspects that she originally took to occultism.

The terrifying contact with an undoubted practitioner of black magic was also the starting point of her later researches into ways and means of combating mental interference and domination by one person, or group, over another. She learnt how to diagnose and counteract the most insidious kinds of psychic attack; and soon developed and mastered the ability to travel in her astral body, to extrude her etheric double, to scry in the spirit vision and similar practices of operative occultism. It was not until she was initiated into an esoteric society, the Hermetic Order of the Golden Dawn, that she was fully healed from her encounter with evil forces. She claims that initiation sealed her damaged etheric body, which since the time of her experience had been leaking energy like a broken vessel. In the Golden Dawn she applied herself systematically to the study and practice of magic, and emerged a fully fledged occultist. Her own group—The Fraternity of the Inner Light—was founded in the 1920s and is still in existence.

Under the assumed name Dion Fortune she wrote widely on the occult, her most important book being *The Mystical Qabalah* (1935); much of her material was related to Aleister Crowley's researches in the sphere of magical correspondences and symbolic affinities. Toward the end of her life these two adepts, both of whom were intent upon reviving the ancient mys-teries exchanged a number of letters.

Like many occultists, Dion Fortune also used fiction as a vehicle for her ideas, well aware that she could disseminate truths otherwise incommunicable to uninitiated minds. Her novels are mainly concerned with the lives of ordinary people who, in the course of their experiences, become so disillusioned through sorrow or suffering that their minds are forcibly turned inward. This introversion taps the memories of previous incarnations; the individuals thus gain insight into the purpose of their present lives and are able to act accordingly.

Black Isis

Two novels, *The Sea Priestess* (1938) and *Moon Magic* (published posthumously in 1957) throw a great deal of light on her magical personality. In them she relates the history of a priestess of Isis who comes to restore paganism to a world that has lost touch with the elemental forces that make life truly dynamic. But it is not the Isis of simple unregenerate Nature, or primal emotional and sensual pleasure, but the power of the Black Isis, the primordial and elemental essence of Woman in her power aspect. Mated to its complement in the male stripped of the accretions of civilization by the realization of inherent divinity, this power is capable of effecting profound transformations in human consciousness.

Black Isis embodies the sakti (power) that destroys all that is inessential and obstructive to the soul's development. It is the power that liberates the spirit of man from the confines of limited experience. The basis of Fortune's practical work involves the bringing through into manifestation of this sakti, by the magically controlled interplay of sexual polarity. This is embodied in the priest, or consecrated male, and the specially chosen female. Together they enact the immemorial Rite and form a vortex in the ether, down which the tremendous energies of Black Isis rush into manifestation.

Dion Fortune believed that her work would form a nucleus enabling the ancient Temple mysteries to operate once more. She was, indeed, a priestess of the Western esoteric tradition, the ground plan of which is the Tree of Life which forms the subject of *The Mystical Qabalah*.

FURTHER READING: Dion Fortune. Psychic Self Defense; Applied Magic; Sane Occultism. (London: Aquarian Press, 1967); The Mystical Qabalah. *(Weiser); fiction:* Moon Magic; The Sea Priestess. *(Weiser, 1981); see also publications of the Society of the Inner Light.*

French Witchcraft

The pattern of witchcraft in Europe, as it emerged in the time of the great persecutions, combined two different ingredients. One was what could be called 'cottage-industry witchcraft', the use of spells and potions to work black magic or white. The second and newer ingredient was the belief that witches were the storm-troops of the Devil. The witch was now not a mere rustic wise-woman, who would provide a healing charm as readily as a poison (though this was what some of the accused witches may have been in reality). She——or he, there were plenty of male witches—was entirely dedicated to evil and had deliberately enlisted in the malevolent service of Satan.

In its early days, this picture of witchcraft was developed largely in France. It drew heavily on the accusations made against earlier heretical sects, and it was confirmed by putting leading questions to accused witches and torturing them until they confessed. They were forced to name other people as witches, who were then interrogated and tortured in their turn. Through the confessions and the books in which the persecutors reported their experiences, a clear pattern of witch behaviour and witch beliefs was built up, a pattern which may have attracted some people to become witches of this type now widely recognized.

The central feature of the new witch religion was the sabbath, the meeting at which the Devil was worshipped. From c. 1425 on, there was an extensive persecution in the Dauphine, spreading eastward from Lyon to Grenoble and Briancon. One old man, Pierre Vallin, who was sentenced in 1438, confessed that he had given himself body and soul to the Devil long before. He had also given the Devil his baby daughter and the Devil had killed her. On the Devil's orders he used to stir up destructive storms by flailing the waters of a stream. He rode to the witch meetings on a stick and there copulated with the Devil, who took the form of a girl for the purpose.

'In the Name of the Devil, Go!'
The confession of a woman named Antoine Rose, a witch of the Savoy who was tortured and tried in 1477, confirms this description and adds some extra details. The first time she was taken to the synagogue she saw many men and women there, enjoying themselves and dancing backward. The Devil, whose name was Robinet, was a dark man who spoke in a hoarse voice.

Kissing Robinet's foot in homage, she renounced God and the Christian faith. He put his mark on her, on the little finger of her left hand, and gave her a stick, eighteen inches long, and a pot of ointment. She used to smear the ointment on the stick, put it between her legs and say, 'Go, in the name of the Devil, go!' At once she would be carried through the air to the synagogue.

At the meeting the Devil would turn into a black dog which they all kissed, under the tail. He ordered them to do all the evil they could and gave them ointments and powders with which they could harm men and beasts. He also told them to worship him and not Christ, and not to adore the consecrated host in church but to

The skeleton of 'La Corriveau', in her iron cage, terrifying a traveler

The Form of a Black Cat
The anonymous *Errores Gazariorum*, written c. 1450 in a French-speaking region of Savoy, gives a more detailed description of the sabbath. It says that a new recruit is taken to 'the synagogue' (an early name for the gathering) by someone who is already a witch. He is presented to the Devil, who takes the form of a man or an animal, usually a black cat. He swears an oath to be faithful to the witch society, to bring in new members, to reveal none of the society's secrets, to kill small children and bring their bodies to the synagogue, to avenge all injuries to the society and its members. After this he worships the Devil, kissing him under the tail. Then the witches feast and dance. The lights are put out and the Devil cries Mestlet, mestlet (mingle, mingle) and there is a promiscuous orgy. Before they leave, in mockery of the Eucharist, the witches urinate and evacuate in a cask.

spit it out. At one meeting a consecrated host was brought and they all trampled on it.

In 1452 a witch tried at Provins, near Paris, said there were only fifty or sixty witches in all France, most of whom carried mirrors in their hats. Five people were promptly discovered with mirrors in their hats, and were arrested. A small boy said that his father and mother had twice taken him to witches' meetings and that if they were stripped and searched, a white mark, the size of a pea or bigger, would be found on their bodies—an early reference to the famous 'Devil's mark'.

The suggestion that there was only a handful of witches in France was contradicted by the poet Martin le Franc, who maintained that in the mountain valleys to the east and south of Briançon anything from 3,000 to 10,000 people attended the sabbaths, and that more than 600 women had confessed to copulating with demons at these gatherings. Alphonsus de Spina, a convert from Judaism who became a Franciscan, wrote a book called *Fortalicium Fidei* in c. 1459, in which he says witches were particularly numerous in Dauphine and also in Gascony, where they met at a rock to worship a boar and kiss its backside. Many of them had been executed and in the house of the Inquisitor at Toulouse were paintings showing their meetings and the punishments inflicted on them.

Pierre de Lancre

French magistrate and witch-finder Pierre de Lancre devoted the latter part of his life to energetically ferreting out evidence, real or imaginary, of devil-worship and witchcraft: he boasted of having consigned 600 witches to the flames. In his *Tableau de l'inconstance des mauvais anges* (Description of the Faithlessness of Evil Angels) he gives a first-hand account of his witch hunt in the Basque region of France

'Satan is shown in the form of a goat preaching from a golden chair; the flame issuing from one of his five horns is to light the sabbath fires. On his right sits the Queen of the sabbath and kneeling before them a witch presents a child she has abducted. Partaking of the sabbath feast are witches and demons: only the meat of corpses, hanged men, hearts of unbaptized children and unclean animals never eaten by Christians are eaten. At the extreme right, poor witches who dare not approach the high ceremonies watch the festivities. After the banquet, the devils lead their neighbours beneath a cursed tree where, forming a ring facing alternately inward and outward, the company dance in the most indecent manner possible. At the left of the picture musicians play in accompaniment to the dancing and below them a troop of women and girls dance back to back in a circle. A group of noble lords and ladies mingle with rich and powerful witches who are disguised or masked to avoid recognition and who conduct the important business of the sabbath. During the sabbath, witches arrive on pitchforks and broomsticks, or on goats with their children whom they will present to Satan. Children with sticks, to prevent toads from getting out of a stream, assist witches to brew poisons: one witch holds serpents and toads, the other skins them and throws them in the pot.'

This insistence, by so many persecutors, on the enormous numbers of witches helps to explain the growing fear of them and the cruelty with which they were treated. The American scholar H. C. Lea commented: 'The world was full of them and no one knew whether his family and friends or anyone whom he might meet was not a sorcerer gifted with the awful powers granted by the demon. That the terror was fantastic and imaginary did not render it less real and it accounts for the craze which devastated Europe in the seventeenth century.'

Another important factor was the belief, found in many primitive societies, that what we regard as accidents of Nature are not accidental at all but are caused by the malice of witches. At Metz in 1456 and 1457 witch hunts were sparked off by unusually bad weather which harmed the crops. Again in 1488 a disastrously cold summer was put down to witchcraft at Metz, and twenty-eight people were burned.

All sorts of natural misfortunes, from minor illnesses to the failure of a harvest, were lumped together as *maleficia* or 'evil doings', and attributed to witches. In 1460 Martin of Aries announced that all maleficia involved an implied agreement to serve the Devil. Nicholas Remy, author of *Demonolatreiae* (1595), maintained that, 'Whatever is not normal is due to the Devil.'

The Witches of Arras

The linking of witchcraft with the worship of the Devil was originally the work of the Inquisition and was later adopted by the secular courts, though in the fifteenth century civil courts in France were still sometimes dealing with cases of witchcraft without bringing the Devil and the sabbath into it at all. By contrast, when a number of witches were examined by the ecclesiastical authorities at Arras in 1460, the suspects were tortured into confessing that they worshipped the Devil and had attended the sabbath. Their master appeared to them in human form but he never showed his face. (Presumably, if he existed at all, he was a man with his head covered or wearing a mask.) He made them all give him the obscene kiss. They feasted luxuriously until all the lights went out and there was a wild orgy.

One of the accused had been cruelly beaten by the Devil when he threatened to leave the society. Another had attended many meetings, holding a lighted candle in the Devil's honour and kissing him under the tail, had signed in his own blood a formal pact making over his soul to the Devil, and had used powders and ointments to harm men and cattle.

Altogether, thirty-four suspects were arrested and twelve were executed. It is interesting that apparently very few people believed in their guilt. One hundred years later the weight of popular opinion would go the other way.

The first work on witchcraft to be written in French was an anonymous pamphlet of c. 1460, 'La Vauderye de Lyonois' (Vauderye from the heretical sect of Waldensians), describing trials at Lyons. The Devil appeared at the sabbath as a man with horns and talons or in a variety of animal forms, and he spoke in a harsh and terrifying voice. The meetings were usually held on Thursday nights. In church, witches would not cross themselves properly but would make a kind of circle. They turned their eyes away at the elevation of the host and took consecrated hosts to the sabbath to be contemptuously fouled.

Full Flood

Almost all the accusations about the witches' behaviour at the sabbath had earlier been made against the heretical sects—including the worship of the

Devil, his animal forms, the obscene kiss, the violent hatred of Christianity, the cannibal eating of babies, the promiscuous orgy. In the early fourteenth century the Knights Templar were accused of worshipping the Devil; trampling on crucifixes, copulating with demons, and obscene kissing. In the fourteenth and fifteenth centuries there were various trials of important personages, notably Joan of Arc and Gilíes de Rais, in which accusations of witchcraft played a part and which helped to create popular belief in the prevalence of witches.

From the end of the fifteenth century the tide of persecution began to run at full flood. Year after year, suspects were nosed out, interrogated, tortured, and condemned. Forty witches were burned at Toulouse in 1557, four at Poitiers in 1568, eighteen at Avignon in 1582. In 1580 the political philosopher and witch judge Jean Bodin published *De la Démonomanie des Sorciers*, in which he observed that burning over a slow fire was an inadequate punishment for a witch, as it took only half an hour or so.

In Lorraine Nicholas Remy condemned 900 witches in a few years after 1581. There were witch hunts in Normandy between 1589 and 1594, and again between 1600 and 1645. In Burgundy Henri Boguet exterminated some 600 witches and wrote the famous *Discours des Sorciers* (1602) which went through twelve editions in twenty years. In 1609 Pierre de Lancre descended on the Basque-speaking provinces north of the Pyrenees and claimed to have executed 600 witches in four months.

In the seventeenth century there was a rash of outbreaks of supposed demonic possession in convents. Staggering confessions of witchcraft and deviltry were poured out by hysterical nuns. Some of these ravings were so improbable that they helped to undermine belief in the reality of witchcraft.

Alombrados Bywater Temple

By about the middle of the seventeenth century the tide had turned. Occasional trials occurred down into the eighteenth century and belief in the old-fashioned type of witchcraft lingered on in country districts. As late as 1885 at Sologne a suspected witch was burned alive by her daughter and son-in-law. But the virtual end of the persecution of witchcraft as the Devil's religion came in 1670, when Louis XIV reprieved twelve witches who had been condemned at Rouen, commuting their death sentences to banishment from the province, and restoring the property which had been confiscated from them. A royal edict of 1682 helped to put witchcraft back into its much older category of 'superstitious practices' and 'pretended magic'.

The Devil's Mass

The Devil was the witches' god, and de Lancre said that they would go down on their knees to him and hail him as 'Great Lord, whom I adore'. A new member of the society would say to the Devil, 'I put myself entirely in your power and into your hands, recognizing no other god, for you are my god.' According to Boguet, before they began their feast the witches said a kind of grace, 'but with words full of blasphemy, making Beelzebub the author and protector of all things.'

A witch named Antide Colas confessed in 1598 that, 'Satan ordered her to pray to him night and morning, before she set about doing anything else.' According to Silvain Nevillon, tried at Orleans in 1614, 'they say to the Devil, we recognize you as our master, our God, our Creator.'

Since witchcraft had been identified as worship of the Devil, it was naturally a stock accusation that witches consciously and formally renounced the Christian faith. De Lancre quoted a girl of sixteen, named Jeannette d'Abadie, who said that she was made to renounce and deny her Creator, the holy Virgin, the saints, her baptism, her father and mother and family, heaven, earth and everything there is in the world.' She also said that she saw the children of witches being enrolled in the Devil's service by baptism at the sabbath. Silvain Nevillon said that the witches baptized babies and anointed their heads with oil, muttering phrases in Latin.

The belief that the witches perverted the Mass into a ceremony in the Devil's honour followed naturally enough from their notorious detestation of Christianity. Boguet said that the celebrant was an apostate priest who wore a black cope with no cross on it. Instead of the host he consecrated a piece of turnip stained black, and the congregation cried out, 'Master, help us!' At Aix-en-Provence, Madeleine de Demandolx accused the priest Louis Gaufridi of inventing the saying of Mass at the sabbath, consecrating the elements to Lucifer and sprinkling the wine on the worshippers, who responded with 'His blood be upon us and our children.'

Silvain Nevillon said that the sabbath was held in a house and he saw there a tall dark man, reading in an inaudible mumble from a book which had black and crimson leaves. Presently he elevated a black host and then a chalice of cracked pewter, 'all foul and filthy'. Another witch of Orleans, Gentien le Clerc, described how the Devil himself said the Mass. He wore a chasuble on which was a broken cross, and turned his back on the altar when elevating a black host and a black chalice. He muttered the words of the service from a book, bound in some soft and hairy material like a wolf's skin, and with red, white, and black leaves.

The Black Goat

The Devil frequently appeared to his followers in animal form, and especially as a goat. At Poitiers in 1574 he was 'a great black goat who spoke like a person.' At Avignon, when he climbed onto a large stone to be worshipped, he turned himself into a great black goat, though normally he appeared as a man. In Puy de Dôme in 1594 he was a black goat with a candle between his horns. He might also show himself as a dog or a cat, a bull or a stag, or even as a pig or a sheep. Many of the descriptions suggest a man wearing a mask and an animal's skin.

The Devil also very often appeared in human form. In 1567 a witch of Amou in the southwest said that they all danced round a great stone on which sat a great black man, whom they called Monsieur. Françoise Secretain in 1598 said that the Devil was a great black man. Barthélemy Minguet of Brécy, tried in 1616, said that he saw the Devil at the sabbath 'in the shape of a man, who held a horse by its bridle, and that they went forward to worship him, each one holding a pitch candle of black wax in their hands.'

How much truth there is in these accounts, and in all the descriptions of the sabbath, is very hard to determine. It is clear that hundreds of innocent

The Black Book of Death

From the sentence pronounced against witches at Avignon, 1582:

. . . you and each of you have renounced the one and triune God, the creator of us all, and have worshipped the merciless Devil, the old enemy of the human race . . . in pledge of the faith professed in the demon you have given him a fragment of your garments; and in order that your name should be removed and obliterated from the Book of Life, by the command of the Father of Lies, with your own hand you have placed your sign in the black book of perpetual death and of the reproved and damned; and, in order that he might bind you more firmly to such great infidelity and impiety, he branded each of you with his mark or stigma, as being his own property . . . you and each of you have bound yourselves by oath to obey his orders and commands, trampling on the cross and the sign of the Lord; and in obedience to him, mounted on a staff and with your thighs anointed with a certain most execrable unguent prescribed to you by the said Devil, you have been carried through the air . . . to the appointed spot on certain days, and there, in the synagogue . . . by the light of a noisome fire, after many jubilations, dancings, feastings, drinkings, and games in honour of the presiding Beelzebub, prince of demons, in the form and appearance of a most black and filthy goat, you have adored him as God, by acts and words . . . asking his aid to punish all your enemies and those who refuse you anything, and, taught by him, inflicting revenge, injuries, and enchantments on men and beasts . . . you men have fornicated with succubi, you women with incubi . . . And what is the most detestable of all, when you receive the most august sacrament of the Eucharist in the church, by instruction of the said serpent ejected from paradise, you have retained it in your mouths and nefariously spit it out on the ground so as to insult our true and holy God . . .

people were harried and tormented into confessing anything whatever that was demanded of them. But it seems quite likely that among the hordes of the innocent there may also have been a few who were guilty.

RICHARD CAVENDISH

FURTHER READING: H. C. Lea. Materials Towards a History of Witchcraft. *(Porcupine Press reprint, 3 vols); R. H. Robbins.* Encyclopedia of Witchcraft and Demonology. *(Crown, 1959); M. Summers.* History of Witchcraft. *(Routledge & Kegan, 1973); J. Favret-Saada.* Deadly Words: Witchcraft in the Bocage. *(Cambridge Univ. Press, 1980); W. Monter.* Witchcraft in France and Switzerland. *(Ithaca: Cornell Univ. Press, 1976).*

German Witchcraft

Always unjustly persecuted, the victim of a witch trial was the defendant in legal proceedings which followed the judicial procedure laid down by the Inquisition; this contained certain features which automatically put the accused at a disadvantage, particularly in that he or she was not allowed a defense. Witches could be seized and imprisoned merely 'on suspicion'—on circumstantial evidence alone.

During local outbreaks of witch hysteria, sometimes leading to hundreds of convictions, many communities erected so-called 'witch towers' or 'witches' houses' which served as special jails for this type of prisoner, and in which incredibly sadistic outrages took place. Defence witnesses were not even admitted to the witch trials and relatives of an accused person were allowed to visit only on condition that they agreed to try and persuade him or her to make a confession of witchcraft activities.

The majority of court records are of a monotonously stereotyped nature. The accused victims made their confessions—usually extracted under torture—according to a standard formula, prepared by the local torturer, and based on those used in the trials against demon-worship dating back to the fourth century. The Emperors Constantine, Valentine, and Valens

The Revelation of St. John: 14. The Whore of Baylon. **One of a series of woodblocks made by the German artist Albrecht Dürer in the late fifteenth century during the height of the so-called 'war on witches' conducted by the Christian Church against the people of Europe.**

had established the use of the Roman penal code against sorcerers, as supporters of a subversive pagan group; the formulae of confession continued to be used by executioners and torturers during both heresy trials and witch persecutions over 1,000 years later.

The sentence was of equally stereotyped severity. In the majority of cases the accused witch was sentenced to death by burning, although he or she might be strangled or executed with the sword beforehand as an act of clemency. If torture failed to produce a confession from the more resolute defendants, they might be sent into exile; this was more common during the later phases of witch persecution, when those permanently invalided by torture were often pushed over the border in carts. The reality of law was experienced as the justice of terror, the essence of which consists in the fact that the terror could not openly be referred to by name.

The principle of suspicion made such a climate of terror possible. To be denounced as a witch was enough to destroy the lives of both rich and poor alike. Merely associating with a witch, or with a relative suspected of witchcraft, was thought to be proof of one's own guilt. Devil-worship was believed to be transmitted to a child either by its godmother, skilled in magic, or through its own mother, shortly after birth.

There is a basic sociological difference between a magic-orientated culture, believing in the existence of men and women gifted with the power of sorcery, and the notorious witch persecutions of the twelfth to eighteenth centuries. It lies in the belief that 'we', as members of an orthodox Christian community, neither wish to nor are able to practice magic, but that there are others, outsiders, apostates, enemies of civilized man, who can perform these arts.

As far as the man in the street is concerned, the victim must have been guilty of witchcraft; otherwise it follows that the Church, the courts, and the government have been accessories in the most terrible murder. But this adoption of the persecution ideology into the public consciousness always remained ambivalent. There was an element of doubt in nearly every individual case, if not in general. This is apparent in one of the first German testimonies, that of Mathias Widman, who was Court Chaplain to the Elector Friedrich von der Pfalz in Heidelberg in 1475. On the one hand Mathias Widman describes the horrible rites performed by witches, and the heretical Gazariorum sect, only to make an exception of those people known personally to him who have been indicted for witchcraft.

Children on Trial

Particularly striking is the adoption of these ideas by children and youths in those areas where the trials had been in process for some time. Gangs of children hounded suspected witches with unusual venom, before the unfortunate victims were finally imprisoned. They accused each other of sorcery and boasted that they could bewitch people as if it were a game, without understanding the serious implications of their actions. They invented imaginary

The impulse which led to the witch trial originated at the lowest level of society and worked its way up.

stories of nightly feasts and revels, reminiscent of delusions caused by fever. The authorities pounced on such tenuous information and children's trials were frequent, at which small children would appear not only as witnesses but also as defendants.

The most comprehensive account of these conditions is given by Friedrich Merzbacher in his book *Die Hexenprozesse in Franken* (Witch Trials in Franconia) published in 1957. He gives a detailed account of the wave of witchcraft trials in the Bishopric of Wurzburg in the seventeenth century, where 900 people were tried in the years 1623–1631 alone, and the even more notorious Bamberg trials of the decade 1623–1633.

It seems highly probable that some of the major figures in this network of persecution were psychopaths and people suffering from paranoia. At the same time, the presence at these trials of credulous and perhaps intimidated local dignitaries, as well as those who commanded the respect of the people—priests of both denominations, lawyers, scholars, and writers—helped

to guarantee recognition of the witchcraft ideology and its perpetuation.

Crime and Corruption

There are, however, many examples of witch-finders being motivated by criminal urges to line their own pockets through blackmail and exploitation. Jakob Bithner, an official of the province of Styria, provides just one example of this corruption. He was originally given the task of ridding the countryside of vagrants, mostly disbanded mercenaries; he took it on himself to include 'those criminals who dabble in sorcery', and eventually became a professional witch-finder. Similarly, a soldier named Geiss of Lindenheim offered his services to the town's officials as a witch-finder, hinting that the church and a local bridge could be repaired by extorting money from the richer citizens. Geiss instituted a regime of terror, until public indignation forced him to flee. The infamous Count Balthasar Voss or Noss, who carried on his activities for fifteen years, boasted that he hoped to achieve 1,000 convictions. In 1603 the Supreme Court of the Holy Roman Empire intervened to put an end to his excesses. Many persecutors attracted a large number of followers, but they required the legitimate sanction of a secular or ecclesiastical body. At Esslingen, near Stuttgart, for instance, the fanatical witch-finder Nagogeorgus was supported in his actions by the judge of the nearby village of Wiessenstein. Sometimes, however, individual itinerant witch-finders were seized by enlightened magistrates and prevented from doing any more harm. An executioner's assistant from Eichstatt, who had started rumours of witchcraft, was punished at Nuremberg. Hans Schock from Furstenfelden in Austria, who had tried to earn money by denouncing witches in

Strasburg and Basle, was sentenced to death by drowning.

The relationship between the men in authority, on the one hand, and their atrocities on the other, was far from simple. The situation was not purely one of induced delusion; there was also the factor of revenge. This is particularly evident in the account of a man named Kothmann in Lemgo. During the first wave of trials in the area, Kothmann's mother was burned as a witch, and he was forced to flee and roam the country as a poverty-stricken law student. When he finally returned to Lemgo he succeeded in being elected to the position of mayor, and set about revenging himself on all those families who had held positions of authority in the town at the time of his mother's death. Kothmann remained in office until his death in 1684 and was responsible for the execution of ninety people.

Repeated efforts to keep the hysteria in check were made by a number of lawyers and others in positions of authority. In 1628 Vice-Chancellor Hahn of Bamberg became a victim because of his known leniency toward witches. The outstanding figure, however, is the Jesuit Father Friedrich von Spee. As a result of his experiences as confessor to the witches of Würzburg, he wrote a book, *Cautio Criminalis*, in which he examined and exposed from his first-hand knowledge the whole process of witch persecution from a sociological standpoint. His work was published anonymously in 1631; he was forbidden to make his views known, and was disposed of discreetly by being sent as confessor to those sick with the plague.

A Sympathy for Witches

Spee sympathized with the predicament of accused witches who were only entitled to the services of a confessor if they first guaranteed that they would not recant their previous confessions. He questioned whether witches really existed and, showing a remarkable understanding of the group psychology which underlay the persecutions, he came to the conclusion that the impulse which led to the witch trial originated at the lowest level of society and worked its way up;

Hexenmeister, Carl Spitzweg (1808-1885)

Hexenküche (Witches Kitchen), Franz Francken (1581–1642)

that the persecutions were engendered by the common people themselves, 'the irrational and, generally speaking, jealous and base rabble'. 'If the authorities did not immediately seize upon baseless rumours' says Spee, 'there would be a great outcry that the officials themselves were afraid for their wives and friends, and that they (the common people) were being hoodwinked by the rich.'

The publication of this book at such a period in history, by a man who had reason to fear for his life, shows that it is possible even in such circumstances to examine the process of terror and to see it clearly for what it was.

WANDA VON BAEYER-KATTE

FURTHER READING: John A. Rush. Witchcraft and Sorcery. (C. C. Thomas, 1974).

Golden Dawn

Many well-known people belonged to the Golden Dawn, which functioned as a kind of occult university in Britain in the 1890s. The Order's modernization of the Western tradition of ritual magic has exerted a lasting influence.

The light of the typical modern occult society shines brightly for a little while before the group splinters into quarrelling and power-hungry factions and vanishes without trace. The Hermetic Order of the Golden Dawn was an exception. Founded in London in 1888, it attracted a very high-powered membership, enjoyed a vigorous life for a dozen years, and exerted a lasting influence on occult and New Age ideas and groups in the West. Israel Regardie, who was Aleister Crowley's secretary for a time and long afterward published the Order's rituals, called it, 'the only [esoteric] Order of real worth that the West of our time has known.'

The Golden Dawn was founded when the tide of the nineteenth-century revival of interest in magic and the occult was rising high. Spiritualism was much in vogue. So was Freemasonry, which was attracting many new members. The Theosophical Society had opened a London branch in 1883 and Madame Blavatsky herself had settled in London in 1887. Where the Theosophists were drawn principally to oriental religion and mysticism, the Golden Dawn emphasized the high magical tradition of the West, rediscovered in Europe during the Renaissance.

Chiefs and Secret Chiefs

The Order emerged from the world of fringe Masonry and purported to be a branch of a mysterious Rosicrucian order in Germany, though in fact the German group did not exist and the documents which linked the Golden Dawn with it were forged. One of the founders was a retired medical man, William Robert Woodman (1828-91), who was Supreme Magus of the Societas Rosicruciana in Anglia, known familiarly as the Soc. Ros. This obscure group, of which the novelist

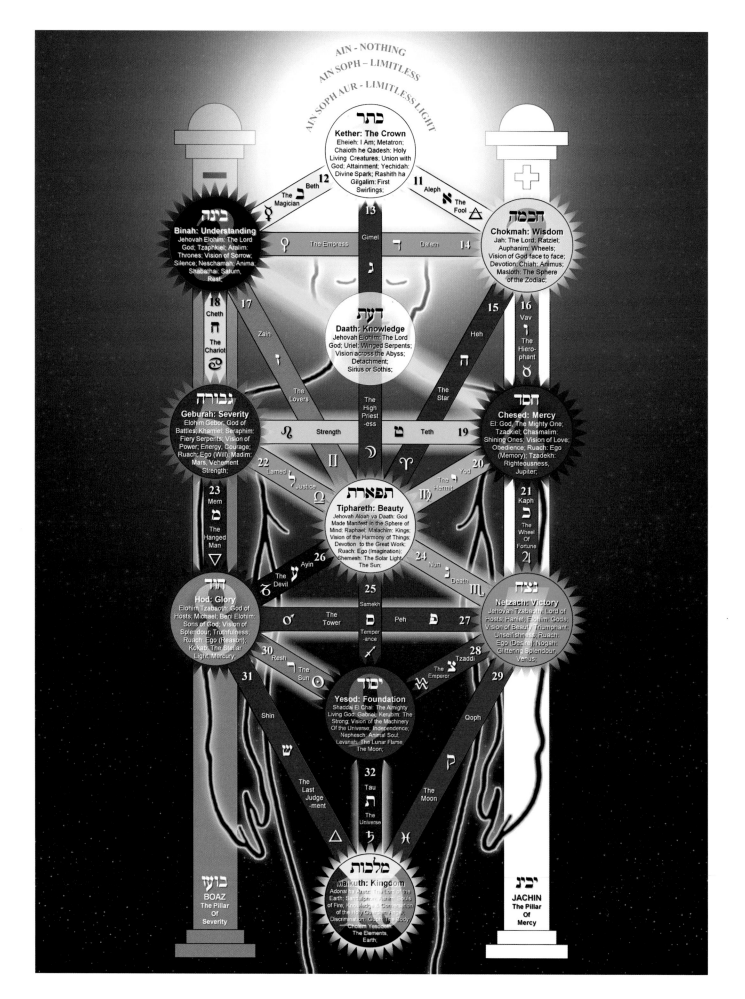

Bulwer Lytton had been Grand Patron, was interested in the Hermetica, the Cabala, the Rosicrucian tradition, and Spiritualism. Another founder was a London doctor and coroner called William Wynn Westcott (1848–1925), who was a member of the Theosophical Society and succeeded Woodman as Supreme Magus of the Soc. Ros.

There was much impressive talk of awesomely mysterious 'Secret Chiefs', in line with the fondness of both Rosicrucians and Theosophists for 'Invisibles' or 'Masters'—great superhuman adepts from whom a group drew its authenticity and authority. In reality, Westcott was the prime mover and the one who forged the Golden Dawn's founding documents, but he was soon eclipsed by his protege, MacGregor Mathers, a more formidable chief than any Invisible. It was Mathers, more than any other single person, who made the Golden Dawn a success.

Samuel Liddell Mathers (1854–1918) was the son of a London clerk and was educated at the grammar school in Bedford. Forceful and commanding, of sternly military demeanour, he was an enthusiast for all things Celtic and an ardent Jacobite, who longed for the restoration of the Stuarts to the British throne. He called himself MacGregor Mathers because he liked to think that he was descended from that clan of romantic Scots outlaws. He also awarded himself the title of Comte de Glenstrae.

In 1890 he married Moina Bergson (1865–1928), sister of the French philosopher Henri Bergson. The new Mrs. Mathers had studied art in London at the Slade School. She met Mathers in the British Museum, where she was studying Egyptian art, and was involved with the Golden Dawn from an early stage.

Opposite page:
Qabalistic Tree of Life in the Golden Dawn tradition.

Aleister Crowley, British occultist, writer, philosopher, and mystic, dressed in one of his character magical robes (April 19, 1934)

Mathers was genuinely learned in the Cabala and he published editions of *The Key of Solomon* and other grimoires. He was also a friend both of Madame Blavatsky and of Anna Kingsford.

University of Magic

Westcott, Woodman, and Mathers were the three Chiefs—the visible ones at least—of the new order. The Golden Dawn was intended from the outset to be a secret society, restricted to an elite membership and concentrating on the Western magical tradition. It was Mathers who wrote the Order's rituals and much of the teaching material which was distributed to its members. In the process he constructed a coherent magical system which embraced the Hermetic and Gnostic texts of the early centuries, the Cabala, the Tarot, alchemy, astrology and divination, Rosicrucian and Masonic symbolism, and ritual magic. The system also emphasized the psychological factors in magic as a technique of self-development. It was a brilliant achievement and one which gave the Golden Dawn

Light of Occult Knowledge

He was waiting without the portal under the care of a sentinel while the Hierophant (Mathers), between the pillars and before the altar, addressed his chief officers and the assembled members. Crowley was clothed in a strange, feminine-looking robe with a hood over his head so that he couldn't see a thing, for the light of the natural world is but darkness compared with the radiance of Divine Light. And he was held by a triple cord, a token of nature's tie which bound him. A voice cried from within the Hall of Neophytes . . . 'Child of Earth! wherefore hast thou come to request admission to this Order?' A voice answered for him. 'My soul is wandering in the Darkness seeking for the light of Occult Knowledge, and I believe that in this Order the Knowledge of that Light may be obtained.'

John Symonds, *The Great Beast*

profound influence on subsequent occult groups.

Recruitment of members began in 1888 and by the end of 1891 more than eighty people, including forty-two women, had been initiated into the Isis-Urania Temple in London, while branches had been established

A Battle of Spells

Crowley and Mathers had fallen out meanwhile, and in 1903 they conducted a ferocious magical battle—or so Crowley said. Mathers allegedly sent a delectable female vampire to seduce him, but Crowley turned her own current of evil against her. According to his friend and disciple, J. F. C. Fuller, the distinguished military historian, the consequences were dramatic. The woman's hair turned white and her skin wrinkled. 'The girl of twenty had gone; before him stood a hag of sixty, bent, decrepit, debauched. With dribbling curses she hobbled from the room.'

Undeterred, Mathers struck Crowley's entire pack of bloodhounds dead at one fell stroke. In reply, Crowley summoned up the arch-fiend Beelzebub with forty-nine attendant demons in hideously repellent forms and ordered them to go at once and chastise Mathers in Paris.

The effects of this alarming visitation, if any, are not recorded, but in 1910, when Crowley began publishing Golden Dawn rituals and teachings in his magazine *The Equinox*, Mathers was sufficiently spry to cross the Channel and obtain a legal injunction to stop him publishing any more. However, Mathers had too little money to contest Crowley's appeal, which the Great Beast won. Mathers must have been desperately disappointed to lose control of the order he had done so much to create and to see it disintegrate. He took to the brandy bottle for solace, and in Crowley's thriller *Moonchild* he is unkindly caricatured as Douglas, Count of Glenlyon, a decrepit old drunk.

Mathers died in Paris in 1918, of unknown causes, though Dion Fortune said he had been carried off by the severe influenza epidemic which swept Europe that year. Ithell Colquhoun, who wrote his biography, hinted that years of contact with the superhuman powers and vitality of the Secret Chiefs was finally too much for his frame to bear. His work survives him in the volumes of Golden Dawn rituals and teachings published by Israel Regardie in the 1930s.

RICHARD CAVENDISH

FURTHER READING: E. Howe. Magicians of the Golden Dawn. *(Routledge, 1972); I. Regardie.* The Golden Dawn. *(Llewellyn Publications, 1978); I. Colquhoun.* Sword of Wisdom. *(Spearman, 1975); F. King.* Ritual Magic in England. *(Spearman, 1970); R. Cavendish.* A History of Magic. *(New York: Penguin Arkana, 1990).*

> *A grimoire contains spells, incantations, and symbols, but the book itself is said to be imbued with magical power.*

Grimoire

Grimoire is from the old French *grammaire*, also the root of the word "grammar"; because of this name, it would have been considered much as we view a grammar book today: a book of instructions or a set of rules. A grimoire is a textbook, or manual, of magic, originally published between the late Middle Ages and the early eighteenth Century, although present day authors have begun calling their works grimoires also, so the word has lost the weight of its original nearly sacred meaning. A grimoire contains spells, incantations, and symbols, but the book itself is often said to be imbued with magical power.

Neo-Masonic magical orders such as The Hermetic Order of the Golden Dawn laid claim to some historical grimoires, notably *The Book of the Sacred Magic of Abra-Melin the Mage* and *The Sixth and Seventh Books of Moses*, said to be two missing books of The Old Testament. Copies of the latter were sometimes found in the possession of practitioners of folk medicine and were said to contain information that the Church fathers had left out of the Old Testament because they did not want commoners to have access to the information they contained, techniques such as how to cure a toothache or ease the pain of childbirth. The thinking was this kept the common man and woman dependent upon the Church and its approved doctors for treatment of their ills. In some grimoires you will find instructions for making protective amulets, how to construct a charm, how to ward off evil or attract true love. Others contain information for summoning demons and fairies or plotting astrological forecasts. Still others are replete with folk medicine, cures, and palliatives for various ills.

Hysterical Possession & Witchcraft

Much has been written in the last 100 years on the psychology of the witch herself. It seems undeniable, on the evidence of trials and personal testimonies, that in every era a number of the people who were accused of witchcraft did believe themselves to be witches. Isabel Gowdie, whose spontaneous confession in 1662 amazed and discomforted her contemporaries is a classic example of this type.

On the basis of this and comparable cases there is now a substantial modern literature which treats the witch as a mental case, a person suffering from a classic psychosis, often associated with senility, characterized by delusions as to her own importance and powers. While there is undoubtedly much truth in this view, it seems important to realize that the insanity was by no means one-sided. Frequently as much emotional abnormality, irrationality, and sheer ill-will was displayed by the witch hunters and the witches' 'victims' as by the witches.

Seen in the context of their own time, not all witches were grossly abnormal nor were all the 'bewitched' constitutionally inadequate or hysterical. Nor indeed were all the judges sadistic and neurotic: many were averagely decent, Christian men of their time, doing what they believed to be their duty. Nevertheless it is undeniable that the rigid, tendentious nature of Church law on witchcraft during the centuries of persecution, with the tendency to regard many circumstantial facts as automatic evidence of sorcery and to consider an accused witch guilty unless proved innocent, rather than the other way round, did load the dice consistently against the accused. This provided the opportunity for the abnormally impressionable or paranoid person, to give full rein to his or her imagination.

In every era there are a substantial number of people who are ready, indeed eager, to believe themselves harmed or threatened. The paranoiac who today believes that 'they' (the police, the government, the Jews, the blacks, the Communists, the Arabs) are conspiring against him or his society, is the same man as the suspicious citizen of past centuries who accused witches. The focus of paranoia changes with regimes and fashions in belief, but the type of emotion remains constant. Moreover most paranoiacs display a dreary lack of originality. The repetitive accusations against witches in the past ('they're cursing my pigs—blighting my crops—laming me') are paralleled today by accusations such as 'they're trying to kill me by radar' (or 'by electricity'), which are familiar to every mental health officer.

Unchanging, too, is the paranoid tendency to ascribe the evil not just to one individual's malevolence but to an organized conspiracy of ill-doers; hence the collective prejudice against a mythical 'secret society'—of witches, or Jews, or people of colour. The belief that the scapegoat-group are physically different in some way from ordinary people, and that they are plotting to multiply their number and gain

Philippe Pinel releasing mental patients at La Salpetriere from their bonds (1796). Hand-coloured, nineteenth-century halftone reproduction of a painting.

control over society also seems to be constant. The probable explanation for this apparent flaw in the argument is that the accuser, having made a particular group into his collective scapegoat, has to justify his persecution of its individual and apparently defenceless members by making out that there is some widespread organization behind them. The judges who followed the dictates of the *Malleus Maleficarum* (1487) and similar manuals would no doubt have found it difficult to condemn many of the simple old hags dragged before them unless they had fixed in their minds the idea that it was the whole secret society of witchcraft they were attacking, not just this individual.

Self-induced Symptoms

It may be felt that accusations made by individual paranoid schizophrenics can hardly account for the large-scale witch persecutions that took place, especially on the Continent, in the fifteenth and sixteenth centuries. In fact, though such clinical paranoia may have been relatively rare, even one isolated case in a town could (and still can) serve to excite the milder, more generalized but equally irrational paranoid tendencies and prejudices found among otherwise sane members of the community. Therefore, although there are probably only a few people in a community at any one time who are convinced that they themselves have been singled out by the scapegoat for evil attentions, there are many more who will concede the possibility of such things happening.

There is also another form of unbalanced behaviour which is in itself less ominous than paranoia but which can be just as devastating in its social effect if it is not recognized for what it is. This is characterized by the production of hysterical ailments, usually believed by the subject himself to be genuine. The prime reason for them seems to be a desire to attract attention and sympathy, but often an accusation is thrown in to substantiate the hysteric's case. The accusation is therefore not an essential part of the syndrome, but when it is made, and believed, the effect is the same as with the primary accusations of the paranoiac.

In short, while the paranoiac develops a rooted distrust of one particular person or group, and only then invents his injuries, often fantastic ones, the hysteric reverses the process. He—or, perhaps more typically, she—produces symptoms of injury, often in great variety and abundance, and only then casts around for a scapegoat on which the blame can convincingly be laid. Usually this process seems to be unconscious, but it also seems possible that in many cases the hysteric does know, at some level, that her afflictions are self-induced, and therefore finds it particularly necessary to have a good story about their origins. There is no doubt that both types of person, the paranoiac and the hysteric, made a substantial contribution to the history of witch-persecution.

Very little was generally known or accepted about the working of the human mind in the Middle Ages or, indeed, until the nineteenth century. At various times individual physicians and scholars preached what we should now regard as sound sense: Agrippa (1486–1535) was one and he narrowly escaped being branded as a witch himself for his pains. His pupil the Dutchman Johannes Wier or Weyer was another, and so were the sixteenth century English squire Sir Reginald Scot and, slightly later, an English doctor named John Cotta. Other writers, such as James I of England in his *Demonologie* (1597) and Joseph

The Bristol Old Vic Company in a scene from Arthur Miller's play *The Crucible*, which told the story of the Salem witch trials and a commentary on the power of hysterical prosecution. (November, 1954)

A Rake's Progress, by William Hogarth

Glanvil in his *Saducimus Triumphatus* (1681), while subscribing in the main to popular prejudice on the subject of witchcraft, were sufficiently intelligent to discount certain aspects of it, or to point out rampant abuses. Glanvil, who was in principle a persecutor of witches, admitted that it was 'very improbable that the devil who is a wise and mighty spirit would be at the beck of a poor hag, and have so little to do as to attend to the errands and impotent lusts of a silly old woman.'

But such flashes of reason have to be set against a background of radical ignorance and prejudice. The ancient belief in possession by devils was entrenched in Christian thought; the

madman in the New Testament whose 'devil' Christ was supposed to have cast out was the prototype for an interminable series of lunatics in the sixteenth and seventeenth centuries whose madness was blamed on the evil attentions of a witch. Inevitably, if society has this basic concept of 'bewitching', the supposed signs of it are taken at their face value without further examination. There was little realization, in the centuries of persecution, that vomiting, pains, disturbance of the menses, impotence, paralysis and indeed 'wasting disease', and fits, could be psychosomatic or hysterical ailments, having their root in the sufferer's own fear or in desire for attention rather than in

any organic interference on the part of another.

Hysteria Due to Repression

One of the oldest charges against witches was that they caused impotence, either (in the most ancient accusations) by stealing the male organ, or by 'impeding the conjugal action of men and women' in some less drastic way. This may be taken as simply one manifestation of the general link between witchcraft and sterility, the distortion of the original fertility cults into a 'black' form. It may also be considered as evidence for an important psychological source of witch-fear, the rejection of the mother figure and the buried, infantile fear that the mother is all-powerful and has the power to castrate. The sexual roots both of certain forms of witch activity and of witch-phobia are obvious, but as time went by the emphasis within this psycho-sexual area changed.

The male accusing the witch of stealing his masculinity largely disappears, and instead there appear in the records numerous women displaying what to modern eyes seem clear symptoms of hysteria due to sexual repression. These they frequently blamed on male demons and, ultimately, on a specific witch, male or female, who was said either to be wishing the demons onto them or, if a man, 'possessing' them, in two senses, in spirit form. The earliest such recorded case occurred among a group of nuns at Cambrai, in France in 1491, shortly after the *Malleus Maleficarum* and the Bull of Pope Innocent VII had alerted the gullible public to the dangers of witchcraft all round them. The nuns had fits in which they showed superhuman strength, barked like dogs and foretold the future. Eventually the nun who had first begun to have fits, and who was therefore the ringleader of the hysteria, was 'unmasked' as a witch herself.

This was by no means the last occasion on which a 'witch's victim' was finally declared to be a witch herself, and this illustrates the confusion that existed on the whole subject of possession. Literally, the root of the word 'possess' implies that the person is being inhabited by an alien spirit sitting within him or her, as distinct from 'obsessed', the linguistic root of which means 'sitting by'. Since witches were commonly regarded as being 'possessed by the Devil', in the sense of owned by him, and also as having

intercourse either with him or with 'possessing' demons in the forms of incubi and succubi, the assertion that one was 'possessed' could be rather double-edged.

'Nay, that I will not do: it shall never be said that I was both a witch and a whore.'

At the same time, since it was also believed that witches could 'shift shape', go forth in spectral form and send their own spirits or those of attendant demons out to inhabit hapless bodies. A plea that one was possessed could also be regarded as a protestation of innocence. 'Involuntary possession' could therefore be a legal defence and a let-out; it was used as such by Johannes Wier when defending accused witches. This doctor of medicine, who has been often called 'the founder of modern psychiatry', was a pious man who subscribed to the established belief in devils but at the same time displayed an admirable insight, common sense, and frequently courage, in judging particular cases, rejecting hearsay evidence and carefully scrutinizing notions of bewitchment. 'The uninformed and unskilled physicians,' he wrote in his book *De Praestigiis Daemonum*, 'relegate all the incurable diseases, or all the diseases the remedy for which they overlook, to witchcraft. In all such cases a good doctor is to be consulted because nothing is more important than to make the clinical situations as clear as daylight, for in no domain of human life are human passions quite so freely at play as in this one, these passions being superstition, rage, hate, and malice.'

Wier's lifetime (1515–1588) was the heyday of possession cases in

Europe, and many of them involved communities of nuns or single young women. Writing at the beginning of the seventeenth century, Guazzo, an Italian 'authority' on witchcraft, noted that 'those especially afflicted were bound by a vow of virginity', but the only conclusion he drew was that 'it was wonderful with what wiles the Devil surrounded them to deter them from chastity'. Elsewhere in his book *Compendium Maleficarum* his list of the symptoms of possession makes one wonder if some of the possessed were suffering not merely from an excess of enforced chastity but from epileptic fits: he notes rigor of the limbs, contortions, rolling eyes, fainting, the appearance of being strangled, palpitations, panting, vomiting, and coma.

Another list of symptoms, drawn up by a priest at Louviers in France, after an outbreak among the nuns there, points more to a purely psycho-sexual hysteria. They included: denial of knowledge of the fits after paroxysm had ended; incessant obscenities and blasphemies; circumstantial descriptions of the sabbat; fear of sacred relics and sacraments; violent cursing at any prayer; lewd exposure and acts of abnormal strength; and finally similar manifestations in others around. A feature of witchcraft outbreaks, this last symptom strongly suggests that the desire for attention played a part in cases of 'possession'.

French nuns, in particular, continued to show signs of being possessed well into the seventeenth century. A company of them at Lille in 1613 claimed to be leading a life which was one long orgy. A similar outbreak in Madrid, in 1628, petered out when the Inquisition dispersed the nuns involved to different convents. Far more lasting in its effects was the most famous case of all, that of the bewitched nuns of Loudun in 1634; even after the execution of the worldly priest Urbain Grandier, who had been charged with causing their demonic possession, the hysteria spread.

In Protestant countries this showy form of mass-possession never seems to have been so popular, partly because the Protestants did not have so many all-female institutions, such as convents, which proved such fertile breeding grounds for this psychosexual hysteria. Protestants also favoured prayer rather than exorcism in cases of possession; a less dramatic and less rewarding treatment from the hysteric's viewpoint. As a modern writer, T. K. Oesterreich, has put it, 'possession begins to disappear among civilized races as soon as belief in spirits loses power'. In England possession was never popular among adults, but there are numerous seventeenth-century English cases concerning children and adolescents.

Snails and Puppy-Dogs' Tails

The pattern of such cases seems to have been based, like so much in English witchcraft, on European prototypes of a generation or so earlier, described by English writers. There was, for instance, Richard Baxter's account of what seems to have been a classic case in Louvain in 1571. A fifteen-year-old girl, Catherine Gualter, took to vomiting 'great flocks of hair, with filthy water, such as in ulcers, and sometimes like the dung of doves and geese, and in them pieces of wood, and those like new chips lately cut off an old tree, and abundance of skins like parchment shavings . . . After this she vomited innumerable stones, some like walnuts, and like pieces broken out of old walls and with some of the lime on them.' The writer added cautiously 'that she was cured by the priest's means does not render the story incredible, though there be many deceits.'

Baxter seems to have suspected,

as a modern reader may, that the girl herself had been deliberately swallowing a variety of unpalatable objects—a symptom not unknown in present-day hysterical psychopaths. It is also possible that she had not really vomited all the matter produced at all, but simply pretended to have done so. No doubt this explains many of the recorded instances of people apparently vomiting an extraordinary selection of things, from pins and needles to snails, puppy-tails and live frogs; and also of some of the related cases of 'bewitched' women giving birth to such creatures as leverets or kittens. Other of these unnatural progeny may have been deformed, aborted human foetuses which were not recognized as such.

In Vienna, in 1583, after a sixteen-year-old girl had complained of abdominal cramps, a group of Jesuits spent eight weeks exorcizing her. In the end they claimed to have expelled from her 12,652 living demons which her grandmother kept as flies in glass jars. The grandmother was then tortured into confessing intercourse with the Devil in the shape of a ball of thread, and was burned to death. If that adolescent's secret motive had been to reject her matriarch, she had succeeded all too well.

The first of a series of such cases in England was the Warboys case, which was also the most discussed witchcraft trial in the land before 1600. In 1589, the ten-year-old daughter of Robert

Engraving showing Urbain Grandier, a French priest, burned alive after being accused of witchcraft

Witchcraft in France: the new sorcerer's apprentices. The prayers and rituals are listed in the *Book of Shadows*, which is still used today by witches.

Throckmorton, a squire of Warboys in Huntingdon, began to have fits. These she blamed on the influence of Mrs Alice Samuel, a respectable, elderly neighbour, and presently her four sisters, aged from nine to fifteen, began to have fits. A local doctor hinted at the possibility of witchcraft, and though the parents were at first inclined to dismiss the whole thing as children's 'wantoness' they reluctantly agreed to confront Mrs. Samuel with the girls. Upon this the fits became more dramatic—though soon the girls reversed their ideas and began to have fits in the old woman's absence so that for a time she was forced to live in the house with them, suffering many indignities.

When this had been going on for nearly a year and had become the talk of the neighbourhood, a distinguished visitor to the house, Lady Cromwell (grandmother of Oliver Cromwell) attacked Mrs. Samuel physically, slashing off part of her hair which she ordered to be burned. The significance of this attack, an example of the custom of 'scratching a witch' to destroy her power, was not lost on poor Mrs. Samuel who cried, 'Madam, why do you use me thus? I never did you any harm as yet'—a probably innocent

however brought before the Bishop of Lincoln and held in custody to await the Assizes along with her husband and her daughter Agnes, whom by this time the girls had also implicated. The fits went on, and now the children began saying that the Samuels had magically murdered Lady Cromwell. By this time the neighbourhood was aroused, and there were additional stories of sorcery. The Assize jury found all three suspects guilty and old Mrs. Samuel confessed to intercourse with the Devil. Agnes, however, refused to confess and further declined to save her own life by pleading pregnancy (a recognized escape route) with the fine remark 'Nay, that I will not do: it shall never be said that I was both a witch and a whore.' All three were hanged. The Throckmorton girls appear to have lived a normal adult life.

Adolescent Fantasies

The case was an important one because, for the first time in England, the families involved were people of considerable education and influence. It was widely reported and this must have helped to spread and confirm popular superstitions and to make them credible to the law-making classes. A series of comparable cases followed over the next two generations. In 1596 at Burton-on-Trent a boy called Thomas Darling had fits in which he claimed to see green cats. He accused a woman called Alice Goodridge, who was convicted and finally died in jail. He was allowed to 'scratch' her, at which she said, 'Take blood enough, child. God help thee.' The child answered, 'Pray for thyself, thy prayers can do me no good.'

Another boy, in Pendle in 1634, accused a number of people, among them Jane Device, daughter of a convicted witch, who as a child had been responsible for getting her own mother executed. He later retracted his statement, but by this time three of the

accused (although not the indestructible Jane) had already died in prison. Yet more children's evidence, at Bury in 1644, brought about the execution of two hitherto respected women, after a trial at which the scholar Sir Thomas Browne gave 'expert' evidence for the prosecution. But many English juries were uneasy about such testimony, even at the height of the witchphobia.

A famous case occurred in 1620, when a boy claimed to be bewitched, to be vomiting oddments and to be voiding blue urine. He was kept under observation and was caught pouring ink into his chamber-pot and also stuffing ink-soaked paper under his foreskin—behaviour not untypical of a neuroti—child in any era. His particular devil was supposed to send him into fits on hearing the first verse of the first chapter of St. John, but those watching the boy were soon to discover that the devil did not apparently understand it read in Greek. The boy was made to apologize publicly to the witch he had accused, and the case was withdrawn. The contemporary comment that the boy had probably been coached in his symptoms by a Catholic priest, sheds a slightly more sinister light on the issues of principle and belief involved in such cases.

Probably no case of witchcraft possession is as famous as that of the 'Witches of Salem' which occurred in the New World in 1692, at a time when the idea of witchcraft was being officially relinquished in Europe. In many respects it comes closest to the Warboys case of a century earlier, in that in Salem, as in Warboys, a group of adolescent girls got the bit between their teeth, and rocked a whole community by their malevolent fantasies and exhibitionism. In Warboys only three people died; in Salem, however, over 150 were arrested of whom thirty-one were tried and sentenced to death. Of these nineteen were hanged, two died in jail, one was

remark which was later made to seem ominous when the 'yet' was emphasized. Lady Cromwell died two years later, when the fits were still going on.

At last, to placate the family, Mrs. Samuel ceremonially ordered the girls to stop. They did so, of course, which was taken as proof that she was a witch indeed. She was nagged by the local parson into 'confessing', but next day retracted her statement. She was, pressed to death and five others made confessions which secured them reprieves. The remainder escaped death for various reasons.

The only reason the holocaust was not much greater was that within a year, the wave of witch hysteria began to pass; the soberer citizens of the New England township were beginning to come to their senses and doubt was cast on the very principle of 'spectral evidence'. Within a generation the whole affair came to be officially regarded as an unfortunate and backward-looking error of judgement, and some paltry restitution was made to the survivors of the trials. The girls responsible went unpunished and only one ever recorded anything like a confession.

Striking contrast is afforded by the case of Jane Wenham in 1712, the last conviction for witchcraft in England, though a witch was burned in Scotland some years later. Jane's accuser, the servant maid of a minister, claimed to suffer from fits, visions of cat-devils, and the vomiting of pins. Jane Wenham, who had long been known as the 'wise woman of Walkerne', was arrested, searched for witch marks, and made a confession. Under her pillow was found 'magic ointment' allegedly made from human fat rendered down, and also cakes of feathers. Clearly Jane thought of herself as a witch, and may have had malevolent intentions. But those concerned with her case had more enlightened ideas. A pamphlet war raged around her in true eighteenth century style and she was reprieved.

It is the treatment of the maid that is most interesting from a modern point of view. A doctor examined this girl, and ordered that she wash her hands and face twice a day, and that she be confined under observation. Her keeper was to be 'a lusty young fellow'. This was done. The fits and other inconveniences ceased forthwith,

and the lusty young fellow later married her. Light, it seems, had at last broken on the true nature of possession and the real needs of many of the possessed.

GILLIAN TINDALL

FURTHER READING: V. Crapanzano and V. Garrison, eds. Case Studies in Spirit Possession. *(Wiley, 1977); T. K. Oesterreich.* Possession. *(Citadel Press, 1974); Sheila Walker.* Ceremonial Spirit Possession in Africa and Afro-America. *(Leiden: E. J. Brill, 1972).*

Inverted Symbols

Symbols which are upside down, backward or the wrong way round, usually connected with evil; inverted crucifixes or other Christian symbols are used in black magic because they deny God and the accepted order of things, and state disorder, abnormality, and evil; prayers are sometimes said backward in the Black Mass and it was long believed that demons write backward.

Italian Witchcraft

La Vecchia—the Old Religion—is still the title given to both black and white witchcraft in Italy and Sicily. Since these practices have their foundations in the beliefs of the ancient colonizers, the name is highly appropriate.

Greek, Etruscan, and Egyptian rites were incorporated into the official Roman religion; and astrology, augury, and divination were employed in imperial policy making. Yet it is important to understand that pagan authority condemned the dark side of magic just as zealously as the Inquisition of Christian times. Frequently, all sorcerers were driven from Rome, accused of harming state or emperor with their evil spells. Nocturnal ceremonies to invoke the infernal deities,

the making of wax images and the tying of knots to cause pain, death, or sexual impotence, and of course the manufacture of poisons (employed to speed up the supernatural processes) were offences punished by crucifixion or being thrown to the wild beasts.

The Roman poet Horace (1st century BC) among other classical writers described the feared magical practices in minute horrifying detail. Apuleius (2nd century AD) gave an account of old and ugly crones and their gruesome art in *The Golden Ass*, story about a young man who is turned into an ass through dabbling in witchcraft. The similarity between their exploits and those revealed under hideous torture during witchcraft trials, some 1,400 years later, is quite startling. Another of his works, the Apologia, made a careful distinction between harmful and helpful magic, the latter including astrology and the conjuration of demons to give the sorcerer advance knowledge of future events. The Roman witch, therefore, named *strix, saga,* or *uolantica*—nocturnal bird, wise woman, or night flyer—was the forerunner of the Italian *strega*, the peak of whose dreadful persecution endured from the fifteenth to the eighteenth century.

In the first years of Christianity all private magical rites were forbidden and only public augury permitted. The Ostrogoths, who invaded Italy under their leader Theodoric in the fifth century, were Arian Christians; they classified divination as paganism, and therefore an offence to be punished by death. In 500 AD all sorcerers were driven from Rome. When in the following century the Lombards reached Italy, they sold magicians as slaves outside their province, irrespective of whether the magic was successful.

Opposite page:
The Witch Salvator Rosa

Pagan Under the Skin

Only fragmentary evidence exists of witchcraft during the Dark Ages. While feudal rulers fought to gain control of the new kingdoms left vacant by the collapse of the Roman Empire, the Church was involved in consolidating her own supreme authority over temporal powers and destroying the early heresies. It took many centuries for the majority of simple folk to absorb Christian tenets. Gradually, pagan temples were rededicated, and St. Apollinarius presided over the healing spring which had once belonged to Apollo. For a long while Christianity must have been only a veneer covering far older customs, especially since the priests were often not much better informed than their ignorant flocks. The evidence produced by the Inquisition shows that paganism and Christianity merged into a curious paradoxical faith.

Though Italy is virtually at the heart of Christian Europe, Italian peasants adhered to their ancient rites and beliefs. In the glades and woodlands set aside for such pre-Christian revels they continued to honour Venus, Bacchus, or Diana Herodias. The last goddess was the evil spirit said in later centuries to lead countless bands of witches on flights through the night. It is reasonable to assume that the pagan gatherings survived in the form of the notorious witches' sabbaths.

Two strands must be distinguished in Italian witchcraft. The wise women dealing in love and healing potions, and their destructive opposites, who told simple fortunes, gathered herbs by moonlight, and muttered charms, were only to be found in country regions. Although sometimes subjected to village lynch laws, the pastoral witch, on the whole, remained unharmed until the hysterical outburst against witch-craft provoked by the Inquisition at the beginning of the fifteenth century.

Her urban counterpart, associated with the major cities of Rome and Naples, was a more sophisticated exponent of magic, a descendant of the classical sorcerers. Such people studied astrology and divination, and their interests extended to alchemy,

The girdle is common to all members of a coven, as is the athame *or black-handled knife.*

medicine, and astronomy in pursuit of a wider knowledge of the universe. Their clients were not an illiterate peasantry but the educated members of the ruling class.

The Church's attitude to sorcery was imprecise and depended upon the varying opinions of her leaders. Among the educated there was a passion for knowledge and desire to see into the future, using part-magical, part-scientific processes. Popes, kings, and learned men studied astrology and thereby indulged in the same grisly practices ascribed to sorcerers. To the superstitious anyone seeking to probe the unknown was disobeying God's laws, approaching heresy, or in league with the Devil.

Poisons and Potions

Throughout history the particular Italian failing seems to have been making and using poisons. With their potions the witches were apparently following the national tradition. One of the earliest examples of secular legislation against such practices was instigated by the twelfth century Norman king of the Two Sicilies, Roger II. He stated that the concoction of love potions, whether they worked or not, was a crime. In 1181 the Doge Orlo Malipieri of Venice also passed laws punishing poisoning and sorcery.

Emperor Frederick II of Sicily (1194–1250), known for his wide learning as *stupor mundi,* 'the wonder of the world,' employed Saracen diviners and invited to his court the Scottish sage, Michael Scot, who was reputed to be a wizard. With Frederick's permission his astrologers practiced the forbidden augury, using flights of birds and victims' entrails, but the Emperor had no real belief in sorcery, despite the reputation his clerical adversaries gave him. He upheld the law made by Roger, and set down that anyone tampering with food or drink to provoke love or hatred must be executed if the recipient died or lost his senses; if nothing happened the would-be sorcerer faced a year's imprisonment.

Throughout the thirteenth century sorcery was in Italy an offence punished in the secular courts. Astrology was not included among the forbidden arts, and papal decisions were sometimes made with the aid of astrologers. Every court in the kingdoms which made up Italy had its resident astrologer. But such practitioners, even though they were respected and believed, walked on thin ice. If, like Peter of Albano and Cecco d'Ascoli, they were led by their studies in heresy, they were in as much danger from the Inquisition as the sorcerers.

The witch mania which swept through Europe reached Italy in the mid-fifteenth century; the northern territories, nearest Germany, were particularly affected. The more the Inquisition sought, the more cases of witchcraft came to light. Papal Bulls, like the one issued by Innocent VIII in 1484, turned the persecution of witches into an uncontrolled epidemic. In the first year of its publication, forty-one people were burned in Como after the zealous investigations of the Dominican Inquisitors.

Fear, ignorance, and superstition, fanned by the desire to stamp out heresy, sent countless innocent people to the stake. Anything out of the ordinary was thought to indicate witchcraft. A woman, neither young nor pretty, who inspired love in a man, would be suspect. The village wise woman who healed, procured abortions, or made love philtres was naturally assumed to have the Evil Eye and to work in conjunction with demons. When children became sick their hysterical parents sought a scapegoat and confused, lonely old women were accused of witchcraft. The most terrible tortures were then employed to extract confessions. Details of witches' sabbaths obtained in this way varied very little from those found in the rest of Europe, which suggests that the Inquisitor, wherever he might be, asked the same questions until the required answers were given.

It is not really surprising that reports were soon circulating which suggested that witches would outnumber the faithful. In 1510, 140 witches were burned at Brescia, and 300 in Como four years later. Fantastic stories spread that at least 25,000 people attended a sabbath near Brescia. At Valcanonica, seventy more people were burned and the Inquisitor claimed to have another 5,000 under suspicion.

Venetian secular authority protested vigorously because the area was threatened with depopulation. In theory, the secular court was supposed to carry out the sentences if they agreed with the findings produced by the Inquisition. In 1521 Leo X issued a Bull which gave the real state of the law, and showed that the secular court was expected to do no more than confirm the proceedings. The Inquisition was given the right to use excommunication and interdict if sentences on

La Volta

One particular characteristic of Italian witchcraft was the dance called La Volta. This was described as having such fantastic leaping steps as to make it incredible to the onlookers. At Como and Brescia children between eight and twelve years old, who had attended sabbaths but been reclaimed by the Inquisition, performed this dance. It appeared so difficult and skilful that the learned men concluded it could not have been learned from human beings.

witches were not carried out.

The Venetian Council of Ten bravely produced a most enlightened reply and suggested proper legal regulations for future trials. They pointed out that the witch hunters' greed for money prevented anyone from being found innocent, adding that if so many of the ignorant peasantry were in error they had need of really good preachers rather than persecutors. Such sensible attitudes were ignored.

More sophisticated magicians turned hurriedly to astrology to prevent being charged with witchcraft, but the Italian sorcerer's reputation was known far afield. When in 1439 a French baron, Gilles de Rais, had wanted to procure gold by supernatural means he had sent to Florence for a priest and necromancer named Francesco Prelati.

Despite his thirst for knowledge, the cultured man of the Renaissance was extremely superstitious. The new classical studies revived interest in magic. Omens were studied. There was a widespread belief in ghosts, and in ceremonies that could evoke devils to do man's bidding. Such attitudes among literate people increased the witch hunting atmosphere.

Devils in the Colosseum

In his autobiography, the great goldsmith and sculptor Benvenuto Cellini wrote of a learned Sicilian priest who invited him to take part in some magical ceremonies to conjure up the spirits of the dead. Accompanied by some friends, Cellini went to the Colosseum. The priest donned sorcerer's robes, drew circles on the ground, and heated perfumes. The rites continued for an hour and a half, in which time Cellini said the Colosseum was filled with legions of devils.

In a notorious case in 1633 the pope himself was the victim of sorcery. A certain Giocinto Centini was told by a prophecy that his uncle, Cardinal d'Ascoli, would be the next pope. In order to shorten the life of the present pope, Urban VIII, Centini hired an Augustinian friar and notorious sorcerer, Peter of Palermo. Two other friars helped cast spells and celebrate a mortuary mass. Their attempts failed and they were all arrested.

A picture of a typical sabbath emerges from the evidence at a witch trial in 1646 when an old woman known as La Mercuria was arrested at Castelnuovo. Long suspected of being a witch, the woman was charged with the offence that, instead of swallowing the host at two Communions, she held it in her mouth to use afterward for some devilish purposes. It was also said that her spells had caused a young noblewoman to miscarry. Under torture La Mercuria named other witches who in turn were tortured. One, Domenica Gratiadei, described the sabbaths at which they feasted, danced, and worshipped Satan. They smeared themselves, she said, with ointments made from dead babies, among other equally appalling ingredients, and then had sexual relations with the Devil, to whom they also gave the hosts they had purloined. When the trial ended in 1647, eight people were beheaded and their bodies burned.

In 1789 Giuseppe Balsamo, known as Count Cagliostro, and his wife set up as sorcerers in a house in the Piazza Farnese in Rome. His illustrious clientele included princesses and priests. Three years later the Inquisition condemned him to death. Pope Pius VI commuted the sentence to life imprisonment and shut Cagliostro's wife in a convent.

At the end of the nineteenth century Charles Leland wrote a book entitled *Aradia*, in which he described practices that were still rife in Italy and Sicily. In most cases witches claimed to be descendants of families where the craft had been practiced for generations. At their sabbaths they wore no clothes, said incantations over meal, salt, honey, and water, and worshipped Diana and her daughter Aradia, or Herodias, as the female messiah. After supper they danced, sang, and had sexual intercourse. Stones with natural holes through them were valued as having special powers, and the witches dealt mainly in the preparation of love philtres.

Almost more than anywhere else in modern Europe, the people of southern Italy and Sicily still retain the customs of La Vecchia. The Evil Eye is feared and the phallic sign invoked to destroy its power. Wax hearts and images are stuck with pins, and wise women consulted for charms to make people fall in or out of love, and to gain lucky lottery ticket numbers.

SANDY SHULMAN

Malleus Maleficarum

'*The Hammer of Witches*,' written by two German Dominican friars, Jakob Sprenger and Heinrich Kramer; first printed in 1486 and frequently republished in the sixteenth and seventeenth centuries, it was generally accepted as the most authoritative work on the behaviour of witches and demons, and on the methods of interrogating, torturing, and convicting witches; it

has been described as 'a perfect armoury of judicial murder'; there is a modern English translation by Montague Summers.

Modern Witchcraft

In recent years much publicity has been given to the activities of people claiming to be 'witches'. With a few notable exceptions these people dress in a normal fashion, earn a living in ordinary jobs, are married and have children and, in fact, show few outward signs of their unusual beliefs.

Yet they firmly maintain that witchcraft is as relevant to the twenty-first century as to any time previously. Modern witches refer to their religion as 'Wicca', the feminine form of an Old English word *wicce*, meaning a witch. Wicca is a largely urban cult drawing principally upon a membership of lower-middle and middle-class people between the ages of thirty and fifty. In common with more orthodox religions, Wicca has worship as its main object, but the additional element of magic lends the cult an illicit and undoubtedly attractive aura. Both male and female members of Wicca

Caroline Tully practices witchcraft at her home on August 2, 2005, in Melbourne, Australia. The Victorian State Government recently repealed the 200-year-old Vagrancy Act under which it was an offence to profess or pretend to tell fortunes or 'use any kind of witchcraft, sorcery, enchantment, or conjuration'. Pro-witchcraft groups had campaigned against the Vagrancy Act on the grounds it discriminated on the basis of religion.

are known as witches, although the cult is mainly matriarchal, the high priestess being looked upon as the personification, and in some ceremonies the incarnation, of the mother goddess who is the principal deity of modern witchlore. In some respects she is not dissimilar to the Virgin Mary of Roman Catholicism; she is Queen of Heaven, and her symbols are the moon and stars. She is light, love, and above all fertility, and is sometimes referred to by the names of old pagan goddesses—the Celtic Arianrhod, the Roman Diana, the Egyptian Isis. Her consort, who is personified by the high priest, is the horned god—Cernunnos, Pan, Osiris—the dark, male factor. Out of the union of the god and goddess came the universe, and between them they control the turning of the seasons, bring fertility to crops and animals, bestow magical powers upon their followers, and generally operate workings of the cosmos.

Wicca is basically a fertility cult and its great festivals are geared to the seasons. They are the spring equinox, on 21 March; May Eve or Beltane, on 30 April; the summer solstice, mid-summer, on 22 June; August Eve, or Lammastide, on 1 August; the autumn equinox on 21 September; Hallowe'en on 31 October; the winter solstice, or Yule, on 21 December; and Candlemas on 2 February. The witch meetings on these dates are known as sabbats, and additional sabbats are also held on the nights of the full moon, in honour of the goddess. Weekly or monthly meetings, less formal affairs at which cult business is attended to and new members initiated, are *esbats*.

Garter and Knife

The basic working unit is the 'coven'. This may comprise any number of members, from four to twenty, although thirteen is considered the ideal number, partly because of tradition and partly because a nine-

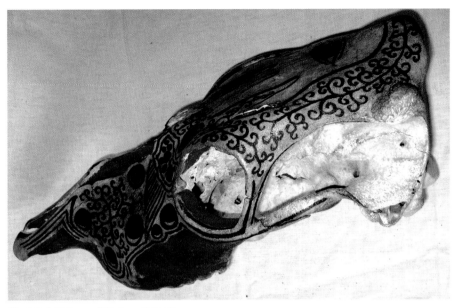

Skull Spirit House Witchcraft tools

foot circle, in which the group operates during its ceremonies, nicely accommodates thirteen people.

Modern witches frequently quote the legend of the founding of the Order of the Garter by Edward III in 1348. According to them, the garter has always been the badge of office of the high priestess of a coven (though there is little or no textual evidence to support this), and the Countess of Salisbury, who dropped hers, could therefore have been a witch. In the days of Edward III ladies at court were unlikely to feel shame at merely losing a garter, and Edward donned the garter himself to show that he too was a witch; he subsequently founded the 'double coven' of the Order of the Garter in the witches' honour.

Whatever the case, the modern high priestess in some covens wears a single garter to show her rank; a priestess who is head of more than one coven may have a silver buckle on her garter for each of her covens, displaying them with pride. On her head, the priestess wears a crescent headdress, symbol of the moon, and around her waist is tied a girdle consisting of three cords, each cord commemorating the degree of her initiation, and symbolizing her bondage to the service of the mother

goddess and her coven. The priestess, like the priest, also carries a sword as a mark of office; on his head the priest wears the horned helmet of the god.

Circle of Power

The girdle is common to all members of a coven, as is the *athame* or black-handled knife. This weapon, inscribed with magic symbols, is presented to each witch on initiation, although ideally it should have been made personally by the witch. It is used to mark out the magic circle and, held point upward, to draw down magical power into the circle. Often, the 'circle' is no more than an invisible boundary drawn around the coven by the high priestess. Sometimes, however, it may be an elaborately drawn affair, with symbols and 'names of power.' In the centre of the circle stands a small altar, upon which are placed the *Book of Shadows,* the liturgy of Wicca, containers for salt and water, a censer, a scourge, a wand, the pentacle or plate, and a chalice: fewer or more items of equipment are used depending on the practice of each coven, and on the nature of the ceremony.

Ceremonial, within the broad outline of Wicca, differs from coven to coven. At the average *esbat,* usually held indoors on a Saturday night, the circle is marked out and four candles are lit, one at each point of the compass. The naked witches stand just inside the circle, with the high priestess at the centre, kneeling at the altar, and the high priest standing with his back to the north, his arms crossed on his breast. Using the point of her athame, the high priestess mingles the salt and water together in a small bowl and then sprinkles the mixture around the perimeter of the circle and upon the heads of the witches present. The water symbolizes purity, the salt life and freedom from corruption. She herself is sprinkled with the mixture by the high priest.

Thus purified, the high priestess takes her sword in her right hand and, arms outstretched, stands at each of the four points of the compass, invoking the 'Mighty Ones' of Air, Fire, Water, and Earth, traditional elements from which the god and goddess created the universe. Air is attributed to the east, fire to the south, water to the west, and earth to the north.

On the nights of the full moon, and at certain of the major festivals, the high priest performs a short ceremony known as 'drawing down the moon' on the high priestess, during which, her followers believe, she becomes the goddess incarnate. The 'power' is generally achieved by a process of dancing and chanting. Witches believe that the build-up of power is achieved much more readily when the participants are naked and a certain sexual tension is present; some claim to have 'seen' this power as a golden conical aura, its base resting upon the heads of the dancers.

Casting the Spells

In this charged atmosphere the witches begin to cast their spells. Only three pieces of magic can be performed at each meeting, they claim, and the spells should always be for good; an evil spell rebounds threefold upon the head of its creator. Sometimes the spell is cast telepathically; for instance, in the case of a spell cast to cure a person of a bad leg, the witches may stand silently and 'will' the leg to heal. On other occasions they might use a doll, or *fith-fath*, to represent the sick person, and bathe the doll's leg with a healing potion, or the high priestess might 'bind' the spell, wrapping her girdle around the blade of her athame in a special way. The spells suitably cast, the circle is closed, the Mighty Ones are dismissed, and the witches settle down to a ceremony with cakes and wine. The wine is consecrated by the high priest and priestess together, the latter dipping her athame into the wine which the priest holds up to her in the chalice—an obvious piece of sexual symbolism. The cakes are then consecrated by having the athame passed over them in the form of a pentagram, and cakes and chalice are passed around to each witch in turn. Despite protests to the contrary, witches claim that the cakes and wine ceremony is not a travesty of the Mass; it is, they say, simply a form of thanksgiving for the grape and the grain.

The motives of modern witches are often thought to be questionable, and certainly a considerable element of sexuality is present at many meetings, although charges that Wicca is an excuse for sexual orgies are hotly denied. The nudity of the coven, the frantic dancing, the incense, and the slightly illicit atmosphere contribute to this, as do certain ceremonial acts. The binding and whipping of a new initiate for 'purification' purposes, for instance, can be highly titillating for those with sadomasochistic tendencies (though the 'whip' is usually of embroidery silk) while the 'five-fold kiss' bestowed by the high priest or priestess on the feet, knees, genitals, breasts, and lips of new members speaks for itself. The 'Great Rite', performed at certain ceremonies and consisting of token or actual sexual intercourse between the high priest and priestess, is justified by witches on the grounds that Wicca is, after all, a fertility cult. Only the high priest may initiate a female member, while the high priestess initiates males.

History of the Cult

In the eyes of Wicca members, the cult is of vast antiquity, predating Christianity by thousands of years. In fact, as a modern cult, Wicca has been in operation for less than a century; it was only with the passing of the Fraudulent Mediums Act of 1951 that it was able legally to present itself to British society at all. This Act, which restricted prosecution only to those who obtained money from the public under the pretext of possessing supernatural power, enabled spirit mediums and astrologers, as well as witches, to practice their arts legally in the open for the first time in hundreds of years.

Some 300 years after the Witch-Finder General, Matthew Hopkins, had terrorized the eastern counties of England, a succession of books appeared which set the scene for the modern reappearance of the ancient craft. Margaret Murray's *The Witch-Cult in Western Europe* (1921) argued that witchcraft had not been an anti-Christian perversion but surviving pre-Christian paganism.

In 1949 Gerald Gardner published a novel, *High Magic's Aid*, which purported to give authentic details of witchcraft practice; this was followed five years later by a nonfiction work, *Witchcraft Today*. In this Gardner claimed to be a witch, and

Witches and Witchcraft

Practices with origins long lost still survive to this day.

maintained that his fellows in the New Forest coven to which he belonged had appointed him their 'publicity officer'. Gardner proselytized for the witches in a further book, *The Meaning of Witchcraft* (1959), and attracted a great deal of largely hostile publicity from the newspapers before his death in 1964. In the absence of any evidence except hearsay, there is a strong case in favour of the suggestion that Gardner invented the cult of Wicca to satisfy his own sense of the esoteric, drawing upon magical texts (he was a great admirer of Aleister Crowley, parts of whose *Gnostic Mass* bear a close resemblance to the rituals of Wicca), Masonic ceremonial, Margaret Murray's theories, and a handful of books about witch lore and assorted mythology—in particular, Charles Leland's

Aradia: the Gospel of the Witches, and Emile Grillot de Givry's *Pictorial Anthology of Witchcraft, Magic and Alchemy.* (The latter, interestingly, was first published in English translation at around the time Gardner returned to Britain after a career in Malaya.) Gardner's rituals appear to have been far more heavily based on sex than the ones most commonly practiced today, and it is reasonable to suppose that Gardner's sexual whims were gratified by the 'religion' he had created.

Gardner's followers in the 1960s and 1970s were often referred to specifically as Gardnerian witches, for during those years they were increasingly superseded by followers of the 'Alexandrian' variety of Wicca, whose leader was a Manchester-born man named Alex Sanders. A plausible talker

with a roguish smile, he referred to himself as 'King of the Witches' and claimed to be descended, through his maternal grandmother, from Owen Glendower, the legendary Welsh chieftain said to have been given the same title by his followers.

Alexandrian witches differed from the Gardnerian variety principally in that they leant far more strongly toward ceremonial magic—although they worshipped the same god and goddess as the Gardnerians and performed the same fertility rituals. The Alexandrians recruited a greater percentage of young people into their ranks, most of them well-educated.

Sanders lost no opportunity of explaining the beliefs of his followers and himself, using any modern medium available. He made numerous radio and television appearances, appeared in several films in Britain, Europe, and Canada, and was the subject of a book, *King of the Witches.*

Nevertheless, the Gardnerians continued to maintain a high profile, largely through the efforts of several of Gardner's female disciples—in particular Patricia Crowther and Doreen Valiente, both of whom produced a succession of books on witchcraft.

In the United States, one or more versions of the cult began to surface at the end of the 1960s. Among the first to publicize modern witchcraft was a certain Dr. Leo Louis Martello, who claimed at times to be a hereditary Sicilian witch, and to have been initiated into four other witchcraft traditions. For years he published book after book, and was responsible for editing the Wicca Newsletter.

Other members of the movement who became active in the United States at that time included Raymond Buckland and Sybil Leek, both English Gardnerian initiates, and Louise Huebner. In the broad-minded climate of the early 1970s, their widespread publication of the 'secrets' of modern witchcraft provoked only mild public interest, but a minor scandal followed the publication of *The Witch's Bible* by Gavin and Yvonne Frost in 1972.

In this book, the Frosts—an Englishman who had become a United States citizen, and his Californian wife—set out the practice of what they called 'Celtic Wicca'. Much of it indistinguishable from Gardnerian ritual, it was in some respects (such as the lack of insistence on nudity) a watered-down version, but what caused an outcry were the instructions for the ritual deflowering of adolescent girls, before their initiation into the coven, with a wooden phallus.

It is not surprising, therefore, that to some people modern witchcraft is a smutty, underground cult whose sole objective is sexual licentiousness

carried out in the name of religion; to others it is healthy and rational, the nudity being a symbol of the stripping away of material things, and the idea of worshipping the creative forces of the universe being the most logical and simple method of worship. Whatever the truth of its claims to ancient roots, its basic aims seem harmless enough, and give a certain spiritual satisfaction to many people whose faith in established religion has flagged.

FRANK SMYTH

FURTHER READING: M. Adler. Drawing Down the Moon; Witches, Druids, Goddess Worshippers *and* Other Pagans in America Today. *(Beacon Press, 1986); Gerald Gardner.* Witchcraft Today. *(Citadel Press, 1970); C. A. Hoyt.* Witchcraft. *(S. Ill. Univ. Press, 1981); Gavin and Yvonne Frost.* The Witch's Bible. *(Nash, 1972); T. M. Luhrmann.* Persuasions of the Witch's Craft. *(Harvard Univ. Press, 1989).*

Modern-day Wiccan spouses

North Berwick Witches

The celebrated case of the North Berwick witches, with its mixture of politics, high treason, and sorcery, is one of the most interesting in the annals of Scottish witchcraft. According to *News from Scotland*, a contemporary pamphlet published in 1591, the existence of these witches was discovered when David Seaton, the Deputy Bailiff of the town of Trenent, noticed that his maidservant, Gilly (or Geillis) Duncan, was behaving rather oddly.

She had taken to absenting herself from his house at night without permission, and she had suddenly acquired a local reputation for healing the sick. When Seaton questioned her about these alleged cures, she refused to answer, and he resorted to torture. The author of *News from Scotland* says that he used 'the pill winks upon her fingers, which is a grievous torture; and binding and wrenching her head with a cord, or rope, which is a most cruel torment also; yet would she not confess anything.' It was not until she had been searched for the Devil's Mark, and something supposed to be that mark had been found upon her throat, that she broke down and acknowledged that she was a witch.

After she had made this confession, Gilly Duncan was committed to prison, and there she named and accused a number of other people. David Seaton must surely have been horrified at the outcome of his examination of a maidservant in his own home, as slowly there came to light, not only the practice of dark magic by bands of local witches, but, more serious still, a murderous plot against the life of James VI.

The instigator of this plot was said to be Francis Hepburn, Earl of Bothwell, who was the King's cousin and had some claim to the throne of Scotland if James should die without an heir. He was suspected of being the 'Devil' of the covens concerned, and of having been present, in ritual disguise, at their meetings.

It is quite possible that both these accusations were true. He and the King were at constant enmity with each other. James's death could have put supreme power within Bothwell's grasp, and he was reputed to be deeply interested in occultism and magic. He may in fact have attempted to clear his way to the throne with the help of the North Berwick witches, as some of the evidence given in the trials that followed suggests. If he did, he escaped the worst consequences of his guilt, although he was eventually forced to flee Scotland and take refuge in Italy, from which he never returned. While he lived there, he seems to have continued to dabble in various forms of sorcery. In his *Relation of a Journey* (1623), George Sandy's makes the interesting statement that, when he was traveling in Calabria in 1610, a man whom he met 'would needs persuade me that

The Witches' Well near Edinburgh Castle on the Esplanade

I had insight in magic; for that Earl Bothel was my countryman, who lives at Naples, and is in these parts famous for suspected necromancy.'

Of those named by Gilly Duncan, only four were brought to trial: Dr. John Fian (or Cunningham), a young schoolmaster; Euphemia Maclean, Lord Cliftonhall's daughter; Barbara Napier, the only one of the four whose life was to be spared; and Agnes Sampson, a midwife of Keith, well known in her own district as a wise woman and healer of the sick.

John Fian appears to have been one of the officers of the North Berwick organization, being, as he acknowledged in his confession, 'clerk to all those that were in subjection to the Devil's service.' He kept a list of their names, took their oaths, and 'wrote for them such matters as the Devil still pleased to command him.' It was stated in evidence that he was always present at the meetings and stood nearest to the Devil, 'at his left elbow'; at the great gathering on All Hallows Eve, 1590, he was the leader of the dance for which Gilly Duncan provided music, playing upon a Jew's harp.

When Fian was first examined, he denied all the charges brought against him, but after being horribly tortured he confessed and signed his confession in the presence of King James. He is said to have implicated Bothwell directly in some of his admissions, and afterward to have bitterly regretted having done so, but this cannot now be proved because the original document has been lost. That night he was left alone in his cell to recover from the effects of the torture. According to 'News from Scotland,' he had sincerely repented his past evil and was anxious to make his peace with God. Next morning, he told his jailers that the Devil had come to him during the hours of darkness, dressed all in black and carrying a white wand in his hand, and had demanded that he should renew his former vows of service. Fian refused, declaring that he had listened to him too much already, and was now utterly undone in consequence. The Devil replied, 'Once ere thou die, thou shalt be mine', and so saying, he broke his white wand, and vanished.

This is an odd tale, of which, at first sight, the most likely explanation

A black toad was hung up by its feet for three days, and its venom carefully collected as it dropped into an oyster shell.

seems to be a nightmare, or delirium caused by the dreadful treatment he had received. Dr. Margaret Murray, however, in *The Witch-Cult in Western Europe*, suggests that the visitor was human, either Bothwell himself or one of his messengers, and that he came to make arrangements for Fian's escape. It is a fact that, after another day of solitary confinement, Fian did escape, but instead of going into hiding he went quietly back to his house, and there remained until, inevitably, he was recaptured.

But by then he was changed. Somehow, in that brief interval, he had gained a new and unshakable courage. He denied all that he had confessed before, declaring that it had been wrung from him only by the fear of pain. He was tortured again most brutally in the hope of breaking down his resistance, but in spite of this he refused to answer any further questions, or to say anything more. He died, still silent, in January 1591, being first strangled and then burned on the Castle Hill in Edinburgh.

Calling Up a Storm

Agnes Sampson was a witness of a to- tally different kind. It is true that, like Fian, she confessed nothing until she had been brought low by torture, but then she spoke freely, being, as we are told in one account, 'grave and settled in her answers, which were all to some purpose.' She acknowledged that she and certain named companions had conspired against the King's life on more than one occasion. When he was in Denmark and about to return from there with his newly-wed wife, she was present at a meeting specially convened for the raising of a great storm at sea, whereby the royal ships might be destroyed. The method employed for this was to christen a cat, pass it three times through the links of the chimneycrook and three times under the chimney, and then bind on to its four feet 'the chiefest part of a dead man and several joints of his body.' When this horrible ceremony had been duly performed, the poor creature was carried to the pier at Leith, and hurled into the sea, as far as the witches could throw it. A storm sprang up immediately, and a boat then coming from Kinghorne to Leith was sunk, but the spell was apparently not strong enough to sink the King's ship which, though much troubled by contrary winds and bad weather, came safely back to Scotland.

The venom of a toad, mixed with other poisons, was tried also. A black toad was hung up by its feet for three days, and its venom carefully collected as it dropped into an oyster shell. The concoction was kept until a piece of old linen which had once been worn or used by the King could be obtained. Upon this it was proposed to smear the venom and so poison the victim through the medium of the cloth that had once been in contact with his body. The plan failed because John Kers, one of James's servants, of whom

Agnes had begged such a fragment, refused to give it. Had he done so, she said, she could have killed the King with such pains 'as if he had been lying upon sharp thorns and ends of needles.'

The witches then resorted to the age-old practice of image-magic. Agnes Sampson told her examiners in Holyrood Palace that she had been instructed by the Devil to make a wax image of the King. This she did, and brought it, wrapped in a linen cloth, to a secret meeting held by night. Only nine other witches were present beside herself, and 'the Devil, their master . . . standing in the midst of them.' She offered him the image for his inspection, and when he had approved it, he returned it to her. It was then passed from hand to hand round the company, each person saying in turn: 'This is King James the Sixth, ordained to be consumed, at the instance of a noble man, Francis Earl Bothwell.' If John Fian had been deeply troubled by the fear that he might have implicated his master in his confession, it seems evident that Agnes Sampson had no such scruples.

From her, and later from Euphemia Maclean and Barbara Napier, the interrogators heard accounts of the great assembly at North Berwick Church on All Hallows Eve. Witches commonly met in the open air, often by standing-stones or some other traditional site, but in winter they sometimes met in houses or, if the gathering was a large one, in the local church.

A considerable number of witches were present, seven score according to Barbara Napier, 200 according to Agnes Sampson. They came by sea, making merry on the way with flagons of wine. They danced round the churchyard to Gilly Duncan's music, singing as they went:

> Cummer, go ye before; Cummer,
> go ye;

Morgan La Fey, witch of Arthurian legend

> If ye will not go before, cummer,
> let me.

When King James heard this, he sent for Gilly Duncan, and made her play the dance tune for him upon a trump similar to the one she had used at North Berwick.

Under God's Protection

The Devil presided over the gathering in the form of a man wearing a black gown and a black hat. He may have worn a mask also, for his face is said to have been terrible, with great burning eyes and a nose like the beak of an eagle. His hands were hairy and had claws on them and his feet were like those of a griffin. Barbara Napier said that he was bearded like a goat, and had a long tail. All made their homage to him, coming and going, saluting him on departure with the posterior kiss. Inside the church, he stood in the pulpit, with black candles burning round him, and called the roll, each person answering to his or her name with 'Here, master!'

He preached to his followers concerning the obedience they owed him and the evil they ought constantly to do; more particularly, he urged them to work evil upon King James, who was the greatest enemy he had in the world. He enquired what success had been achieved by the melting of the waxen image Agnes Sampson had made, and when an old ploughman named Gray-Meill tactlessly remarked that 'Nothing ailed the King yet, God be thanked', he struck him a fierce blow with his clawed hand. When some of the witches asked how it was that all their magic had so far failed against the King, though it had not against others, the Devil rather curiously replied that it was because James was a man of God.

To all this, and much else that was marvelous and improbable, the King listened until, suddenly losing patience, he declared that the witches were 'all extreme liars'. Then followed one of the most extraordinary incidents in this very odd case. Agnes Sampson said she did not wish him to think that her words were false, and to convince him of their truth, she would tell him something that he could not doubt. And drawing him a little aside, she whispered to him the words that had passed between him and his bride, Anne of Denmark, when they were alone on their wedding-night in Oslo.

No one knows why she did this. His incredulity must have seemed like a door opening on the hope of pardon and release, and that door she deliberately closed upon herself and her fellow-prisoners. She was, as far as we know, quite sane, nor does she appear to have been one of those individuals who will confess to anything. The startled King acknowledged that what she told him was quite true, and that she could not have known it by any normal means. 'All the devils in Hell,' he said, 'could not have discovered the same'; nor is it clear, even now, how she came by her secret knowledge.

The effect of the disclosure was, of course, fatal. James, forced to accept one part of her confession, was now ready to accept the rest. She was convicted and, in due course, executed on Castle Hill, and so, some time later, was Euphemia Maclean. Barbara Napier was condemned also, but was eventually released. With the subsequent flight of Lord Bothwell, the North Berwick case ended, for though many others were involved, and their names were known to the authorities, none was brought to trial thereafter.

CHRISTINA HOLE

FURTHER READING: Margaret Murray. The Witch-Cult in Western Europe. *(Oxford: Clarendon Press, 1967 reprint).*

Old Age and Witchcraft

All generalizations are subject to exception, but Reginald Scot's verbal cartoon of the sixteenth century English witch as 'lame, blear-eyed, pale, foul, and full of wrinkles' seems to have had wide European currency. In his examination of Spanish witchcraft materials, J. C. Baroja noted that the Evil Eye was more particularly found in elderly spinsters. Perpetuated by German and Scandinavian folklorists, the stereotype of the witch as a malign old woman has found contemporary reaffirmation in Disney films.

But the bent old hag, whilst she may indeed have typified the European witch, is not a universal symbol. Anthropologists would admit that those arraigned for witchcraft in Africa, although they are usually women, are by no means typically elderly. In fact in most African communities the old are revered rather than rejected. If one accepts the idea of the witch as a special personality, it would be logical in terms of modern sociological theory to interpret her as a function of the society or culture that produced her. With this concept in mind, the differences between African and European witchcraft beliefs may be instructive.

African society is organized around the 'extended family', which consists of several generations and a number of kinsfolk living together. In the extended family, which tends to be found in rural and agricultural communities, the position of each member is defined with some clarity and the elderly retain both status and respect. Contrasted with this type of family organization is that typical of the Western world, the nuclear family, which consists of mother, father, and their children. Members of the older generation tend to be found both intrusive and disruptive in the nuclear family, and for these reasons, often to be excluded.

Since even in modern Europe examples of the extended family still survive, it is not an unreasonable supposition that earlier European society very closely resembled the social organization found today in Africa and Asia. Furthermore, one might suggest that in the evolution of the European nuclear family from its original form

A representation of old women using common powers to defeat the Devil

as an extended family, outbreaks of witchcraft accusation could be expected to coincide to a large extent with those periods of social change when elderly women in particular had become a burden that the emerging social structure was unable to support.

Since Europe at the end of the Middle Ages lacked adequate welfare mechanisms to cope with the widespread plight of the aged, it looks as though unconscious forces first isolated the old and then destroyed them by fire for witchcraft. Later generations were to use the gas chamber with a different set of rationalizations.

One of the problems encountered in the study of medieval European witchcraft is that the research worker has to rely on people living centuries ago to supply him with materials. And of course these people perceived their world in ways often very different from ourselves. There is always the danger therefore, in reinterpreting observations made in past centuries, one may lose valuable significances. Nevertheless, as one examines the bizarre evidence of the witchcraft trials, one is struck by the psychotic flavor, not only of many of the accusations but of the confessions. One wonders to what extent many of those found guilty of witchcraft were, in fact, elderly people whose minds had degenerated into some form of schizophrenia. Edmund Spenser in *The Faerie Queene* noted—and misunderstood—the typical schizoid withdrawal of the witch:

> *So choosing solitary to abide*
> *Far from all neighbours, that her*
> *   devilish deeds*
> *And hellish arts from people she*
> *   might hide,*
> *And hurt far off, unknown, whom*
> *   she envied.*

While one must be careful to discount many of the confessions, which were extracted under the most callous torture, there nevertheless remains a catalogue of delusion that calls for re-examination. The stress on sexuality, the claim to be directed by voices, and the alleged ability, after stripping, to be able to fly, all provide a pattern which modern research may help us to interpret.

As a recent Anglo-Scandinavian study was able to demonstrate, many of the characteristics of the witch can also be identified in the schizophrenia of old age. It is interesting to notice that of the sample studied, more than half were unmarried women and over forty percent were living alone. Almost without exception these were women who until comparatively recently had regular employment and who, now in retirement, had been reduced to straitened circumstances. Modern

An Arrest for Witchcraft in the Olden Time, John Pettie (1839–1893). The oil painting shows a group of people in a courtyard surrounded by old buildings. A man is leading away an old woman dressed in black and wearing a white covering on her head. Other people in the crowd are trying to stop the woman being taken away.

studies of the mental condition of some of the aged not only confirm the findings of this particular research project but closely resemble surviving accounts of witch behaviour. Discussing the onset of paraphrenia (a type of schizophrenia found in the aged) the authors comment: 'The first signs are manifested in an increasing quarrelsomeness or unprovoked abuse of those living near. Oddities in speech appearance or other aspects of behaviour are noticed. The patient may seclude himself, refuse callers, break off contact with tradesmen, and wander outside or move about the house at night, talking, laughing, or crying out.' Modern society considers such people need medical attention rather than the stake, but one hesitates to think what the seventeenth-century Witch-Finder General, Matthew Hopkins, would have decided. And it is by no means unheard of in medical case histories to find elderly women complaining that men who have hitherto shown not the least interest in them have sexually molested them—an allegation not without parallel in the strange erotica of European witchcraft.

The Role of the Outcast

The danger of so much anthropological analysis is that it merely permits the substitution of one system of labeling for another. Undoubtedly many witches were insane. But if the value of modern research lies in the insight that it may give into historical events, so too the value of past events such as the massive witch hunts of the sixteenth and seventeenth centuries, lies in the light they can shed on our contemporary life. The fact that old people today are committed to hospital, rather than burned, does not really remove the underlying social pressures which continue to produce aged outcasts.

It is generally accepted by psychiatrists that an emotionally disturbed person is to some extent satisfying the

The old crone in the woods is a common character throughout European folklore.

unconscious needs of the immediate family or its equivalent. In fact, the family is itself in part responsible for unconsciously demanding and unconsciously rewarding the sort of behaviour now labeled as psychotic. And this implies that the family, although it is not consciously aware of the fact, has an emotional investment in the abnormal behaviour which, if maintained, must militate against the patient's recovery. In this interpretation of insanity, as to some extent an expression of the needs of others, lies the reason why many modern psychiatrists like to include the whole family in the therapeutic strategy.

While this particular theory does not exclude hereditary factors, it does assert that the particular form (and possibly the depth and duration) in which insanity will manifest itself is determined by social conditions. Scattered studies of schizophrenia in Africa, and particularly of *ukuthwasa*, or witch doctor's disease, support these contentions. *Ukuthwasa* is a type

of schizoid condition regarded as an essential characteristic of a would-be witch doctor, which, because of differences in social attitude, has usually quite a different course and outcome from that of schizophrenia in a white European community.

The problem under consideration is the extent to which witchcraft can be seen as a role that satisfied unconscious group expectations—just as contemporary expressions of insanity may be seen as responses to unconscious group needs.

The extraordinarily complex interaction of the individual with those with whom he is associated helps us to see abnormal behaviour as at least partially determined socially. Hollingshead and Redlich, examining the social origins of psychotics, found that most schizophrenics came from families who were semiskilled, partially educated people, suspicious, individualistic, self-centred, and hostile to formal education. These are traits that lead to further isolation and discrimination.

'Such people in our society,' Hollingshead comments 'tend to be dropped by their families as injured limbs are cast off by some organisms.'

The gradual reduction in sharpness of sight and hearing in old age may well have the effect of further emphasizing an isolation already partly produced by social forces. Changes in behaviour due to a reduction of communication are likely to follow. Modern studies of conditions of sensory deprivation show that strange and sometimes irreversible changes can be induced in the personalities of people subject to solitary confinement.

Naked to the Sabbath

Artificially created sensory deprivation has been used as one of the main techniques in 'brainwashing' political prisoners, and similar experiences have been noted in people exploring the polar regions or lost in great deserts. Admiral Richard Byrd, for example, isolated in Antarctica for several months, noticed that after the twelfth week he was in a state of deep depression, which was succeeded by a loss of identity during which he felt that he was floating like a disembodied spirit; this would have been evidence enough to convince the authors of the *Malleus Maleficarum*, Heinrich Kramer and Jacob Sprenger, that they had another case of witchcraft on their hands. Christine Ritter subjected herself to periods of up to sixteen days of isolation in the polar wastes and recorded an almost overwhelming desire to run naked into the snow. If this calls to mind witchcraft evidence concerning women who stripped and went naked to some sabbath, the monsters which the hallucinated Christine Ritter saw seem to rival the bestiary of witch annals.

Alone, socially rejected, with failing sight and hearing, the medieval old woman must have suffered to a pitiful degree. If in addition her faculties were

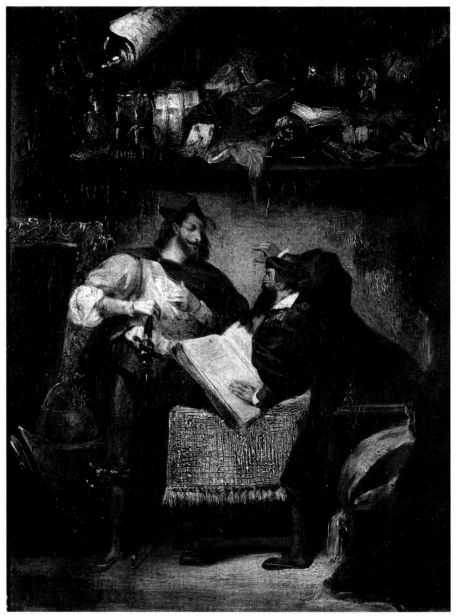

Faust and Mephistopheles in the Studio, Eugène Delacroix (1798–1863)

frequently weakened by hunger and cold, it is no small wonder that she responded to rejection with bemused and antisocial reactions.

The study of witchcraft raises far more than an image of a bumbling old hag; for behind her is the society that created her. Eventually one is left wondering who are the more pitiful, those condemned for witchcraft or those who accuse of witchcraft. After considering the legal and religious armoury of the Middle Ages piled up against the frail, short-sighted old woman, one is inclined to wonder how much of our modern legislation will not

come to be regarded as a monument to our own less reputable desires.

BRIAN W. ROSE

Pact

The pact with the devil bulks large in the history of witchcraft and also in Western literature. It is based on the belief that the Evil One hungers for human souls and that every Christian on whom he can fasten his talons is the spoil of a triumphant campaign in the war which he has waged against God and man ever since he was expelled from his high seat in heaven. He therefore offers his services to greedy magicians and groveling witches in return for their souls and bodies. The formal agreement with him may be made verbally or in writing and, if in writing, may be signed in the sorcerer's blood, the blood which carries his life-energy and so conveys his life into the Devil's hands. The pact may last for the whole of the signer's natural life or for a limited number of years, at the end of which the Devil will come to claim his victim.

Scriptural authority for the possibility of a pact with the Prince of Darkness was found in Isaiah 28.15. This verse originally had nothing to do with any bargain with the Devil but the Vulgate translation suggested that it had: *percurrimus foedus cum morte et cum inferno fecimus pactum*, 'we have signed a treaty with death and with hell we have made a pact'. The early Christians tended to believe that magicians and diviners obtained their effects through the assistance of demons and the main impetus to belief in the Satanic pact came from St. Augustine, who (in *De Doctrina Christiana*) condemned sorcery, astrology, and other occult arts, 'from the pestiferous association of men with demons, as if formed by a pact of faithless and dishonourable friendship.' This passage, quoted by later authorities, became part of Church law.

Stories began to circulate about people who had sold themselves to the Devil. An early one is the tale of Proterius, a servant who fell hopelessly in love with his master's daughter. To win her, he appealed to the Devil and signed a paper renouncing his baptism and faith in Christ, and promising to share the horrors of hell with his new master. The Devil kept his part of the bargain by causing the girl to fall in love with Proterius but the latter was

saved from hellfire by St. Basil (bishop of Caesarea in Asia Minor, in the fourth century), who forced the Devil to return the signed paper. This story already has the element of 'having your cake and eating it' which is typical of many pact tales. The Devil demands a formal contract to make sure that the bargain cannot be broken but, although he keeps his part in it, the contract is broken through the intercession of some high spiritual authority and the signatory gets the best of both worlds.

The same thing happens in the story of Theophilus of Adana, which has been traced back as far as the sixth century and was included in *The Golden*

> ...but then the Devil tells her that this is not enough, for she must give herself to him, body and soul, forever.

Legend, which was a thirteenth-century collection of legendary lives of saints extremely popular in the Middle Ages. Theophilus was a Christian who was persecuted by his bishop, and resented it. He consulted a wicked Jew, who took him in the middle of the night to a place where they saw a crowd of creatures in white robes. They carried candles and seated among them was their prince, the Devil, who demanded that Theophilus 'deny the son of Mary and those things which are offensive to me, and let him set down in writing that he denieth absolutely.' Theophilus did so, sealing the writing with wax (though by at least the thirteenth century he was said to have signed the statement in his own blood).

The fortunes of Theophilus spectacularly improved after this but he began to be depressed by the terrible prospect of an eternity in hell. He wailed and

bemoaned himself so noisily that the Virgin Mary heard him. She took pity on him, obtained divine forgiveness for him and recovered the written pact. It was publicly burned after Theophilus had made an open confession.

In some stories the human signer of the pact intends trickery from the beginning. An example is the case of Roger Bacon, the thirteenth-century scientist and philosopher, who was said to have promised the Devil his soul unless he died neither in the Church nor out of it. The Devil readily agreed but lost his prey because Bacon constructed a cell in the wall of a church, neither inside nor outside it, and took care to die there.

But the Devil is not always cheated and, psychologically, if you believe in him, perhaps, once summoned, he is not so easily got rid of. There was a well-known medieval legend that the brilliant Gerbert of Aurillac, who became Pope Sylvester II in 999, was a sorcerer who had signed a pact with Satan. A speaking brazen head, which he had made with the Devil's assistance, told him that he would not die before he celebrated Mass in Jerusalem. Gerbert naturally decided to go nowhere near the Holy Land but one day, in the year 1003, he was saying Mass in a church when he felt his strength draining away from him and sensed the presence of an army of gloating demons. He discovered that the church was dedicated to the Holy Cross of Jerusalem, and just had time to confess before he died.

The pact was important in prosecutions for witchcraft because it was evidence of heresy, of the repudiation of Christ and deliberate enlistment in the ranks of the Enemy. According to the *Dialogus Miraculorum* of Caesarius of Heisterbach (thirteenth century), about the year 1200 two heretics came to Besançon, in eastern France, and worked all sorts of marvels and miracles. It was discovered that they carried written pacts with the Devil concealed in the skin of their armpits. The documents were removed and the heretics were burned to death.

In 1320 an inquisitor in Carcassonne, in southern France, was instructed to proceed against people who worshipped demons and gave them writings and made pacts with them. *Errores Gazariorum*, written in Savoy c. 1450, says that becoming a witch involved swearing an oath of fidelity to the Devil, who then drew blood from the neophyte's left hand and wrote with it on paper, which he kept. In 1460 one of the Arras witches confessed to signing a pact in his own blood and Antoine Rose (1477) said she had kissed the Devil's foot in homage and renounced the Christian faith, and then the Devil put his mark on her.

The Malleus Maleficarum (1486) says that when a new witch joins the cult, the Devil asks her 'whether she will abjure the Faith, and forsake the holy Christian religion and the worship of the Anomalous Woman (for so they call the Most Blessed Virgin Mary), and never venerate the sacraments.' The new witch duly swears this with upraised hand, but then the Devil tells her that this is not enough, for she must give herself to him, body and soul, forever. The Malleus also quotes from an earlier work, John Nider's *Formicarius* (c. 1435), which says that the new recruit swore 'to deny the Christian religion, never to adore the Eucharist, and to tread the Cross underfoot whenever she could do so secretly.' From the same source the *Malleus* quotes a Swiss witch as saying that the neophyte entered a church on a Sunday with the leaders of the group and in their presence denied Christ and the Church: 'and then he must pay homage to the Little Master, for so and not otherwise do they call the Devil'.

Evidently, a written pact signed in blood was not always necessary, though a Basque witch burned in 1619 showed Pierre de Lancre the pact she had made with the Devil, scrawled in menstrual blood. A written pact which is still preserved is the one allegedly signed by Urban Grandier and produced against him in evidence at his trial in 1634, together with a reply signed by the chief princes of hell. The pact reads:

My lord and master Lucifer, I acknowledge you as my god and prince, and promise to serve and obey you while I live. And I renounce the other god and Jesus Christ, the saints, the Roman Church and all its sacraments, and all prayers by which the faithful might intercede for me; and I promise to do as much evil as I can and to draw all others to evil; and I renounce chrism and baptism, and all the merits of Jesus Christ and his saints; and if I fail to serve and adore you, paying you homage three times a day, I give you my life as your own.

In reply the lords of darkness promised him a life full of carnal delights for twenty years, after which he would join them in hell.

In England, Anne Chattox said that 'a thing like a Christian man, for four years together, did sundry times come to this Examinate, and requested this Examinate to give him her Soul, and in the end this Examinate was contented to give him her said Soul, she being then in her own house, in the Forest of Pendle.' The phrasing of this confession suggests another source of the firm belief in the pact, the tendency of lawyers to rejoice in set forms and due process, and their assumption that the Father of Lies must do so too.

The pact has little importance in the textbooks of ceremonial magic. *The Grand Grimoire* does include an unimpressive ritual for making a pact with a subordinate demon named Lucifuge Rofocale in order to borrow money from him, but the grimoires are mainly concerned to dominate evil spirits, to quell them and reduce them to obedience, and the mentality of the sorcerer who bargains his soul away to obtain the Devil's services is foreign to their view of the overwhelming power of the master magician.

RICHARD CAVENDISH

FURTHER READING: E. M. Butler. The Myth of the Magus. *(Cambridge Univ. Press, 1979); H. C. Lea.* Materials Towards a History of Witchcraft. *(AMS Press reprint, 3 vols); R. H. Robbins.* Encyclopedia of Witchcraft and Demonology. *(Crown, 1959); M. Summers, ed.* Malleus Maleficarum *(Weiser);* Guazzo's Compendium Maleficarum. *(Muller, London, 1970 reprint).*

Plants & Witchcraft

From the early days of man's habitation on earth, women were charged with the task of gathering nuts, berries, and other plants. Not only did they search for food plants, they also learned that many plants had medicinal qualities as well. Thus it came about that women in particular became adept at using these plants to heal the sick, relieve pain, aid in childbirth, and more. Eventually, a few of these powerful and wise healers realized that anything strong enough to cure illness might have power of a different sort. Some of the plants useful in healing were also hallucinogens and toxins. That which was useful in healing had other, less benign uses; some of the drugs could be used to sicken, even kill, and they could be administered in secret. Of course, those that were hallucinogens were thought to provide transport to another realm or to the spirit world, and the shamans and witches saved some of the best of those for themselves.

Witches were accused by the establishment of flying off to gather in covens and meet the Devil, but perhaps this charge is not so preposterous as it seems; they used so-called 'flying ointments' made with psychotropic plants, and they truly believed that when they did this they could not just fly off to the next county but enter unknown worlds while in the trancelike state that resulted.

Poisoning has long been associated with witchcraft, and historically, when someone died from a cause that was not obvious, often witchcraft was suspected and a guilty party was sought.

The image we have of witches riding broomsticks is based in fact. Specifically, witches used ointments containing the tropane alkaloids obtained from plants of the Solanaceae family. They applied these ointments to their armpits and genital or anal areas, and thus achieved a hallucination of flying.

In the case of the Irish Lady Alice Kyteller, accused of witchcraft in 1324,

investigators found: 'a pipe of oyntment wherewith she greased a staffe, upon which she ambled and galloped through thick and thin.'

Later, in the fifteenth century, Jordanes de Bergamo wrote:

'But the vulgar believe, and the witches confess, that on certain days or nights they anoint a staff and ride on it to the appointed place or anoint themselves under the arms and in other hairy places.'

Many of the plants (henbane, belladonna, mandrake, and others of the *Solanaceae* Family) used by witches, or 'wise women,' throughout the world contain tropane alkaloids, specifically, hyoscine, which are hallucinogenic as well as antispasmodic. Hyoscine is used today to treat menstrual cramps,

In the upland regions of Homolje from time to time people consult fortune-tellers, always elderly women who have learned the arts of fortune-telling, magic, and witchcraft from a close relative. They practice these beside a hearth, on the threshold of a house, by a woodpile or a dunghill, or in the place where poultry alight. The means used range from spells and incantations to dropping molten lead into water, examining dead embers, and 'reading' dried beans or maize, like this elderly fortune-teller near the village of Ravniote.

Hyoscyamus niger (black henbane)

irritable bowel syndrome, and muscle spasms in the bladder.

Solanaceae, or the Potato Family

Belladonna, Datura, Henbane, Mandrake, Nightshades, members of the *Solanaceae* family, all of which are found in flying ointment recipes, have been used as medicine for millenia to treat anything from skin ulcers to headaches to the plague. These drugs were included in the recipes of most flying ointments, tinctures, or salves, which were applied topically and which made the users able to fly . . . or so it seemed to them. Tropane alkaloids are readily absorbable through the skin, particularly sweat glands and mucus membranes, so the early witches and others who used them were taking a drug, although they didn't realize it. The flying ointment usually contained both a tropane alkaloid and an opium alkaloid, so belladonna and morphine mixed together with some form of fat was absorbed through the skin and caused a hallucination of flying.

The *Solanaceae* family includes peppers, tomatoes, tobacco, and petunias as well as the more dangerous plants used as medicines and in witch-craft; the same alkaloid ingredient that gives hot peppers their piquancy is present in greater concentrations in the more harmful plants in the *Solanaceae* family.

Atropa belladonna, or deadly nightshade, is known by many common names, including dwale, death's herb, and sorcerer's berry. It is named for Atropos, one of the three Fates; she is the one who cut the cord of life causing death to all humans. It's name, belladonna, or beautiful woman in Italian, stems from its use as a cosmetic. Belladonna drops were placed in women's eyes to make their pupils dilate, which was considered attractive.

Belladonna is used as a doorway between worlds, and it was a key ingredient in the witches' flying ointments. In witchcraft, belladonna is used to enter deeper levels of trance and dream states. It is both toxic and hallucinogenic.

Bittersweet nightshade, also known as bittersweet, felonwort, garden night-shade, scarlet berry, snakeberry, staff vine, or woody nightshade is not a hallucinogen, but the whole plant is toxic. This plant was used to heal bruises, swellings, sprains, corns, and sores. It can be combined with chamomile to ease soreness.

Black nightshade is found wild in the woods and hedges. It is not a hallucinogenic, and when boiled, the berries are said to be safe to eat, but only an experienced practitioner should try it. All parts of the plant are toxic. Black nightshade is not in widespread use in witchcraft. In witchcraft, nightshade is associated with hiding and revealing secrets.

Various species of datura, or angel's trumpet, are known by such common names as devil's apple, devil's trumpet, jimsonweed, sorcerer's herb, stramo-nium, and thorn apple. Datura is dangerous even to touch and is both toxic and hallucinigenic. It can be mixed to form an ointment that is used for healing and for out of body travel. Datura also had widespread use as a poison and hallucinogen.

In witchcraft, datura is one of the hexing herbs, that include datura, belladonna, mandrake, henbane, and hemlock.

Henbane, or *Hyosycamus niger*, is also called black henbane, devil's eye, henbells, jupiter's bean, poison tobac-co, and stinking nightshade. Henbane is highly toxic and hallucinogenic and was used in flying ointments and aphrodisiacs. Henbane was used

Atropa belladonna (deadly nightshade)

by men to attract a wife or burned outside to bring rain. It has sedative effects and was used in love potions and in incense to call up the dead.

In witchcraft, henbane is believed to be useful in blocking or stopping communication, interrupting lies, or interfering with gossip.

Mandrake, or alraun, is also known as brain thief, circeum, circoea, djinn's eggs, golden apples of Aphrodite, Mandragora, Mandragor, Mannikin, sorcerer's root, witches' mannikin, and womandrake.

This root, which can resemble the shape of a man, is used in love potions. It may have been one of the plants responsible for making men act like beasts, leading to legends of werewolves and shapeshifters. It is less toxic than others in the *Solanaceae* family, but it is hallucinogenic. Mandrake is another of the 'hexing herbs' used in flying ointments. It is also an ingredient in fertility spells and love potions.

In Greek mythology, Medea used mandrake root in a flying ointment for Jason so he could infiltrate Hecate's garden and steal the golden fleece.

The roots of the mandrake and the shape of its bulb make it look as if it's shaped like a man. It is associated with mastery in witchcraft.

Other Plants Associated with Witchcraft

Hemlock is a member of the *Apiaceae*, or carrot, family. Other plants in this family are parsley, parsnip, carrot, celery, and the flowering roadside plant Queen Anne's lace. Hemlock is known by such common names as poison hemlock, devil's bread, poison parsley, spotted hemlock, and others.

The spirit of hemlock is said in witchcraft to be a spirit of reparation, and it is used to bring about reconciliation and to set things right.

Foxglove, or digitalis, a member of the Plantaginaceae family, is a beautiful flowering plant, which is used as an ornamental garden plant. It has been used medicinally as a treatment for some heart conditions since the late eighteenth century.

In witchcraft, floxglove is said to be associated with communication with the otherworld and can be used to restore passion between lovers.

Aconite is also known as wolfsbane or monkshood. It is a member of the buttercup family. Aconite is second only to mandrake in power; both are associated with humans. Aconite was the poison of choice for elf darts. In the folklore of early Europe, an elf dart was supposedly responsible for someone being suddenly taken by a stroke or heart attack. The real reason was unknown to primitive people, so they attributed the suddenness of the 'attack' to a dart thrown by an invisible elf. Witches and others later used aconite to coat the points of tiny darts, and surreptitiously pricked their victim with the dart. If done in a crowded place, no one suspected, and the victim fell to a seeming stroke, a victim, it seemed again, of attack by an elf.

Mushrooms are associated with the moon and its power. Their seeming ability to pop out of the ground overnight is mysterious to simple people, and the toxic and hallucinogenic qualities of some mushrooms make them of particular interest to the witch. In European folklore, fairy rings, or hexenrings, were thought to have been created by the energy left after witches had danced in the woods. A fairy ring of mushrooms was a sign to common folk that they should stay away from a particular area of the woods.

Pricking

The theory that a witch could be identified by a special mark, a bodily blemish representing the seal which Satan had set upon his followers, led to the practice of pricking the suspect's body in order to find this proof of her pact with the Devil. The 'Satanic compact' was held to be one of the worst forms of heresy, since it committed the witch to a denial of God and to the frustration of his angels and servants, and the search for the Devil's mark became standard witch hunting procedure.

The mark was supposed to be made by Satan's teeth, tongue, or claw, and in some cases it was actually called the 'Devil's claw.' It might be in the shape of a spider, a dormouse, or 'the likeness of a hare,' while according to some early medieval authorities it could be compared with the imprint of a cloven hoof.

Opinions varied as to where it was most likely to be found. The great majority of witch hunters looked for the mark near the pubic area of a female suspect, or the anus of a male. Michael Dalton, in his *Country Justice*, a guide to witch hunting published in 1618, makes it clear that the 'marks be often in their secretes parts and therefore require diligent and careful search.'

The hunt for the Devil's marks was conducted by skilled witch hunters who had acquired, as the result of long and careful study, an ability to distinguish between ordinary bodily blemishes like moles, warts, old scars, and piles, and genuine Devil's marks, which had the peculiar characteristic of being insensitive to pain and incapable of bleeding. It is difficult to determine how this theory could have arisen in the first place, but such an assumption might have been based upon cases of stigmatization, which sometimes occur among hysterics. Bleeding can also be halted on occasion by shock or suggestion.

A suspect's naked body had to be completely shaved to ensure that no protective charm lay concealed among the hairs. With a woman this work was occasionally delegated to a committee of honest matrons, but in the vast majority of cases a highly skilled searcher, usually a man, was responsible for the whole operation because of the possibility that a demon might be lurking in the pubic regions. The entire body was then exhaustively inspected for possible Devil's marks, every wart, pile, or mole being thoroughly prodded with a long bodkin which pierced the flesh right down to the bone. The effusion of blood and the screams of the prisoner generally bore testimony to a clean record so far as witchcraft was concerned, but the witch hunter usually prodded on until some old scar that was insensitive to pain provided the evidence he needed.

There were occasions, of course, when even a comprehensive searching and pricking failed to produce proof of witchcraft, and the theory that the Devil's marks could be invisible began to find favour among witch hunters. It seemed reasonable to suppose that the Devil would protect his slaves by imprinting upon their bodies a mark that could not be seen, and it therefore became necessary for the witch hunter to prod every inch of the victim's body, even if it was completely free from blemishes. Even then the Devil's mark might still elude the searching bodkin, and the suspect would be handed over to the torturers.

In Switzerland in the seventeenth century, Michelle Chaudron strenuously protested her innocence although she was searched for Devil's marks until her whole body gushed blood from the wounds she received; but when she was tortured she readily confessed her guilt. This kind of treatment was justified by a declaration made by the Jesuit Martin Del Rio, that a Devil's mark was not invariably insensitive to pain; it was recognized that even a true witch might occasionally experience agonies when pricked.

Paid by Results

In countries where torture was not commonly practiced, or was forbid-

Witch burning in Switzerland, sixteenth century

den by law as in England and Wales, the witch-finder sometimes had to cheat in order to ensure a conviction. A false bodkin, consisting of a hollow shaft with a retractable needle, would be pressed against the body of the prisoner who, since he or she betrayed no symptom of pain, could then be presumed to be guilty.

Throughout the seventeenth century, the witch hunters continued their search for the Devil's marks. In the case of Father Louis Gaufridi, of the notorious Aix-en-Provence affair, no less than three such marks were discovered upon his body. Scotland at one time had a number of witch-prick-

ers who were paid by results, one of whom was hired by the magistrates of Newcastle-on-Tyne at a fee of twenty shillings for every witch he brought to book, plus his traveling expenses. As a result of his activities, fifteen victims, all but one of them women, were sent to the gallows.

During a witch hunt in 1649, one of the magistrates, a Lieutenant Colonel Hobson, challenged the authenticity of the tests. A woman, her clothes pulled over her head, was being examined by a witch-finder. He 'ran a pin into her thigh, and then suddenly let her coats fall, and then demanded-whether she had nothing of his in her body, but did not bleed.' Because she had felt nothing, the woman would have been sent for trial had not the magistrate ordered the witch-finder to run his pin into the same place again. This time the wound gushed out blood, and the 'pricker' had no alternative but to release her.

'Like a Little Spot'

Closely allied in the popular mind with the Devil's mark were the 'biggs' or teats with which witches were supposed to feed their familiars with blood. These naturally became objects of great interest to the witch-prickers. In a typical case which came to light during the time of Matthew Hopkins, Margaret Bayts, a housewife of Framlingham, Suffolk, was found guilty of feeding a familiar by means of two teats concealed in her 'secret parts'. Another English victim was Elizabeth Sawyer, a one-eyed and blasphemous witch of Edmonton. When searched by 'three grave matrons', she was discovered to have a 'thing like a teat', the size of her little finger, in the region of her buttocks.

It is obvious from the writings of John Bell, an eighteenth-century Scottish clergyman, that there was a common confusion between the two blemishes, as he describes witches' marks as being 'sometimes like a little spot, or a little teat, or red spots like flea-biting, sometimes also the flesh is sunk into a hollow'. Many people have supernumerary nipples, which are frequently hereditary—as the powers of a witch were also frequently believed to be.

The examination of women for witches' marks seems to have continued into the eighteenth century, although the old belief in the Devil's marks disappeared. Jane Wenham, the last person to be brought to trial for witchcraft in England, was thoroughly searched for marks without success in 1712, and it was finally found nec-

essary to indict her for 'conversing familiarly with the Devil in the shape of a cat'. She was found guilty of this offence, but later pardoned. During her interrogation Jane Wenham was subjected to the ordeal of witch-pricking, a pin being plunged into her arm six or seven times to start with, and then, when no blood came, 'a great many times more'.

Sabbath

In Goethe's *Faust*, Mephistopheles takes Faust to the witches' sabbath on the Brocken, a peak of sinister reputation in the Harz Mountains which was traditionally the place where all the witches of Germany gathered to hold high revel on Walpurgis Night. The pair struggle up into the hills, with Mephistopheles suggesting that they would be better off equipped with a broomstick or a he-goat to fly on. The wind raves and hisses round the rocks and trees, through the clefts and chasms there gleams a dull red light,

and they hear the cries of the witches hurrying through the storm-tossed air to the summit, where they dance to the point of madness in sensuous riot.

Goethe did not take the witches' sabbath very seriously, and on their way up the mountain Faust and Mephistopheles agree that they have entered a world of enchantment, of dream. There is, in fact, a dreamlike air about some of the accounts of the sabbath which were extorted from accused witches.

Witch hunters themselves were struck by this and Nicolas Remy, who hunted down hundreds of unfortunates in Lorraine in the 1580s, said that he was quite willing to agree with those who thought that the witches' meetings sometimes existed only in their dreams. He quoted a witch named Catherine Prevotte as saying that 'sometimes witches are fully awake and actually present at these assemblies; but that often they are merely visited in their sleep by an empty and vain imagination'—though he went on to make it clear that in either case

The Legendary Faust in his Study with Mephistopheles. **They are surrounded by the apparatus of witchcraft, a cauldron, skulls, spiders, and numerous animal familiars. A winged demon shows Faust the image of a beautiful woman as a temptation. (c. 1500)**

Flugbatt Zauberey (Witches Sabbath) (1626)

witches were equally the confederates of the demons.

Besides the Brocken, there were other places in Europe where witches were believed to gather like evil shapes in a nightmare: the Blocula in Sweden, a place in the mountain range of Amboto in the Basque country, or the famous walnut tree of Benevento in Italy. The picture of a huge gathering of hags and wizards where every animal passion was let loose by the light of black candles and smoking torches, with the great black goat looming darkly on his evil throne, obviously owes a good deal to overexcited human fantasy. The real sabbath, if it existed at all, must have been far smaller in scale and altogether less romantically sinister.

Whether there ever was such a thing as the witches' sabbath is crucial to the whole question of the existence of witchcraft as an organized movement or cult, as distinct from the activities of individual witches, charmers and magicians, acting alone. The evidence is unsatisfactory and incomplete but, putting it cautiously, it seems quite possible that groups of witches did exist, if only in small numbers, and that they met regularly for organized ceremonies. At all events, it was most certainly believed that they did.

Straws in the Wind

The name *sabbath* seems to have been applied to the witches' meetings through association with another fiercely hated and persecuted group, the Jews, for in the early accounts the meeting is frequently called the 'synagogue'. (The word *sabbat*, which some modern writers insist on, is merely the French spelling of 'sabbath'.) Early references to the meeting bring out the sexual and animal elements in it. The witch submits her body to the Devil and to other witches, the Devil appears as a goat or some other animal—presumably represented by a man dressed up—and he is saluted with the 'obscene kiss' on his backside.

Later accounts suggest that the meetings were usually, though not always, held at night and in the open air, with smaller gatherings sometimes held in a house or in a church. The atmosphere of dream and fantasy enters the picture at once with the question of how the witches went to the meeting. Very often they seem to have used perfectly normal means, walking or riding, but it was an old belief that among the uncanny powers of the witch was the ability to fly. Once it was firmly established that being a witch meant being in league with the Devil, it was widely accepted that he enabled his servants to ride through the air to the sabbath on demonic animals, broomsticks, reeds, or wisps of straw.

In 1664 in Somerset a woman named Julian Cox told how one evening, about a mile from her house, she saw three people riding toward her on broomsticks, four to five feet above the ground. Two of them she knew, a witch and a wizard, the third she did not: 'he came in the shape of a black man'. Two years earlier, in Scotland, Isabel Gowdie said that she would make a 'horse' of a straw or a beanstalk, putting it between her legs and saying, 'Horse and hattock in the Devil's name', and then flying away wherever she liked, as straws blow along a road in the wind.

Out of the Body
The ointment which the witches smeared on themselves may have caused delusions of flying, and some of the accounts may even have something to do with what we would now call 'astral' or 'out-of-the-body' experiences, but some suggest dancing, in

the manner of 'ride a cockhorse to Banbury cross', rather than flight. In other accounts it is the staff which is smeared with ointment, not the witch.

Whatever the truth may have been, most writers on witchcraft remained convinced that, with the Devil's aid, witches really flew through the air, and their lack of humor allowed them to accept even the most comically far-fetched tales. Guazzo's *Compen-*

Pierre de Lancre was told that the witches danced back to back and hand in hand, led by the black goat himself.

dium Maleficarum (1626) quotes with impassive solemnity and approbation a story about some soldiers at Calais who heard voices emanating from a black cloud in the sky. One of them fired a bullet at the cloud and from it there dropped a very fat, naked, drunken female of mature years, hit in the thigh. When they questioned her, 'she pretended to be feeble minded'.

Descriptions of what happened at the sabbath, and in what order, vary from area to area and author to author, but it generally seems to have begun with the witches acknowledging the Devil as their god and giving him the obscene kiss as a mark of their utter subjection to his will. They reported the acts of magic and malice they had done since the previous meeting and received instructions and guidance: 'at what time,' says King James's Demonology, 'their master enquiring of them what they would be at, every one proposes unto him what wicked turn they would have done, either for obtaining of riches, or for revenging them upon any whom they have malice at, who granting their demands (as no doubt willingly he will, since it is to do evil)

he tea-cheth them the means whereby they may do the same'.

Next, new recruits would be formally presented to the Devil to renounce Christianity and swear allegiance to him, and there might be weddings between members to be celebrated or baptisms to be performed. According to the French witch hunter Pierre de Lancre, 'witches were accustomed to have their children baptized more often at the sabbath than in church, and presented more often to the Devil than to God.'

A Foul and Horrid Fire
In making obeisance to their master, the witches are reported to have adopted curious postures. Guazzo says: 'When these members of the devil have met together, they generally light a foul and horrid fire. The devil is president of the Assembly and sits on a throne in some horrid shape, as of a goat or a dog; and they approach him to adore him, but not always in the same manner. For sometimes they bend their knees as suppliants, and sometimes stand with their backs turned, and sometimes kick their legs high up so that their heads are bent back and their chins point to the sky . . . they turn their backs and, going backward like crabs, put out their hands behind them to touch him in supplication. When they speak, they turn their faces to the ground; and they do all things in a manner foreign to the use of other men.'

Reversing the normal order of things is appropriate to the worship of the Devil as the great rebel against God and against Christian values, and approaching him backward may have been an example of this, like the candles offered to him, which were black instead of white. The candles also fit his role as Lucifer, 'light-bearer', and he was sometimes said to have had a lighted candle on his head, between his horns, from which worshippers lighted their own candles.

The obscene kiss is another example of the reversal of accepted values. According to de Lancre, one witch of southwestern France said that the Devil had the form of a goat and beneath his tail he had a second face, which was black, and it was this which she kissed.

The next part of the meeting seems to have been the feasting and dancing. Descriptions of the feast vary considerably. Sometimes the witches are said to enjoy a substantial meal, like the Lancashire witches who sat down to beef, bacon, and roast mutton. The Somerset witches ate meat and cakes, and drank wine or beer. The 'man in black' sat at the head of the table with his favourite female witch beside him. Isabel Gowdie described the Devil presiding at the head of the table: 'and when we had ended eating, we looked steadfastly to the Devil, and bowing ourselves to him, we said to the Devil, We thank thee, our Lord, for this.' Madeleine de Demandolx followed popular tradition in saying that the witches feasted on bread and malmsey wine, and the cooked flesh of young children. They took no salt with their meal, salt being a preservative and therefore hostile to the nature of demons, which are agents of corruption.

But many authorities believed that all things connected with the Evil One must necessarily be 'foul and horrid'. Remy says in his Demonolatry that all who have attended the Devil's table agree 'that his banquets are so foul either in appearance or smell that they would easily cause nausea in the hungriest and greediest stomach . . . And for drink he gives them in a dirty little cup wine like clots of black blood.'

'I am Always Caressed'

Dancing was evidently a vital element in the sabbath, and Remy regarded this as a survival from pagan times. 'The dances which were in ancient days performed in the worship of demons [pagan deities] are still used today at their nocturnal assemblies.' He says that they danced in a ring, back to back, and one witch told him that they always moved to the left widdershins, or contrary to the course of the sun. They carried their dancing to a point 'little short of madness' and on returning home found themselves utterly exhausted.

Pierre de Lancre was told that the witches danced back to back and hand in hand, led by the black goat himself and usually moving to the left. Guazzo says that they formed 'a frenzied ring with hands joined and back to back; and so they dance, throwing their heads like frantic folk, sometimes holding in their hands the candles which they have before used in worshipping the devil'.

The main purpose of the dancing seems to have been to create a state of wild emotional intoxication that culminated in the frenzied sexual orgy in which the sabbath reached its peak. The Devil himself pleasured many of the witches and it was said that all restraints of sex, age, and relationship were swept away in an ecstatically abandoned revel that included virtually every conceivable heterosexual and homosexual perversion. Many writers insisted that, far from being pleasurable, the Devil's attentions were frightening and painful. A French witch tried in 1594 was quoted as saying that when the goat copulated with her she found it painful, and that his semen was cold as ice. A girl named Jeannette d'Abbadie, aged sixteen, told de Lancre that she had been carnally known by Satan many times: 'she feared coupling with the Devil because his member was scaly and caused intense pain; and his semen was extremely cold, so much so that she had never been made pregnant by him, or by the other men at the sabbath.'

Accounts of the Devil's genital equipment and the coldness of his emission, as well as his remarkable powers of endurance, suggest the use of an artificial phallus. One of the rare notes of humour in the

History of the Lancashire Witches is in the John Rylands Library in Manchester.

ehemaliger Richtplatz
in Erinnerung an die Opfer
der Hexenverfolgung
im 17.Jh.

horrifying annals of the witch persecutions is in another confession reported by de Lancre, that of Marie de Marigrane of Biarritz, aged fifteen, who said that 'she had often seen the Devil couple with a multitude of women, whom she knew by name and surname, and that it was the Devil's custom to have intercourse with the beautiful women from the front, and with the ugly from the rear'.

The experience was not always described as unpleasant. The Italian witch judge Paulus Grillandus said that several women told him that they enjoyed the Devil with 'the greatest voluptuousness'; a French witch said, 'I will not be other than I am; I find too much content in my condition; I am always caressed'; and Isabel Gowdie enjoyed what may have been a perverse mixture of pleasure and pain, saying that the Devil was 'heavy like a malt-sack; a huge nature, very cold, as ice' but also that 'he is abler for us that way than any man can be'.

Several witches, despite the pressure brought to bear on them to repent their ways, insisted that the sabbath was an occasion of joy and delight. One of them told de Lancre that 'the sabbath was the true paradise, where there was more joy than could be expressed. Those who went there found the time too short because of the pleasure and happiness they enjoyed, so that they left with infinite regret and longed for the time when they could go again'. Another, a very beautiful woman aged twenty-eight, said that 'she had more pleasure and happiness in going to the sabbath than to Mass, for the Devil made them believe him to be the true God, and that the joy which the witches had at the sabbath was but the prelude of much greater glory'. In England, Elinor Shaw and Mary Phillips were asked to say their prayers before execution, but they laughed, 'calling for the Devil to come and help them in such a blasphemous manner, as is not fit to mention . . . and as they lived the Devil's true factors, so they resolutely died in his service'.

The Murray Theory

In *The Witch-Cult in Western Europe* (1921), Margaret Murray advanced the theory that the witches had preserved the old pagan religion of pre-Christian Europe. 'The evidence proves that

> *This god was the master of life on earth, not a distant being in a far-off heaven.*

underlying the Christian religion was a cult practiced by many classes of the community, chiefly, however, by the more ignorant or those in the less thickly inhabited parts of the country. It can be traced back to pre-Christian times and appears to be the ancient religion of western Europe.'

This brilliantly ingenious theory has persuaded a good many writers on witchcraft and has greatly influenced modern witches (and the theory's attraction for the modern mind is itself an interesting fact). But the evidence does not really support the view that through centuries of Christianity a pagan cult survived in the assemblies of witches, especially as none of the witches or their investigators ever said that it did. It looks as if the views of people at the time were nearer to the truth: that the real witches, as distinct from the many who were bullied or tortured into making false confessions, were worshipping, not the pagan god of a hypothetical 'old religion' but the Devil of Christianity as the opponent of the Christian God and the lord and master of all sensual pleasure and fleshly delight.

This gives point to the accusation that the culminating orgy of the sabbath came at the end of a religious ceremony which was a parody of the Mass, degrading and blaspheming the Christian ritual and turning it into an act of worship of the Devil. Paulus Grillandus said: 'Those witches who have solemnly devoted themselves to the Devil's service, worship him in a particular manner with ceremonial sacrifices, which they offer to the Devil, imitating in all respects the worship of Almighty God, with vestments, lights, and every other ritual observance, so that they worship and praise him, just as we worship the true God.' In 1678 there was a meeting of the witches of Lothian in Scotland, at which a deposed Presbyterian minister took the part of the Devil and preached a sermon. 'Among other things, he told them that they were more happy in him than they could be in God; him they saw, but God they could not see; and in mockery of Christ and his holy ordinance of the sacrament of his supper he gives the sacrament to them, bidding them eat it and to drink it in remembrance of himself.'

Another account of the same meeting says that the Devil 'adventured to give them the communion or holy sacrament, the bread was like wafers, the drink was sometimes blood, sometimes black moss water. He preached and most blasphemously mocked them, if they offered to trust in God who left them miserable in the world, and neither he nor his son Jesus Christ ever appeared to them when they called on them, as he had, who would not cheat them.'

Survival of an Idea

There were certainly pagan survivals in witchcraft, as there were in Christianity itself, but this is not the same thing as the continuance of a pagan cult. That the god of the witches was Cernunnos, the Celtic horned god, or Pan, or Dionysus, are enticing but not finally convincing proposals. What seems more likely than the survival of any particular pagan god is the survival of an idea. The witches were, after all, practitioners of magic, and they seem to have shared the magical sense of the value of the animal in man. The frenzied dancing and the orgiastic worship of a god in animal form imply the letting loose of all the animal elements of human nature, which in magical theory is a step toward the achievement of wholeness, toward the liberation of the real inward self, and so toward achievement of the divine.

The witches may have believed that they attained the divine in the sabbath, especially in the sexual union with the god. This god was the master of life on earth, not a distant being in a far-off heaven. 'Him they saw, but God they could not see.' This was a god through whom they could achieve release, power and divinity in the flesh, and through the flesh, who had not gone away and left them behind, 'miserable in the world', and who, they thought, would not cheat them.

RICHARD CAVENDISH

Salem Witches

The Salem witch hunt of 1692 is perhaps the most famous of its kind, at least in the English-speaking world. It was the greatest in scale, continuance and numbers of people involved of any witch hunt to take place in the United States, and therefore has naturally attracted much attention from Americans. By comparison with central European countries, however, the proportions of the outbreak were not remarkable, and the unique feature of the Salem scare is that it ended as

suddenly as it began. There was a public revulsion of feeling during the later trials, none of the later suspects were punished, and a heated controversy broke out on whether there ever had been any witchcraft in the community at all, or whether the whole affair had been a tragic delusion.

Because of this controversy, the whole story is unusually well known; but it has to be realized that more is known about Salem than about most such cases precisely because it was untypical. The panic arose in Salem Village, Massachusetts, a rural community some distance out of Salem proper (and since renamed Danvers). It began among a group of eight girls,

aged eleven to twenty, who in the winter of 1691–1692 used to meet in the back premises of the minister's house, in the company of the minister's slave, Tituba. Everybody has always assumed, reasonably, that Tituba, who came from Barbados, stuffed their impressionable heads with tales of African magic. Unfortunately there is no trace of any specifically African, or West Indian, superstition in the stories the girls told later.

These sessions ended by driving Abigail Williams and Ann Putnam, aged eleven and twelve, into what was evidently a hysterical illness. Abigail, the youngest of the eight girls, was related to the minister,

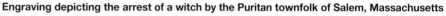

Engraving depicting the arrest of a witch by the Puritan townfolk of Salem, Massachusetts

Samuel Parris, and lived in the house, so she was more exposed to Tituba's influence than the others. The two girls moaned and shrieked for no apparent reason, grovelled and writhed on the ground and occasionally acted as if they believed that they had been transformed into animals.

The Accusations Begin

These symptoms began to spread through the child population of the settlement. The adult community seem to have agreed at once that the girls were bewitched, but Mr. Parris (who was doubly involved, in his private and his religious capacity) was unable to discover who was bewitching them. Eventually, however, at the end of February 1692, Abigail and Ann were able to name three of their tormentors: Tituba, Sarah Good, and Sarah Osburne. The two last, like most accused early in the witch hunt, seem to have been unpopular in the settlement and already distrusted by the Puritan leadership. Later, the children seemed careless whether their accusations were plausible.

At this stage, everybody in authority was disposed to take them seriously. The magistrates had the women arrested on 1 March, and examined them in the presence of their accusers at a public session, for which they borrowed the church. The two Sarahs denied everything, but Tituba produced an imaginative confession in which she named several more people as instruments of Satan. The afflicted girls duly went into paroxysms in the presence of the people named as witches.

Parody of Holy Communion

Tituba's confession probably saved her life. She was never brought to trial, though she was confiscated from Mr. Parris and eventually sold to defray

The Witch No.1 lithograph

Rebecca Nurse Homestead, Danvers, Massachusetts

court costs. Sarah Osburne died awaiting trial. Meanwhile the list of suspects grew. Abigail and Ann were still the most active accusers, but other girls were joining in, and some of the accused followed Tituba's example. None of those who confessed, and implicated others, was executed. Those who protested that they were innocent included some whose innocence, in the ordinary way, would have been taken for granted. They included a minister of religion, George Burroughs, Martha Corey, who was a church member in good standing (not a particularly common distinction in early Massachusetts), and Rebecca Nurse, of unsullied reputation. Naturally there were a few old villagers who had always been suspected of witchcraft; Bridget Bishop and Susanna Martin had old suspicions brought against them when they were tried.

A special commission of judges was appointed by the governor, Sir William Phips, to sit in the town of Salem (not the village) in June. Bridget Bishop was condemned and executed at once (one of those later rehabilitated), and then the court got to work detecting the tormentors of Abigail Williams and Ann Putnam. The girls were thrown into fits by the near neigh-

bourhood of any witch, but could be temporarily relieved by a touch of her hand. Early on, Rebecca Nurse, against whom there was no evidence at all, was found not guilty; but the court went to the unheard-of length of overruling the jury. She was hanged, together with Sarah Good, Susanna Martin, and three others, on 19 July.

Others besides the jury had misgivings, but those who expressed them were likely to draw accusations down on their own heads. This was probably the real offence committed by Martha

A girl bewitched at a Salem trial in 1692

Corey, Rebecca Nurse's sister Mary Easty, and the deputy constable John Willard, who refused, shortly after the beginning of the trials, to make any more arrests. All three were executed. Salem Village, that summer, was in the full grip of panic, and the fever was spreading. Abigail and Ann had taken to accusing people at a distance whom they knew only by name. One of these, a Mrs. Cary of Charlestown, did not wait to be arrested but came to Salem with her husband and sat among the public in court. The children were quite unaffected by her presence until they casually learned who she was, when the usual fits followed. (She was arrested, but survived the panic and was released.) The authorities of the town of Andover invited some of the children to visit the place and see if any of the local inhabitants were witches. They found several.

The court naturally wanted to find out what witches did, besides throwing children into fits. In this it was not very successful, presumably because the star witnesses were interested in little else. Part of the case against George Burroughs, however, was that he had performed an infernal parody of a Puritan Communion service—a

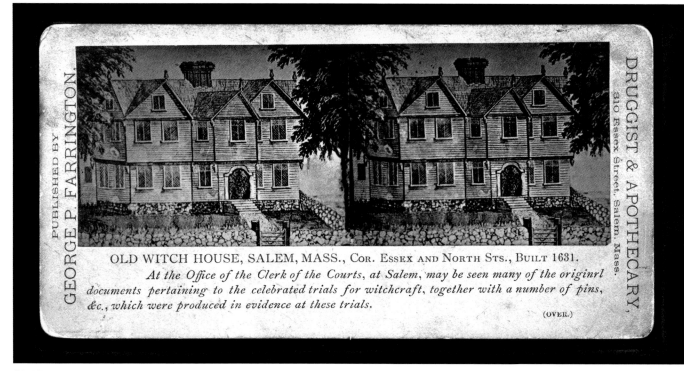

Old Witch House, Salem, Massachusetts

faint, distant echo of the European tales of the sabbath and Black Mass. He was executed on 19 August along with John Willard and the first of the Andover witches. The General Court of Massachusetts passed a special Act of Attainder to deprive him of his clergy status—a procedure nearly, if not quite, unique on American soil.

Pressed to Death

Another incident, believed to be unique in American history, occurred in September when Giles Corey, Martha's husband, who was then over eighty, was pressed to death for refusing to plead to the indictment. Under common law at that date, a prisoner could not be tried until he consented to plead. If necessary, he was induced to do this by being tied on his back on the floor of the cell while weights were piled on his chest. If he died under this treatment he died uncondemned, his goods were not forfeit to the state and his will could be executed. Martha, with Mary Easty and six others, was hanged a few days later on 22 September. By this time the death toll was twenty, and some 200 people

had been arrested. The girls were still producing new names, but they had run out of people they knew and were reduced to accusing people they had merely heard of—including colonial notabilities such as the governor's wife and the president of Harvard.

Governor Phips had been away from the colony for much of the summer, and came upon this situation when he returned. In October he cancelled the special commission and the hearings came to an end, the remaining prisoners being remanded until December, when the majority were acquitted and the governor pardoned the rest. The revulsion of public feeling was apparently complete. The General Court repealed the Act of Attainder on Burroughs. In Salem Village, the magistrates who had begun the inquiry made an admission of error amid general tears and lamentations. Colonial America never again dared to carry out the death sentence for witchcraft.

There had been some bold doubters all along; now there were many. Traditionally, Thomas Brattle, a merchant of Boston, has been remembered as the leading champion of reason. It should

be realized that nobody, or hardly anybody, as yet disputed the reality of witchcraft. Brattle's main contention was that people under diabolic influence were unreliable witnesses. There had been argument before the court on the extent of Satan's powers and how they could be tested. There was argument back and forth on whether Satan could assume the form of a human being who was not in his service. At first it was held that he could not, and one John Proctor was convicted and hanged largely on the evidence that he had appeared to plague a child in her dreams. Later it was realized that such appearances proved too little, and this kind of evidence was ruled out before the end of the trials.

As soon as people were brave enough to say so, it also became clear that Abigail Williams and Ann Putnam could have been inventing their accusations and simulating their afflictions, and if this were so it would explain some of their blunders, such as their failure to identify Mrs. Cary after accusing her by name. Scepticism was growing, even if by modern standards it was very limited.

This alarmed the illustrious Cotton Mather, who published *The Wonders of the Invisible World* (1693) as a counterblast. He had written in denunciation of witchcraft before the Salem scare started, and had probably helped to form the opinions of the local preachers and magistrates. He took an active interest in the persecution, and after it was over he was concerned to defend it. He was prepared, eventually, to admit that there had been miscarriages of justice in individual cases; for instance, he agreed that the evidence of apparitions, which had hanged John Proctor, had been given too much weight. He insisted, however, that Satan had really been specially active in Salem Village that summer, that on the whole the afflicted were genuinely afflicted and the accused justly accused; and that the effect of the persecution was beneficial in purging the community of evil elements and winning for it the favour of God. Mather had started a literary debate on what really happened in Salem Village and why it happened that has never completely ended.

ELLIOT ROSE

FURTHER READING: P. Boyer and S. Nissenbaum. Salem Possessed: the Social Origins of Witchcraft. *(Harvard Univ. Press, 1974); Chadwick Hansen.* Witchcraft at Salem. *(New American Library); G. L. Kittredge.* Witchcraft in Old and New England. *(Atheneum, 1972); Marion Starkey.* The Devil in Massachusetts. *(Doubleday, 1952).*

Somerset Witches

'On Thursday night before Whitsunday last, being met they called out Robin. Upon which instantly appeared a little man in black to whom all made obeisance, and the little man put his hand to his hat, saying, How do ye? speaking low but big. Then all made low obeisances to him again.' This description of a polite exchange between the Devil and his followers, and most of what is known of the Somerset witches in the 1660s, comes from Joseph Glanvill's *Sadducismus Triumphatus,* first published in 1681, a year after his death. Glanvill, who has been described as 'the father of modern psychical research', was a Fellow of

Examination of a Witch, Thompkins H. Matteson (1853)

the Royal Society and a former vicar of Frome in Somerset, who believed in the reality of witchcraft and had earlier published an account of the case of the Drummer of Tidworth in Wiltshire.

The witches tried in 1665 seem to have belonged to two separate groups or covens. The Wincanton group numbered fourteen, six women and eight men, headed by Ann Bishop and including Elizabeth Style and Alice Duke. The other group, at Brewham, numbered eleven, ten women, and one man, and included four women named Green, who were perhaps related, and three named Warberton.

The Devil was described as 'the man in black' or 'a man in blackish clothes' and Elizabeth Style said he was handsome. He presided at the open-air meetings of the Wincanton group, sitting at the head of the white cloth spread on the ground, with his favourite, Ann Bishop, beside him, while they all feasted merrily on wine and beer, cakes and meat, which he had provided. He spoke a grace before the meal, but none after, and his voice was audible but very low. Sometimes he played a pipe or a cittern (an instrument like a guitar) and 'they danced and were merry', according to Elizabeth Style, 'and were bodily there and in their clothes.'

The other side to this peacefully rustic picture comes out in the description of the use of wax images, which the witches called 'pictures', to harm people. The doll was brought to the meeting and the man in black baptized it, with himself as godfather and two witches as godmothers, anointing its forehead and saying, 'I baptize thee with this oil', so as to create an additional link between the image and the victim whose name was given to it. Then they stuck pins into it and said, 'A pox on thee, I'll spite thee.' Margaret Agar, of the Brewham group, 'delivered to the little man in black a picture in wax, into which he and Agar

Wookey Hole witch interviews. Helen Chadfield from Bath, England, with her four-year-old raven, 'Bran', before auditioning for the job of a traditional green wicked witch at Wookey Hole Caves, near Wells, in Somerset, England.

stuck thorns, and Henry Walter thrust his thumb into the side of it; then they threw it down and said, There is Dick Green's picture with a pox on it' (and Dick Green died soon after). They were fond of the phrase 'A pox take it', which they used as an all-purpose cursing formula.

To go to the meetings, the witches smeared on their foreheads and wrists a greenish oil, which the Devil gave them, and were quickly carried to the meeting-place, saying as they went, 'Thout, tout, a tout, tout, throughout and about'. When it was time to leave again, they cried, 'A boy! merry meet, merry part', and then each said '*Rentum, tormentum*' and another word which the witness could not remember, and was swiftly carried back to her home.

They said they were sometimes 'really' present at the meetings, 'in their bodies', but at other times they left their bodies at home and attended in spirit form, and it is interesting that the word trance occurs in Glanvill's account of their familiar imps. Alice Duke's familiar, in the form of a little cat, sucked her right breast, 'and when she is sucked, she is in a kind of trance'. Christian Green said that the Devil had what would seem the incon-

siderate habit of sucking her left breast at about five o'clock in the morning in the likeness of a hedgehog: 'she says that it is painful to her, and that she is usually in a trance when she is sucked.' When Elizabeth Style wanted to do someone harm, she shouted for Robin, and when the familiar came as a black dog, she said, 'O Satan, give me my purpose', and told him what she wanted.

Alice Duke said that, eleven years before, Ann Bishop had taken her to the churchyard, where they walked backward round the church three times. The first time round, they met a man in black clothes. On the second circuit a great black toad jumped up at them, and on the third round they saw something like a rat. Then the man in black spoke softly to Ann Bishop and they went home. It was after this that Alice joined the coven, and the Devil made his mark on her by pricking the fourth finger of her right hand, between the middle and upper joints.

The same mark in the same place was seen on the hands of Christian Green and Elizabeth Style. Elizabeth said that when the Devil first came to her, he promised her money and that 'she should live gallantly' and enjoy the pleasures of the world for twelve years, if she would sign in her blood a written pact giving him her soul. When she signed, with the blood he pricked from her finger, he gave her sixpence and vanished with the paper.

'Lead Us Into Temptation'

A little earlier, in 1663, a woman named Julian Cox, aged seventy, had been tried at Taunton Assizes, accused of bewitching a servant girl who had refused to give her money. She had appeared to the girl in ghostly form, invisible to others, and had forced her to swallow several large pins. Evidence was given that she could transform herself into a hare, that she had a toad as a familiar, that she had driven a farmer's cows mad, and that she had been seen to fly in at her own window. She was found guilty and executed.

It was Julian Cox who gave the curious account of seeing two witches and a 'black man' flying toward her on broomsticks 'about a yard and a half from the ground.' An interesting feature of her trial was that the judge attempted to test the belief that a witch could not say the Lord's Prayer. Julian Cox tried several times and repeated it correctly, except that she said 'And lead us into temptation' or 'And lead us not into no temptation' which, if she was really a member of the Devil's congregation, is the form of the prayer to which she might have been accustomed.

FURTHER READING: C. L'Estrange Ewen. Witchcraft and Demonianism. (Muller, 1970 reprint); M. A. Murray. The Witch-Cult in Western Europe. (Oxford: Oxford Univ. Press, 1967 reprint).

Spell

A word, set of words or procedure, frequently of a relatively minor kind, believed to have magical effect: an enchantment, as in the case of a person or country which has been placed under a spell.

Montague Summers

Students of witchcraft everywhere have reason to be grateful to the Rev. Montague Summers (1880–1948), whose many books included edited translations of the principal classic works in this field: the *Malleus Maleficarum* of Sprenger and Kramer, the *Compendium Maleficarum* of Guazzo, Bovet's *Pandaemonium*, and Remy's *Demonolatry* among them.

He was born into a prosperous banker's family at Clifton, near Bristol, where he was schooled, and after graduating at Trinity College, Oxford, he attended Lichfield Theological College from 1903 to 1905 and was ordained deacon in 1908. The following year, however, he and another clergyman were accused of pederasty, and he turned to the Roman Catholic church; here he was not raised to the priesthood, due to apparent lack of vocation, but finally achieved some kind of priestly ordination at the hands of Ulrich Herford, Bishop of Mercia and Middlesex in the Evangelical Catholic Communion.

For much of his life Summers was a schoolmaster, but he managed at the same time to produce a succession of scholarly books (as well as some pornography). Apart from his interest in witches and demons—which resulted in such works as *The History of Witchcraft and Demonology* (1926), *The Geography of Witchcraft* (1927) and *The Werewolf* (1933)—he was an expert on the Gothic novel, while his rediscovery of the plays of the Restoration dramatists had a profound effect upon theatre in the 1920s and 1930s.

He claimed that, in researching *The Vampire in Europe* (1929), he had carried out investigations at firsthand, and it was rumoured of him that he had seen the Devil. Asked if the Prince of Darkness really had a goat's head, horns and a forked tail, he replied in his characteristic high-pitched lisp: 'No tail, my dear'.

When he died in 1948, Summers was buried (as he had requested) in his violet-coloured vestments, with amice and alb, together with his biretta, ivory crucifix, rosary, and breviary—and the coat of his deceased pet dog.

Swedish Witchcraft

By contrast with Germany, France, England, and Scotland, the Scandinavian countries were comparatively free of organized witch hunts. But that fear of witches existed and could arouse hysteria and panic is shown by the case of the witches of Mora in Sweden, who were accused of taking children to a mysterious place called the Blocula and there enrolling them in the service of the Devil.

In July 1668 the Lutheran pastor of Elfdale in central Sweden, an area with a suitably evocative name in view of what was to happen, reported to his bishop that a girl named Gertrude Svensen had learned the art of magical incantation from a servant, Marit Jonsdottter, and had stolen several children of the district for 'the evil genius', the Devil. Her activities had been detected by a boy of fifteen, Eric Ericson, who also accused several others of stealing children for the Devil. One of them, a woman of seventy, admitted that the accusation was true, but the others denied it. Officials of the royal government had investigated and discovered that the accused had stolen consecrated wine from the church, the implication being that they could only have a diabolical use for it.

The accusations caused great uproar

locally. Rumours spread that hundreds of children had been delivered into the Devil's hand, and that the evil genius himself had been seen going about the countryside. In May 1669 the royal government (King Charles XI was then aged thirteen) instructed the bishop to appoint worthy ministers to join members of the royal council in a commission to restore peace and order, without the use of imprisonment or torture. In June the bishop was told to order public prayers throughout his diocese to ward off the Devil's wrath, and this may perhaps have made the panic worse, for when the commission met, on 13 August, 3,000 people came flocking to hear its deliberations.

After an investigation lasting till 25 August, the commission found that 300 children had been involved, and identified seventy witches. Far from being treated mildly, twenty-three who freely admitted their guilt were promptly beheaded and their bodies then burned to ashes. The other

forty-seven were sent to the town of Falun, where they were later executed in the same way. In addition, fifteen of the children were executed, thirty-six aged between nine and fifteen were made to run the gauntlet and condemned to be publicly beaten on the hands with rods every Sunday for a year, and twenty more, aged under nine, were to be beaten on the hands on three successive Sundays.

Man in Grey

The atmosphere of dream or fantasy so often found in the confessions of accused witches hangs thickly round the Mora case. According to the evidence given to the commission, the children were dressed in red or blue clothes and carried by the witches to the Blocula, riding on goats or sticks or cooking spits or on the bodies of men who were fast asleep. The Blocula itself sounds like a place from a dream. It was 'situated in a delicate large meadow, whereof you can see no

end'. There was a gate, painted in various colours, and behind it a smaller meadow and a house. The beasts the witches rode were left in the smaller meadow and the bodies of the sleeping men were propped up against the wall of the house. Inside, in one huge room there was a very long table at which the witches sat down to feast, and near it was another room, 'in which there were very lovely and delicate beds'.

Every witch had to take a child with her, such was the Devil's dubious fondness for young souls, and he bullied them and whipped them if they did not. Some of them took as many as fifteen or sixteen children with them. The children were made to deny God. They were baptized anew by the Devil's priests and their names were written in blood in the Devil's book.

The Devil appeared as a man. He had a red beard and he usually dressed in a grey coat, a high-crowned hat with linen of various colours wrapped round it, and stockings of red and blue

This is the place in Tjörn, Sweden, where eight people accused of witchcraft were burned on 27 January, 1672.

with long garters. When they sat down to eat, those who stood highest in the Devil's favour were placed nearest him. The children stood by the door and the Devil himself gave them their food and drink.

Afterward the witches danced, careering round and round astraddle on halberds (weapons which were a combination of a spear and a battle axe), while the Devil roared with laughter and played the harp with fingers which were like claws. The dancing culminated in a mixture of fighting and copulation. The Devil had children as a result of sexual intercourse with the witches, but they bore toads and snakes through their intercourse with each other.

The witches also said that they used to meet at a gravel pit which was near a crossroads, and there they would cover their heads with garments and dance. On the beasts or instruments which the Devil provided they would be carried over churches and high walls. He gave them ointment which they smeared on themselves, and a saddle to ride on. He would give a witch a purse in which were shavings filed off a clock. It had a stone tied to it, and the witch would drop it into water, saying, 'As these shavings of the clock do never return to the clock from which they are taken, so may my soul never return to heaven.'

The panic spread beyond Elfdale. In 1670 commissions of investigation were appointed in the Uppsala area and in Helsinki, in the Swedish province of Finland. In 1674 and 1675 a royal commission inquired into allegations of witchcraft in the parishes of Thorsaker, Ytterlannas, and Dahl, and there was another holocaust.

In 1676 there were investigations in Stockholm and six women were executed. Many more were imprisoned, and many of them insisted that they

were guilty. A Finnish woman named Magdalen Mattsdotter was accused by several children and servant girls, and her own two daughters said they had seen the Devil standing beside her. She denied the accusations and was burned alive, her younger daughter walking all the way to the stake with her trying to persuade her to confess. Later it became clear that the servants had accused her out of envy and malice, and they were condemned to death in

The practitioner of white magic is compelled to be rigidly disciplined in his day-to-day affairs, as he may otherwise fall from grace and his spells may fail to work.

their turn. The case contributed to a revulsion of feeling, Charles XI banned all further accusations, and the hysteria died away.

Christian Thomasius, a German lawyer and author of *De Crimine Magiae* (1701), who was head of Halle University (which his opponents nicknamed Hell University), said that he met one of the Swedish officials appointed to investigate accusations. The official told him that he and the other lay judges easily saw through the evidence, which was based on the lies and fantasies of children. But the Lutheran ministers, who dominated the proceedings, were convinced that the Holy Spirit spoke through the children and would never allow them to tell lies in such a case, citing the text 'out of the mouths of babes and sucklings' (Psalm 8, Matthew 21.16). After many innocent people had been put to death, one boy accused a man everyone respected. One of the commissioners offered the boy money to admit that he had made a mistake and had really meant to accuse somebody else. This the boy readily did, and the

ministers on the commission decided that the Holy Spirit did not speak through the children after all. They gave the boy a beating and abandoned the inquiry.

Fighting in Germany during the Thirty Years War, Swedish generals had put a stop to witch trials in areas under their control, on the orders of Queen Christina, who believed that persecuting supposed witches simply entangled increasing numbers of people in 'an inextricable labyrinth', a conclusion which all the European evidence bears out. H. R. Trevor-Roper has commented (in *The European Witch-Craze in the 16th and 17th Centuries*) that the subsequent persecutions in Sweden itself followed on the new intolerance of the Swedish Lutheran Church in the 1660s. 'Like the established Calvinist Church in Scotland, it had shaken itself free from other, more liberal Protestant parties, and its Puritan leaders prepared to advertise their purity by a great witch hunt.'

FURTHER READING: H. C. Lea. Materials Towards a History of Witchcraft. (Yoseloff, 1957 reprint, 3 vols); M. A. Murray. The Witch-Cult in Western Europe. (Clarendon Press, 1967 reprint); R. H. Robbins. Encyclopedia of Witchcraft and Demonology. (Spring Books, 1959).

White Magic

Described as an 'ancestral science' and also as 'the art of compulsion of the supernatural', magic is in practice a human technique designed to control the environment. It is based on the belief that the forces of Nature can be recruited to serve man's interests. In many primitive societies the control of these forces was one of the most important functions of priesthood, and it is only comparatively recently that magic has become divorced from religion.

The battle between good and evil or light and darkness, between white magic and black, may have existed only in the imagination, but it has always been conducted by dedicated individuals who were assumed to have access to psychic powers. The practitioner of white magic may have been a priest, magician, or psychically endowed layman, but he always insisted that his supernatural operations were dedicated to the service of man, a claim that led to a great deal of contention. Both priests and magicians insist that they and they alone have the qualifications to perform their role. This is why the clergy so often attacked magicians as agents of the Devil.

Magic has its positive and negative aspects, its active and passive principles. Similarly, magical practitioners may be divided into two basic personality types. One is the seeker after power, who strives to overcome his personal deficiencies by dominating others. The other is the seeker after wisdom who, driven by the same unconscious impulses, attempts to find the key to the hidden treasures of truth. The white magician, traditionally, calls upon God, angels, and elemental spirits to supply the power he needs for his operations. The black magician is supposed to derive his particular powers from devils, and to have ghouls and other night monsters as his agents. Black magic should not be written off for it can implant a degree of terror in a victim that may seriously harm him.

The history of the conflict between black magic and white suggests that in the main it is not the highly specialized magician who is held responsible for psychic attacks, but ordinary individuals, usually neighbours, who are thought to have the Evil Eye or 'evil mouth', and to be involuntary agents of evil. Among people who believe in

bewitchment, the fear of being caught by it, unprotected, is ever present; drowsiness, for example, is supposed to be a vulnerable state which must be avoided at all costs unless one has taken steps to protect oneself by white magic, such as by wearing an amulet. The gospel of St. John hung on a cord around the neck was thought to be effective for this purpose, as was the Lord's Prayer inscribed on a piece of paper and kept in one's shoe. The charm bracelet, which has become universally popular as a luck-bringer since its introduction well over 100 years ago, is probably the last of the traditional protective devices, but many people observe eccentric rites to which they resort when agitated. An unexpected example which I came across recently was the wearing of a violin 'D' string around the waist in order to benefit from its favourable vibrations. In the past, whenever personal systems of protection failed to put the mind at ease, a white magician was called in, in much the same way that a psychiatrist is consulted today.

In the country the white magician used to be a kind of general practitioner, the village Cunning Man or conjuror, while his urban counterpart, particularly in the upper ranks of society, tended to specialize in one particular art, such as astrology. In fact, the role of white magician will always remain important in a community that fears magic, or in one that has been convinced by its clergy of the presence of devils.

Doctor, Vet, and Detective

It is not generally realized that in its heyday white magic involved a wide variety of socially useful activities which are not readily associated with sorcery. The country magician was likely also to be the local veterinary surgeon, treating sick animals with a combination of muttered spells and a sound knowledge of animal diseases.

The name of God was frequently on his lips when he supplied his human patients with simples or ointments, or exorcized their ghosts and devils. When cross-examining someone who had asked him to divine the whereabouts of a lost object, he would combine incantations with painstaking interrogation. The white magician's status was sustained by the awe with which he was regarded in his community and, unless he was driven underground by persecution, he survived for just as long as people had need of his services, and while they accepted his peculiar version of reality.

An inveterate enemy of the clergy, whom he tended to regard as presumptuous interlopers, the white wizard in Europe assumed a semidivine authority, comparable with that of the African witch doctor. This might be conferred upon him during his initiation, or it might be based upon some unusual circumstance of birth—in England, for instance, he might be the seventh son of a seventh son—or on an inherited power.

In medieval Germany and nineteenth century North America the charmer whispered or sang his patient back to health. At Castel Mellano in southern Italy, a small village which is regarded as a centre of witchcraft by people for many miles around, the maciara or sorceress treats her emotionally disturbed clients by tying knots in a length of string which is buried in a cemetery at the conclusion of the ceremony. The spirit of evil is destroyed by this ritual 'killing'. In nineteenth century England a wizard of Amersham in Buckinghamshire was reputed to have cured a sick child by instructing its parents to 'take the length of the child with a stick, measure so much ground in the churchyard, and there dig and bury the stick'.

The Spanish village of Mojacar, famous for its witches, was the home of a celebrated Almerian wise woman

Princess Takiyasha summoning a skeleton spectre to frighten Mitsukuni at her father Taira Masakado's ruined palace at Soma. Utagawa Kuniyoshi (1797–1861)

Tia Carrica, until about fifty years ago. She achieved some remarkable cures by tracing a cross with a finger on the foreheads of sick clients. She would then enter into a trance state during the course of which the sickness passed from her client's body into her own. She often recited the following spell over individuals suffering from the Evil Eye:

Three have done evil to you.
Three have to be taken away.
Who are the three persons of the
Holy Trinity?
Father, Son and Holy Ghost.
Shepherd who came to the fountain
And came from the fountain,
Take away the Evil Eye
From whom you put it on.

The white magician in medieval England confronted with the same type of case used a very similar technique and recited:

Three biters hast thou bitten
The hart, ill eye, ill tongue.
Three biters shall be thy Boote,
Father, Sonne and Holy Ghost
    or God's name.
In worship of the five wounds of
    our Lorde.

Magic as a force can probably best be defined as the interaction of one mind upon another, with suggestion as its primary mechanism; psychic power is nothing more nor less than a peculiarly effective type of thinking. In Africa the witch doctor is believed to possess an indwelling power which

MAN, MYTH, AND MAGIC

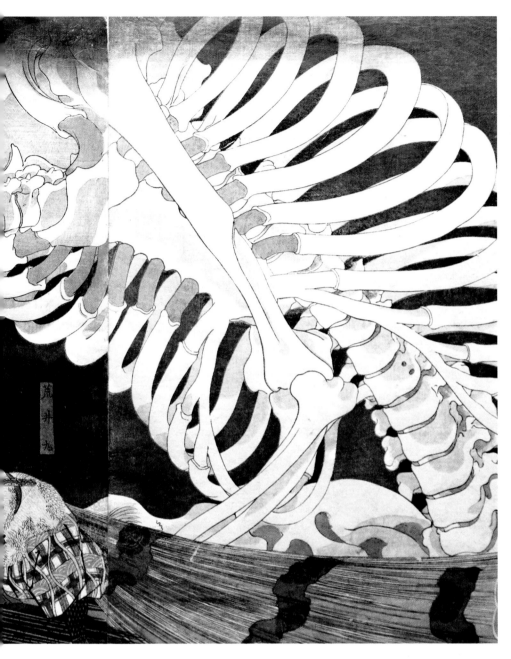

leads to a permanent state of tension, which is in itself a sign of instability, a measure of the emotional disturbance common to 'possessed' people. It is a widely held view today that the witches of the past were often people who would nowadays be classed as suffering from some form of mental illness, and the same could be said of witch doctors. The Siberian shaman became frenzied as he entered the trance state, and it is well known that many white magicians have been emotionally disturbed.

The social value of the white magician was to some extent counterbalanced by the dangers inherent in his methods of treatment. In his extremely informative book *Scared to Death*, Dr. J. C. Barker devotes considerable attention to this problem. There are cases in which fortune tellers have implanted troublesome thoughts and eroding fears in the minds of clients, with disastrous results. It is a curious situation when the sick are treated by the sick, and when the rustic psychiatrist who sets up shop to abreact the community's traumas could be said to be in need of treatment himself.

Another aspect of witch doctor practice, which led to many tragedies, was the execution of so called black witches at the instigation of white ones. Isolated examples have occurred in the twentieth century. Some seventy-five years ago, for instance, the Pow Wow men of Pennsylvania were indirectly responsible for the murders of a number of innocent victims of popular prejudice. More recently, similar cases have been reported from Germany, where the belief in magic is today even stronger than in prewar years.

Aura of Responsibility

Although the definitive history of white magic in the British Isles has yet to be written, it is clear that much of it is of Germanic origin. The white

enables him not only to heal the sick but also to identify witches in the community. This consciousness of an inner force is common to most psychic healers and white magicians, and they usually believe that it can be preserved only if they observe an extremely strict code of conduct. If the witch doctor submits to the temptation to practice magic for illicit ends his power will leave him, or he will become a witch himself.

English folklorists report a similar moral code among the Cunning Men of the past. It seems that they always refused to work for reward since they believed that this would result in a subconscious pandering to the client's wishes, and that they would tell him what he wanted to hear rather than what he needed to know. Such insight, though rare, is not uncommon among white magicians.

The practitioner of white magic is compelled to be rigidly disciplined in his attitudes to day-to-day affairs, as he may otherwise fall from grace and his spells may fail to work. This

St. Cyriacus Exorcizing the Daughter of Emperor Diocletian, Matthias Gruenewald (1470–1528)

magicians and healers of Anglo-Saxon times treated their patients with a combination of prayer, magical incantations, and herbal medicines, based on the Doctrine of Signatures, the principle that 'like cures like.' They healed by touch, breath, and suggestion, and this in their day was probably the best type of medicine available. Medieval healing charms were often supplemented by a type of amulet that goes back to prehistoric times, and which is still used today to bring luck. This is the flint arrowhead or the holed stone, sometimes called a fairy stone, which protected both the byre and the bedroom from demonic attacks. The consecration of a fairy stone was an elaborate affair, and included the following incantation:

*I conjure thee, by all Hosts
    of Heaven,
By the Living God, the True God,
By the Blessed and Omnipotent God*

At the conclusion of the ceremony the magician cried out: 'May it protect you against all evil forces and curses, Amen.'

Such a blasphemous combination of paganism and Christianity was a constant affront to many Christians and gave offence to the ecclesiastical authorities, but there seems to have been very little they could do about it. Basically there appears to have been little difference between the magicians' claims that sickness was the work of evil spirits, and the Church's belief that Satan was responsible.

White magic was apparently sanctioned, if not sanctified, because it was socially necessary. Given the choice between the faith healing of the Church and that of the more skilful wizard, the outcome was generally predictable. Love magic, a primitive type of marriage guidance, was in constant demand by all classes in spite of the fulminations of the bishops. Geomancy and many other divinatory arts had the same meaning for medieval man as the newspaper astrologer has for his modern counterpart. Where anxiety exists, measures will always be taken to allay it. The law of supply and demand applies to every type of human need.

The white magician of medieval days competed successfully with the clergy for the exorcism of ghosts and devils, transferred the evils of sickness from the living sufferer to inanimate objects which were then ritually buried, and at the same time maintained his aura of respectability by insisting that God, Christ, and the twelve Apostles were on his side. This is probably the reason why English white magicians were allowed to operate relatively unimpeded.

From a study of modern white

magic it is possible to reconstruct some of the techniques used by healers until well into the nineteenth century. Magic circles with cabalistic symbols were drawn in order to conjure up what would now be described as psychic energy. Modern witches call this process creating the 'cone of power', and insist that it be directed to social ends. A variety of spells were used to combat black witchcraft, the most remarkable being the witch bottle, which was used when the identity of a witch was unknown to her victim. A bottle which was often made of glass but sometimes of welded iron, and which contained blood, hair, nail parings, urine, and excreta from the bewitched person, was heated on the hearth fire at midnight; at the same time the assembled company intoned the Lord's Prayer backward. The witch was presumed to be undergoing excruciating agonies while the contents of the bottle boiled, with all the blood in her body afire, and this pain continued until she had removed her spell. If the bottle exploded she was expected to die. Witch bottles are not unknown, even today. It is possible that a few hysterics may have been cured by this bizarre rite, but it is doubtful that it could have had much effect upon organic diseases.

From White Magic to Black Box
The state's attitude toward semiheretical magicians began to harden after the Reformation, despite the sympathy directed toward white magicians by the community generally. A few eminent European jurists, such as Paulus Grillandus, a sixteenth century writer on witchcraft who was a papal judge in the witch trials in Rome, were even prepared to tolerate white magic, at a time when witches generally were being persecuted, provided it was socially useful. However, strict adherence to the law of God, particularly to the command in Exodus 22.18,

which is translated in the Authorized Version of the Bible as 'Thou shalt not suffer a witch to live', made it imperative that every kind of witch should be eliminated. The Bible also decreed that 'There shall not be found among you anyone who . . . practices divination, or a soothsayer, or an augur, or a sorcerer, or a charmer, or a medium, or a wizard, or a necromancer. For whoever does these things is an abomination to the Lord' (Deuteronomy 18.10-12).

Religious purists instituted witch hunts to eliminate both black and white sorcerers. The Scots tortured and burned both classes indiscriminately, but elsewhere in the British Isles white magicians were awarded minor punishments unless it could be proved that they were heretics. These prosecutions were at their fiercest during the reign of Queen Elizabeth I, and gradually died down during the following century. As late as 1651 John Lock of Colchester was placed in the pillory for setting up as a diviner of lost and stolen property, and many other white magicians were sent to prison. Jane Wenham, the last woman in England to be found guilty of witchcraft, who was tried and pardoned in 1712, was a

A plaque commemorating the last executions for witchcraft in England. Bideford, Devon, England

former white magician whose clientele had turned against her.

Although the Witchcraft Act of 1735 abolished the death penalty for witchcraft, practitioners of white magic were theoretically liable to be put in the pillory and sent to prison. However, there is no evidence that legal proceedings were ever taken against white magicians.

The traditional type of white magic is still dispensed in the Channel Islands by bone-setters and healers, who often claim to be seventh sons of seventh sons. On the mainland the older type of magician had almost disappeared by the beginning of the twentieth century, although a report published by the British Medical Association just before the World War I revealed that a few healing witches still survived in remote places.

Today the successors of the white magician may be found in the sphere of unorthodox or 'fringe' medicine. The 'Black Box', for instance, which it is claimed can diagnose disease in the absence of the patient, so that it can be treated on homoeopathic principles going back to Paracelsus, has become a vogue in the present century; and there are even radionic instruments which are said to be able to 'broadcast' treatment from a distance. Healing by the laying on of hands—by ordinary men and women rather than priests—is as popular today as it was in the Middle Ages. Astrologers and diviners of every kind dispense their psychic powers in cities and towns, while in the countryside wart charmers and rustic healers have their following. Yet

Rudy Alderette's altar in his Fresno, California, home includes a cauldron with a pentagram, a wand, chalice, statues of the Wiccan god and goddess, and incense holder.

another manifestation of white magic in Britain is in the form of witch covens which flourish in some cities. Modern witches insist that they are the only true heirs of the old magical healers. Needless to say, the Church looks on their activities with a jaundiced eye.

There is a certain similarity between the methods used by modern psychiatrists and those of the old magicians, and in recent years psychiatry has begun to examine sympathetically the functions of witchdoctors, medicinemen, and shamans. If white magic may be defined as the power of the imagination to effect changes in mental states by helping the sufferer to relive his past experiences, and by this means externalize his problems and reduce them to manageable proportions, the comparison becomes obvious.

The Evil Eye may have ceased to trouble civilized man, but the 'evil mouth' in the shape of adverse news continues to assault his peace of mind and to require the ministrations of the healer. Although white magic can have no effect on the objective world it profoundly influences the way in which it is seen. In an age of anxiety the white magician in one form or another can still perform a useful role; for this reason, white magic is likely to be with us for the foreseeable future.

ERIC MAPLE

FURTHER READING: G. Knight. A History of White Magic. (Mowbrays, 1978); David G. Phillips. White Magic. (Scholarly, 1981); E. Maple. Magic, Medicine and Quackery. (A. S. Barnes, 1968).

Wicca

The word 'wicca' is an Old English word meaning a male witch or wizard, sorcerer, or magician. It was first used in modern times by Gerald Gardner in his book *Witchcraft Today*, published in 1954, to describe those who practice the art of witchcraft. Gardner is viewed as the father of the modern movement known as Wicca.

Wicca is a modern form of what Gardner described as the Old Religion; he claimed to have stumbled across practitioners of the ancient art in the New Forest area of southern England about 1939, and he based his later writings on this New Forest coven, which he thought were surviving Witch-Cult members.

Previously, in the 1920s, Margaret Murray, an anthropologist and Egyptologist, claimed that witchcraft was a product of a Pagan pre-Christian Nature religion of western Europe and England that survived into the present and that the witch trials of the Middle Ages were an attempt to eradicate any remnants that survived the Holy Roman Empire's conquest of Europe.

Murray argued that the witches who had been persecuted during the Witch Trials of the sixteenth and seventeenth centuries were practitioners of an actual religion, a Pagan belief system, which she called the Witch-Cult. Her theories have since been refuted, but a few years after her work was published in the 1920s, some people in England had begun to practice the rituals, folk magic, and beliefs based on her books.

Later, in the late 1930s, Gerald Brosseau Gardner was spending time near the New Forest in England where he joined a local Rosicrucian Order which combined elements of Rosicrucianism, Theosophy, and Freemasonry. About that same time, he met a coven of witches (also members of the Rosicrucian Order) who Gardner claimed were descendants of the Witch-Cult Murray had written about.

Gardner joined the coven and began a campaign to bring back what he considered to be the old Pagan religion. In all probability, he built upon what he found in the coven in New Forest, adding a few touches from his experience in the esoteric Order of Rosicrucians, perhaps even borrowing from the writings of Aleister Crowley and others, to create a new religion based upon what he believed the old Pagan one to be.

During Gardner's initiation into the coven, he heard the word 'wicca' for the first time, as it was used in its original meaning, 'male witch,' referring to Gardner himself as he was taken into the coven. It was the first time he had heard the word, which he would use to name his belief system.

The Druid Order Ceremony at Tower Hil, London, England, on the Spring Equinox of 2010

Gardnerian and Alexandrian Wicca (the latter based upon the Gardnerian movement and founded by Alex Sanders), collectively called British Traditional Wicca, came to the United States from England in the 1960s. Three years after the British witchcraft laws were repealed in 1951, Gardner wrote *Witchcraft Today* and, five years later, *The Meaning of Witchcraft*. The repeal of the laws, which had been in effect since 1653, cleared the way for publication of these books and brought the Wicca movement to the attention of the public just in time to be adopted by the free thinking generation that was already advancing feminism in the United States. It is for this reason that Wicca today has a distinctly feminine tradition as well as having its roots in the old earth-centred pantheism.

In any case, by the 1960s, the movement had become a religion with practitioners following in Gardner's footsteps and building upon his writing to devise a Neo-pagan religion. Wicca may be based upon old Pagan beliefs, but it is a twentieth century institution.

Theological Structure

Wicca is a religion, and like other religions, such as Christianity, Islam, and Judaism, there are varied ways of practicing it. Some adhere to the original Gardnerian and Alexandrian beliefs. Alexandrian Wicca differs from Gardnerian Wicca in that it includes aspects of the Kaballah, which its founder Alex Sanders had studied.

Some Wiccans practice in a coven, but most are solitary practitioners.

Most Wiccans have the following principles in common:

1. They are in tune with nature and observant of the phases of the moon and the seasons of the year.
2. They have a responsibility to the environment and seek to live in harmony with nature.

Handfasting using a braided cord

3. They acknowledge a power that is greater than that apparent to average person.
4. They conceive of the Creative Power in the universe as manifesting through polarity—as masculine and feminine.
5. They recognize both outer and inner worlds, or psychological worlds sometimes known as the Spiritual World, the Collective Unconsciousness, etc.

6. They do not recognize any authoritarian hierarchy within Wicca, but honour those who share their greater knowledge and wisdom.
7. They see religion, magic, and wisdom in living as being united in the way one views the world and lives within it.
8. Calling oneself 'witch' does not make a witch. Neither does heredity, nor the collecting of titles, degrees, and initiations.

9. They believe in the affirmation and fulfillment of life . . . giving meaning to the Universe.
10. Their only animosity toward Christianity or any other religion is to the extent that its institutions have claimed to be 'the only way' and sought to deny freedom to others and to suppress other ways of religious practice and belief.
11. They are not threatened by debates on the history of their craft, the origins of various terms, or the legitimacy of various aspects of different traditions. They are concerned with their own present and future.
12. They do not accept the concept of absolute evil, nor do they worship any entity known as Satan or the Devil as defined by Christian tradition. They do not seek power through the suffering of others, nor do they accept that personal benefit can be derived only by denial to another.
13. They believe that they should seek within nature that which is contributory to their health and wellbeing.

Whether Wicca is a nature religion or an attempt to reclaim the Stone Age and Celtic Pagan practices and rituals of worshipping a goddess and a horned god, is a matter of interpretation by various movements and covens within the various 'sects' of Wicca.

It is a religion that is close to nature. The Wheel of the year is divided into eight segments, each marked by a season or an astronomical event. Many Wiccan holidays are Celtic or Gaelic in origin and are associated with agricultural societies. Those holidays, their meanings, and the Christian and secular holidays now associated with some of them are:

Samhain, which marks the end of the harvest, usually celebrated on October 31, midway between the autumn equinox and the winter solstice. Ad-

The sculpture of the Wiccan Horned God at the Museum of Witchcraft

opted by the Christians as All Hallow's Eve, or Hallowe'en. Associated with the Day of the Dead on November 1.

Yule, or the Winter Solstice, which is associated with a winter hunt, marked on December 21. This holiday too was adopted by the Christians and celebrated as Christmas, or Christ's birth day.

Imbolc, marks the beginning of spring. Imbolc is Old Irish for 'in the belly' and refers to the pregnancy of the ewes becoming noticeable. It is celebrated sometime between January 31 and February 2, midway between Yule and Ostara. This holiday was adopted by the Christians as St. Brigitte's Day, and then transformed

into Groundhog Day among German descendants in the United States.

Ostara, or the Spring Equinox, associated with a fertility goddess and dawn. Ostara is celebrated on the day of the spring equinox. This holiday and its theme of new beginnings, symbolized by eggs, was adopted as the Christian holiday of Easter, the celebration of Christ's resurrection.

Beltane, the May Day festival, held April 30—May 1, midway between Ostara, or the spring equinox and Midsummer Eve, or the summer solstice. This holiday was adopted by the USSR as a major holiday and so fell out of favour in the United States during the Cold War.

Litha, Midsummer Eve, or Summer Solstice, celebrated on June 21 or 22, although it should rightly be celebrated on the longest day of the year. Also marked as St. John's Day in the Christian calendar.

Lughnasadh, or Lammas Day, marks the beginning of the harvest season. August 1, midway between summer solstice and autumn equinox. Also known as Harvest Home.

Mabon, or the Autumn Equinox, celebrated around September 21. It is the middle of three harvest holidays, the one associated with giving thanks to the god and goddess.

Wiccan ritual altar

Widdershins

Or *withershins*, the direction contrary to the sun's apparent course, to the left, or anticlockwise; deliberate movement in this direction is sinister, associated with witches and worshippers of the Devil, because it reverses the normal and proper order of things.

Lighting of a candelabra to be placed on the graves of ancestors

The Witch of Endor

Saul, King of Israel, about to do battle with the Philistines, sought God's guidance but God did not answer him. Having previously driven all the necromancers and mediums out of the land of Israel, Saul nevertheless sought a medium to consult.

Saul disguised himself and went to see 'a woman of Endor' who 'had a familiar spirit.' At first the woman refused and accused Saul of laying a trap for her because he himself had forbidden the practice of necromancy, but eventually she agreed, and Saul asked her to bring him the spirit of Samuel.

The woman brought Samuel's spirit from the dead to be consulted by Saul. Samuel told Saul that he and his sons were all doomed to die the next day.

There is nothing to indicate that the Witch of Endor was actually a witch. In the story, she seems to be a medium, or necromancer, but she has come to be known as The Witch of Endor.

Witchcraft

In most English dictionaries *witchcraft* and *sorcery* are roughly synonymous. In anthropological usage they have acquired distinct meanings because an African tribe, the Azande, are more precise in their categories of the supernatural than we are; and E. E. Evans-Pritchard, the anthropologist who studied them and wrote what has become a classic on the ethnography of witchcraft and similar belief systems, found the existence in English of these two words a useful means of translating the Zande distinction.

Witchcraft and *sorcery* are words referring to systems of belief centred on the idea that certain human beings in a community may harm their fellow men by supernatural means. According to the Zande usage now adopted by most of the anthropological profession, both witches and sorcerers are believed illegitimately to kill others or make them ill, to cause them to fall victim to accident or other misfortune, or to destroy their property. 'Both alike are enemies of men,' as Evans-Pritchard puts it.

King Saul seeks the services of a witch, even though he'd made a point of banning such practitioners.

They differ, however, in method and motivation. The techniques of the witch are 'more supernatural' than those of the sorcerer in that they are beyond the comprehension of ordinary folk, whereas those of the sorcerer are acts of destructive magic that are well known and reasonably accessible to most adult members of the community. As to motive, witches are believed to be slaves of aberration and addiction; thus considered, they are weird, sometimes tragic characters. Sorcerers, on the other hand, are considered to be ordinary people driven by understandable, if disapproved, urges such as malice, envy, or revenge, which are part of everyone's experience.

Powers and Spells

The propensity to be a witch is usually attributed to heredity or at least is con-sidered constitutional, in the sense of having been implanted at an early age through mother's milk or, as among the Cewa of Central Africa, through a child's having been magically inoculated by a senior relative against the dermatitis believed to result from eating human flesh, an activity attributed to Cewa witches. Sorcery, on the other hand, usually demands no special personal attributes and is believed to be practiced by anyone who can acquire the necessary magical substances (in Africa) or spells (in Oceania).

Most anthropologists see the advantage of agreement on the meanings of these terms as outlined; but there are some, particularly those writing on Oceania, who treat the term 'sorcery' as socially or morally neutral, using it for all forms of destructive magic regardless of whether it is socially approved—as it may be in property protection for instance—or considered illicit. Similarly, and this applies to historical studies of European witchcraft, the term 'witch' does not invariably have a sinister or evil connotation, especially if it is qualified by the adjective 'white', in which case it may be used in reference to those who cure people rather than kill them, or who help to find lost possessions rather than destroy them. However, in most societies, more often than not, witches, like sorcerers, are believed to be agents of evil and misfortune.

The self-styled witches of modern society usually emphasize that they are not involved in any such antisocial practices as black magic or the casting of malevolent spells. This makes doubtful their inclusion in the anthropologist's definition of either sorcerer or witch. Their continued existence is as much a tribute to the inventive genius of Margaret Murray or of Gerald Gardner as it is to the strength of any continuing tradition.

The Universal Witch

Beliefs in witchcraft (which from this point will be used in a generic sense to include sorcery) have been so widely observed that it has been suggested that the more important elements were probably common to Paleolithic man and spread with him to most of the presently inhabited parts of the world. There are certainly close resemblances between the beliefs in witchcraft revealed by the studies of modern anthropologists and those shown, by historical and literary sources, to have been characteristic of classical and medieval Europe. As Philip Mayer remarks, 'Shakespeare, writing in seventeenth-century England about medieval Scottish witches, makes them recite a list of creatures that would be just as appropriate to witches in primitive Africa. Or again: the Pueblo Indians in Mexico say that witches go round at night carrying lights that alternately flare up and die down; exactly the same thing was said to me in Western Kenya by the Bantu tribe among whom I worked.' These widely dispersed elements would also have been familiar to Lucius Apuleius, author of *The Golden Ass,* a useful source for witch-beliefs in classical times.

Many of the works on European witchcraft, dealing with the early modern period, are concerned with a phenomenon very different from the witch-beliefs of surviving primitive societies or those of classical or medieval Europe. In the Dark Age, as Trevor-Roper puts it, 'there were witch beliefs, of course—a scattered folklore of peasant superstitions, the casting of spells, the making of storms, converse with spirits, sympathetic magic . . . but on the whole the medieval Church

succeeded in containing them.' But the sixteenth and seventeenth centuries saw so great an upsurge in Europeans' preoccupation with witch-beliefs, with the craze encouraged 'by the cultivated Popes of the Renaissance, by the great Protestant Reformers, by the saints of the Counter-Reformation, by the scholars, lawyers, and churchmen of an enlightened age', that Trevor-Roper is led to summarize: 'If these two centuries were the age of light, we have to admit that, in one respect at least, the Dark Age was more civilized.'

Servants of Satan

This means that the witch-beliefs of primitive peoples and those of early

modern Europeans are in many ways not comparable. The first represent a chronic state, active but kept unremarkable by a society's normal mechanisms of tension management. The second reflect times of profound change when witch-beliefs, as sensitive symptoms of social strain, became intermingled with the religious, political, and economic conflicts that punctuated the very rapid emergence of modern European society from feudalism.

For this reason the events relating to witchcraft in early modern Europe might more appropriately be compared with the cult movements which, since the second half of the nineteenth century, have been reported from virtually

Modern-day witch doctor with wood mask

every part of the world where native peoples have had to adjust themselves suddenly to the advent of Western ways of life. Just as the cargo cults of Melanesia, the ghost dance and peyote movements of North America ,and the antiwitchcraft crazes of Central Africa represent, as Worsley has put it, 'desperate searchings for more and more effective ways of understanding and modifying' a confused environment, so may the witch scares of Europe and of Old and New England have played a similar role in blasting away the creaking and groaning remnants of an outdated social structure.

The most important respect in which the epidemic character of European witch beliefs made them differ from those of nonliterate societies was the fact that they were taken up in the conflicts of the late medieval Church, the Reformation and the Counter-Reformation. An early mistaken identification of witches with heretics had the effect of marshalling a pre-Christian moral indignation against those who failed to conform with official Christianity. This fact probably prompted Margaret Murray's now discredited theory that European witches were the lingering adherents of a pagan religion. However, it also accounts for the fact that, whereas in all societies witches personify evil, in the society of early modern Europe they did this in a very specific way, being regarded as the earthly representatives of the Prince of Evil. In the course of time the chief criterion for identifying a witch in Europe or New England came to be whether he or she had made a compact with the Devil. Evidence of such a compact included the presence of a 'Devil's mark' on his or her body.

Witches were often accused of appearing in spectral form to tempt and torment their believed victims. In the Salem trials in New England in 1692, the screaming teenage girls, who were the main witnesses for the prosecution, regularly claimed to see—in the very courtroom—the specters of the accused. The idea that the Devil could not use the spectral counterparts of people without their connivance was an important principle in establishing the guilt of the accused. It was sufficient for an accuser to state that he had seen the accused witch's specter; and it was only when theological opinion questioned this principle that the rate of conviction by the courts declined.

A man accused of sorcery is exorcized in a church of Kinshasa on October 9, 2010, after a 'child witch' reportedly cursed him. Thousands of new fundamentalist Christian sects in Kinshasa make money out of identifying 'witches'. For a fee they investigate the children and confirm they are possessed. For a further fee they take the child and exorcize them, often keeping them without food for days, beating and torturing them to chase out the devil. Many—if not most—children accused of witchcraft are rejected by their families. Today, more than 20,000 children live in the street of Kinshasa, a city of about 10 million; more than a third have been accused of witchcraft.

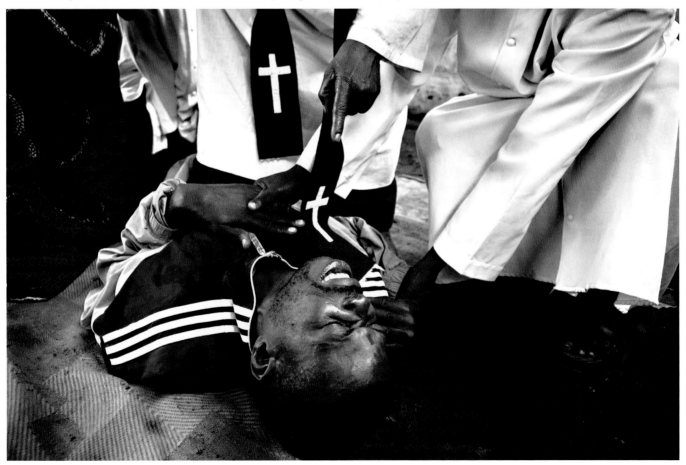

Witch doctor Josephina Rakobela sits in her shop in Lebowa in the Northern Transvaal Province of South Africa, May 1994. Belief in witchcraft and the practice of tribal justice is still on the rise and is one of the problems facing South Africa's government as it continues to strives to combine traditional African culture and modern democracy.

The Hoot of an Owl

Although the epidemic character and the religious entanglement of European witch-beliefs make them different from the beliefs anthropologists have discovered among existing nonliterate tribes, there are still many points of parallel. The ethnography of witchcraft, the description of this complex of beliefs in relation to the total way of life of the people or the period, has shown many similarities between societies separated in space and time.

Wherever beliefs in them are found, witches are conceived as having supernatural powers, antisocial tendencies, and disgusting practices. They are believed to travel around at night by flying through the air on broomsticks (in Europe) or in saucer-shaped winnowing baskets (in Central Africa), or to move over the ground by

riding on the backs of animal familiars such as baboons (in southern Africa). The range of animals and insects they are believed to induce to run their evil errands for them is wide, and includes dogs and cats in Europe and hyenas, owls, nightjars, and red ants in Africa. In the Cewa language an owl's hoot is heard, not as a meaningless inanity such as 'To wit-to woo!', but as a clear and sinister 'Muphe! Muphe! Nimkukute!' ('Kill him! Kill him! That I may munch him!'), and this inevitably links this weird bird with the necrophagous sorcerers who, the Cewa believe, bring them a large share of their misfortunes, such as illness, death, and accident. Witches are usually credited with extra-sensory powers approaching omniscience, knowing by a sixth sense where a death has occurred and consequently where the next ghoulish

feast will be held.

European beliefs reflect the medieval concern over sins of the flesh; for witches appeared to men as voluptuous succubi and to women as seducing incubi. A somewhat similar treatment of illicit sexual relationships occurs in the beliefs of the Pondo of southeastern Africa: their beliefs seem to be related to the fact that custom excludes large categories of individuals living in the same neighbourhood from marrying or flirting with one another. The less sex-ridden but more food-conscious Nyakyusa of southwestern Tanzania, on the other hand, consider witches as being motivated by greed rather than by lust.

From one society to another, ideas vary regarding the relationships between witches and their familiars, whether these be spirits, mythical creatures, or animals. Among the southeastern Bantu-speaking tribes of Africa, including the Pondo, witches are believed to have sexual relationships with their familiars, particularly with a dwarflike creature called *tokoloshe* or *tikoloshe*. Although familiars are usually regarded as the servants or the messengers of witches, they are sometimes believed to urge their masters and mistresses on, giving their aberrant addiction a more feasible, comprehensible and somewhat tragic character.

Even where no sexual relationship is postulated between witch and familiar, some kind of mystical link may be claimed. It was said of a reputed sorcerer among the Cewa that, when he had imbibed heavily, drunken hyenas were to be found in his house and that, when he died, his hyena-familiars died with him.

Attributed with special powers, witches are believed to be particularly difficult to bring to terms. Eternal vigilance and protective medicines have to be employed while they are at large and, once they have been caught, special methods of killing them have to be followed, such as burning them alive or driving stakes, pegs, or nails into various parts of their bodies. Such practices, of widespread occurrence, are probably related to the belief that witches have special spirit helpers or that they possess elusive souls, though not all those who follow these procedures are explicit about their reasons for carrying them out.

Supernatural Terrorists

Owing to their supposed deviant and often revolting practices, witches are everywhere looked upon as beyond the pale of decent living. They provide moralists with shorthand concrete descriptions of evil and parents with effective bogymen. To accuse anyone of witchcraft is a condensed way of charging him with a long list of the foulest crimes, and this action throws into sharper relief the moral precepts of the society to which he belongs.

The fact that the witch is used to make children more circumspect about their conduct is no doubt related to the tendency in many societies for beliefs in witchcraft to provide plausible points of backward reference in the explanation of misfortune. If someone falls ill or has an accident, both he and his fellow men can usually find some incident in his prior social interaction which will explain why someone had reason to have a grudge against him and why he should now be the victim of witchcraft. He may have quarreled with someone of dubious reputation, or he may have failed to discharge an obligation toward someone who, though in a superior moral position, is now believed to have resorted to an immoral form of retribution.

This leads to the paradox that, though witches provide mainly negative instances of conduct, they may also play positive moral roles in being the points of retrospective projection for the Victim's feelings of guilt resulting from acts of foolishness and meanness. This moral import of beliefs in witchcraft can be illustrated from all those societies, contemporary and historical, on which data on such beliefs exist, and this represents an important convergence of the findings of historians and anthropologists. Witches are unmitigated supernatural terrorists in all societies in which beliefs in them occur; and sufferers of misfortune find in the witches' actions the means of expressing their feelings of guilt.

Another anthropological finding has been more difficult to substantiate from historical materials. It has been found that, in contemporary nonliterate societies, accusations of witchcraft and believed instances of attack by witches occur typically between persons whom the social structure throws into uncontrolled competition and tension, for instance rivals in love or in politics. Accusations, which represent crises in the relationship between the alleged witch and the accuser, may thus be regarded as 'social strain-gauges', indicating where the tensions and role conflicts in the social structure lie. Believed instances of attack, involving the relationship between alleged witch and believed victim, have a similar significance but, since all witchcraft and most sorcery exist in the uneasy minds of their believed victims, they are on a different plane of reality and illuminate the society's own model of strained social relationships rather than the anthropologist's.

These two models often differ from one another and either may differ from the accepted picture. For instance, people in most societies where beliefs in witchcraft exist usually claim that witches are almost invariably women; yet, if the anthropologist keeps a tally of actual instances of accusation or of believed attack, he is likely to discover that men, who are generally more socially involved and more in competition for positions of leadership, form a much higher proportion of those accused or suspected than informants' general statements would suggest. In our society, statements about women drivers are a parallel case.

Until recently the nature of the historical materials made it difficult to apply the 'social strain-gauge' hypothesis to European data. The historical sources that have been analyzed have often not revealed enough specific information about the relationships between the important triad of accuser, accused witch, and believed victim; nor have they always thrown light on the nature of the issues between them. However, with Macfarlane's recent meticulous combination of the latest

Opposite page:
Brujas à Volar **(Witches Preparing to Fly),** Francisco de Goya (1746–1828)

A veteran of Haiti's disbanded army sings as a buckling is sacrificed in a voodoo ceremony, in Mariani, Haiti (May 18, 2013). The soldiers believe that slashing the throat of a young goat and drinking its blood is a sacrifice that will help to restore the armed forces. After the ceremony the veterans marched through the Mariani streets, commemorating the 210th anniversary of the country's national flag. The group of ex-soldiers continue to press for the restoration of Haiti's disbanded military. The National Armed Forces of Haiti was abolished in 1995 because of its history of toppling governments and crushing dissent.

techniques of English local history and the theoretical orientations of social anthropology in his study of witchcraft in Essex between 1560 and 1680, an ever closer convergence in this field is promised.

In any society that uses witchcraft as a regular explanatory principle, two features may be expected to be prominent. Firstly, there will be practices such as consulting diviners and oracles, and submitting suspects to ordeals. Secondly, prevailing thought processes will be closed, in the sense that misfortunes, witch-beliefs and the techniques of witch finding form a circular sequence in which each case of misfortune that is attributed to witch-craft reinforces the belief in witchcraft and renders a skeptical escape from the sequence unlikely.

As yet we have no satisfactory explanation of how some societies, including our own, have broken from

Instead of having everyone in the community breathing intimately down our necks, we manage in our modern way of life to escape, even if momentarily, the prison of personal relationships, with their high potential for influence and control of our conduct, for love and hate, and, in general, for the ingredients of those delusions which in the right social setting become standardized and infuse the world with fellow humans wielding supernatural power. It is significant that, in most reports of accusations and believed instances of witchcraft, the main characters, like most of those involved in crimes of violence in even our impersonal society, have been intimately acquainted with one another.

An Open Society

Though modern people may have given up the more specific beliefs in witchcraft, they have retained many of its associated tendencies. They have not yet completely escaped from the charmed circle of taboos and magical beings that confines primitive peoples, and moved into an open society in which they have no qualms about adjusting their social institutions in the light of rational analysis. Some twentieth-century movements have many of the characteristics of a sixteenth-century European or a contemporary primitive witch-scare. An accusation of political deviance may, like an accusation of witchcraft, prove an infallible means of destroying a reputation or a career. Arthur Miller's play *The Crucible*, which attacked Joseph McCarthy's anti-Communist cult in the idiom of seventeenth-century Salem, brought out this parallel with brilliant insight.

M. G. MARWICK

FURTHER READING: Apuleius. The Golden Ass. *(Indiana Univ. Press, 1962); J. C. Baroja.* The World of Witches. *(Univ. of Chicago Press, 1965);* C. Larner. Witchcraft and Religion. *(Basil Blackwell, 1984); A. D. J. Macfarlan.* Witchcraft in Tudor and Stuart England. *(Harper & Row, 1970); M. G. Marwick.* Sorcery in its Social Setting: a Study of the Northern Rhodesian Cewa. *(Humanities, 1965); R. H. Robbins.* Witchcraft. *(Kraus Intl., 1978); John Middleton and E. H. Winter ed.* Witchcraft and Sorcery in East Africa. *(Praeger, 1963); H. R. Trevor-Roper,* Crisis of the Seventeenth Century: Religion, the Reformation and Social Change *(Harper and Row, 1967) and* The European Witch Craze. *(Harper & Row, 1969).*

this closed circle and abandoned beliefs in witchcraft. Part of the answer seems to lie in the larger scale of modern societies with their related tendency to specialization, not only in economic processes, but also in human relationships, with some of the latter personal and others impersonal.

Glossary

Alchemy The part-scientific, mystical, and philosophical study of the elements, particularly know for efforts to turn common metals into gold.

Blasphemers People who speak out or act against something sacred, such as a deity or doctrine.

Calumny Making false accusations or statements about someone or their actions.

Chalice A special cup for drinking wine used in ceremonies, especially in religious rites.

Charlatan One who falsely pretends to be an expert, usually with the purpose of taking someone's money.

Confectionery Collective term for sweets, chocolates, and candy.

Confiscation The process of collecting and taking away someone's belongings or property, usually as a result of laws being broken.

Denounced Having been openly or publicly accused of evil or criminal action.

Desecration The act of mistreating a sacred place or disrespecting a religious rite.

Dolmens Three or more large stone slabs or rocks, positioned upright with at least one placed horizontally across the others that served as a tomb in prehistoric times, especially in the British Isles.

Ecclesiastical Pertaining or relating to an established church, generally referring to Christian ones.

Enmities Feelings of opposition and ill will toward something or someone.

Excommunication Formal dismissal from an established, usually Roman Catholic, religion.

Extant Still in existence, a remaining example of something begun long ago.

Gibbet A grisly tool of public torture or execution, also known as a hanging cage.

Hapless Unlucky and unfortunate, even to the point of being doomed.

Heinous The quality of being especially awful, evil, or in any way extremely offensive.

Heretic One who holds views contrary to an established—usually religious—belief system.

Impervious Not feeling or reacting to a given stimulus, such as pain.

Incantations A set of words spoken in reverence or ceremony which call upon the supernatural.

Incubus A male demon that has sexual relations with women while they sleep.

Inquisition When capitalized, a formal judging body of the Roman Catholic Church in Europe that sought out nonbelievers and heretics to the point of persecution.

Malevolent Having the quality or intention of doing wickedness, harm, or evil.

Nefarious Describing an action or intention that is illegal, wicked, or evil.

Negligible Of very little influence, amount, or account.

Obduracy The quality of adamantly refusing to change an opinion, belief, or behaviour.

Perpetrated Having committed a crime or any wrong-doing.

Phenomenon Something that, when it occurs, is definitely seen or felt by the senses.

Providence An intervention, usually good, into the events of people and world events by a deity or divine nature.

Schismatic Having the quality of splitting a group of believers into separate groups, based on opposing viewpoints about particular issues or doctrine.

Solemnized Performed with reverence in a ceremony

Succubus A demon in female form who visits men in the night for sexual purposes.

Taciturnity Total silence or absence of a stated opinion on a matter.

Talisman An object, usually worn or kept close to the body, that has magical powers and provides good luck and security against evil.

Unguent A prepared lotion or balm used for the treatment and healing of wounds.

Index

Author List

Contributors to *Man, Myth, and Magic: Witches and Witchcraft*

J. C. Baroja is the author of *The World of Witches.*

Wanda von Baeyer-Katte was in the Department of Psychology, University of Heidelberg.

Richard Cavendish is a leading authority on the history of ideas, whose books have been acclaimed for their combination of clarity and insight on both sides of the Atlantic. He is author of *The Black Arts*, a study of the European tradition of magic; *The Powers of Evil; The Tarot; A History of Magic; Visions of Heaven and Hell; King Arthur and the Grail;* and *The Great Religions*, a study of the major religions in the world and their central beliefs. He is also the editor of *The Encyclopedia of the Unexplained; Mythology — an Illustrated Encyclopedia;* and the *Encyclopedia of Legends.*

Max Gluckman was a Professor of Social Anthropology, Manchester, and his books include *Custom and Conflict in Africa; Order and Rebellion in Tribal Africa; Politics, Law and Ritual in Tribal Society.*

Christina Hole was an honorary editor of *Folklore*; books include *English Folklore; English Custom and Usage; English Folk Heroes; A Mirror of Witchcraft; Witchcraft in England;* edited the *Encyclopedia of Superstitions.*

Eric Maple is the author of *The Dark World of Witches; The Realm of Ghosts; The Domain of Devils; Magic, Medicine, and Quackery; Superstition and the Superstitious.*

M. G. Marwick was a Professor of Sociology, Stirling; Marwick previously held chairs in Social Anthropology and Sociology at the University of the Witwatersrand and Monash University, and is author of *Sorcery in Its Social Setting.*

Brian W. Rose was the head of the Department of Education, Johannesburg College of Education, and author of *No Mean City; Lines of Action,* and others.

Elliot Rose was Associate Professor of History, Toronto, and author of *A Razor for a Goat.*

Sandy Shulman is a novelist, and the author of *Dreams.*

Frank Smyth is the author of *Modern Witchcraft.*

John Symonds is a novelist and writer of children's books; he's the author of *The Great Beast; Madame Blavatsky: Medium and Magician,* co-editor (with Kenneth Grant) of *The Confessions of Aleister Crowley;* and member of the Editorial Board of *Man, Myth, and Magic.*

Gillian Tindall is a novelist and journalist, and the author of *A Handbook on Witches.*